Mapping Fairy-Tale Space

Series in Fairy-Tale Studies

Series Editor

Donald Haase, Wayne State University

A complete listing of the books in this series can be found online at wsupress.wayne.edu.

Praise for *Mapping Fairy-Tale Space*

"*Mapping Fairy-Tale Space* brilliantly synthesizes and expands crucial ideas of connection and relatability that enliven contemporary fairy tales. Christy Williams offers fairy-tale studies a compelling gift that rewards attentive engagement. Fans and scholars need this book."

—Jill Terry Rudy, Brigham Young University

"*Mapping Fairy-Tale Space* is an exciting book. Williams guides us skillfully through contemporary fairy-tale landscapes, exploring their storyworlds' geography and tracing the continued appeal of the genre 'as a map for lived experience.' As she traces metafictional critiques and narrative strategies that popular fairy tales in print and on TV share, Williams invites us to revisit the practices of seriality and pastiche in relation to fairy tale and to recognize how opening up narrative borders revitalizes the genre. Richly layered, persuasive, and insightful, this is a study I will keep returning to."

—Cristina Bacchilega, co-editor of *Inviting Interruptions: Wonder Tales in the Twenty-First Century* (Wayne State University Press, 2021)

"Christy Williams's book demonstrates her expert, expansive knowledge of fairy tales and their criticism as well as their role in popular and literary culture. This writing is lively and accessible yet sophisticated in its theoretical understanding of narrative and its interactions with geography. Williams is the first critic to bring such an erudite lens to some of the most popular recent incarnations of the classic fairy tales, such as Disney's *Once Upon a Time*, and her analysis is invigorating. Her understanding of how narrative creates geography and how connections across borders create narrative is welcome food for thought in these times."

—Veronica Schanoes, author of *Fairy Tales, Myth, and Psychoanalytic Theory: Feminism and Retelling the Tale*

"*Mapping Fairy-Tale Space* is a fascinating study that reconceptualizes fairy tales as geographical locations that can be mapped out and that can also have borders artificially imposed upon them. It illustrates how the paths fairy-tale characters follow, the trails of breadcrumbs they take, function as life maps that guide them and which they also contest. Each chapter adeptly showcases fairy-tale texts in which storyworld boundaries are challenged, collapsed, and stretched to accommodate new meanings in new sociohistorical contexts. Christy Williams provides us with an exciting and dynamic theoretical framework to rethink the fairy tale in terms of narrative geographies."

—Anne E. Duggan, professor of French at Wayne State University and co-editor of *Marvels and Tales: Journal of Fairy-Tale Studies* (Wayne State University Press)

Mapping Fairy-Tale Space

Pastiche and Metafiction in Borderless Tales

Christy Williams

Wayne State University Press
Detroit

Copyright © 2021 by Wayne State University Press, Detroit, Michigan 48201. All rights reserved. No part of this book may be reproduced without formal permission.

ISBN (paperback): 978-0-8143-4383-8
ISBN (hardcover): 978-0-8143-4827-7
ISBN (ebook): 978-0-8143-4384-5

Library of Congress Control Number: 2020945841

Published with the assistance of a fund established by Thelma Gray James of Wayne State University for the publication of folklore and English studies.

On cover: *An Ancient Mappe of Fairyland: Newly discovered and set fort*, designed by Bernard Sleigh, printed by W. Griggs & Sons, Ltd., Peckham, London, S.E. (London: Sidgwick & Jackson, 1918). Courtesy of the David Rumsey Map Collection, David Rumsey Map Center, Stanford Libraries (https://purl.stanford.edu/zn126px1047).

Wayne State University Press
Leonard N. Simons Building
4809 Woodward Avenue
Detroit, Michigan 48201-1309

Visit us online at wsupress.wayne.edu

for my mother

Contents

Acknowledgments • xi

Introduction: Remapping a Genre: Fairy-Tale Pastiche as Critical Mode • 1

Part I. Mapping Fairy Tales

1. Genre and Geography: ABC's *Once Upon a Time* and the Mapping of a Fairy-Tale Land • 27

2. Genres Overlaid: Serialization and Hybridity in Marissa Meyer's *The Lunar Chronicles* and Seanan McGuire's *Indexing* • 64

Part II. Fairy-Tale Maps

3. Asking for Directions: Metafiction and Metaphor in the Korean Drama *Secret Garden* • 107

4. Following Footsteps: Redrafting Fairy-Tale Maps in Kelly Link's Short Fiction • 137

Conclusion: Collapsing Borders in the Age of the Internet • 169

Notes • 175

Bibliography • 183

Index • 197

Acknowledgments

I AM VERY FORTUNATE to be a fairy-tale scholar and to have found a group of colleagues and friends who build community and support each other. This project has been guided and helped along the way by so many people that I am sure to forget some, but I will try to name as many as I can. Jennifer Orme helped me to conceive of this project by pointing out that all of my disparate ideas and random conference papers were actually connected. She and Sara Thompson offered invaluable feedback on early sections in the Fierce Fairies writing group. Donald Haase was in the audience when I delivered the first conference paper that would become part of chapter 1 and encouraged me to continue working with it. Veronica Schanoes, Claudia Schwabe, Jeana Jorgensen, Brittany Warman, and Sara Cleto read sections as part of a writing and support group, the Coven des Fées, and they, along with Linda Lee, have been in the audience of almost every conference paper that found its way into the project and have always offered interesting ideas and helpful critiques.

The International Conference on the Fantastic in the Arts has been my conference home for several years, and presenting sections of this project at ICFA has resulted in a great many conversations with colleagues that have informed this book, including those with Theodora Goss and Amanda Firestone. I have also presented sections at the conference Thinking with Stories in Times of Conflict: A Conference in Fairy-Tale Studies, the conference of the American Folklore Society, and the American Comparative Literature Association Conference, all of which were productive and thoughtful experiences. Anne Duggan, Pauline Greenhill, and Jill Terry Rudy have been supportive and inspiring colleagues to work with. And I am blessed with my own fairy godmother, mentor, and friend, Cristina Bacchilega, who suggested I think about the doctoral program at the University of Hawai'i, Mānoa and has encouraged me to think with stories every day since.

I was supported in the writing of this project by grants from Hawaiʻi Pacific University, including travel grants to attend conferences and research leave to complete the manuscript, and I am grateful to the colleagues who made that leave possible. My colleagues and friends Deborah Ross, Micheline Soong, Angela Gili, and Phyllis Frus have helped me work through difficult passages and, more importantly, reminded me that I could do this.

The team at Wayne State University Press has been a pleasure to work with, and I am grateful to Annie Martin, Marie Sweetman, Emily Nowak, Jamie Jones, Kristina Stonehill, Kristin Harpster, and Carrie Downes Teefey, as well as freelance copyeditor Sandra J. Judd and freelance indexer Rachel Lyon, for producing this beautiful book.

Finally, no project I undertake would be successful without the support of William Williams, who makes everything else work so that I can write. He has read practically every word of this book and helped me work through its concepts. He and Heather Willard listen to me talk about fairy tales long after they are ready to move on. Maeve Williams ensured I met my deadline for this book because she was due the week after the manuscript was, and Luna Belle Williams told me to write a thousand words every day when she left for school.

Introduction

Remapping a Genre: Fairy-Tale Pastiche as Critical Mode

MARINA WARNER BEGINS *Once Upon a Time: A Short History of the Fairy Tale* by asking readers to "imagine the history of fairy tale as a map" (xiii). She describes the contours of this map from the "prominent landmarks" of Charles Perrault and the Brothers Grimm to "a whole web of routes from points further east" and north before asking readers to reimage the map as an advent calendar with windows into scenes of storytellers, writers, and folklorists and movie screens into scenes of directors, screenwriters, performers, and artists all working hard on creating fairy tales (Warner xiii–xiv). Warner's map is one of a shifting landscape of fairy-tale history, an Ocean of Story in changing light with migrating tales that traverse place and medium (xv). It is a beautiful metaphor, and she ends by illuminating the "many unexplored corners and much terra incognita" (Warner xvi). Warner's metaphor attempts to help readers visualize the historical, time-based relationships among fairy tales and their creators, and it relies on an understanding of the genre as interconnected.

Warner's map is complemented by Cristina Bacchilega's "fairy-tale web," described in *Fairy Tales Transformed? Twenty-First-Century Adaptations & the Politics of Wonder*. Bacchilega envisions fairy tales as a system of interconnected links with no true center; the web "reaches back in history and across space to intersect with multiple story weaving traditions" (20). She builds on the weaving and spinning metaphors employed in earlier discussions of fairy tales by Karen E. Rowe, who traces the connection of tale-telling with weaving and spinning in tales themselves in "To Spin a

Yarn: The Female Voice in Folklore and Fairy Tale," and on an understanding of the World Wide Web and hypertextual linking explored by Donald Haase in "Hypertextual Gutenberg: The Textual and Hypertextual Life of Folktales and Fairy Tales in English-Language Popular Print Editions." Bacchilega explains that "when it comes to storytelling in practice, we are now very familiar with the idea that all texts—oral, written, visual, and social—participate in a web of intertextual relations" (19). Bacchilega's web, with its multiple centers, necessarily decenters the European fairy-tale tradition marked by Warner's prominent landmarks of Perrault and Grimm. Just as Warner's map extends beyond these fairy-tale monuments, Bacchilega's web expands far beyond the European canon. Central to her metaphor is the idea that "in the twenty-first-century fairy-tale web, links are 'hypertextual,' as Donald Haase put it—that is, not referring back to *one* center" (Bacchilega 27). There are "competitive authorities and the awareness of multiple traditions" that make the fairy-tale web not only "intertextual, multivocal, and transmedial" but a web of interconnected webs, and Bacchilega explores the sociopolitical ramifications of this decentering of European fairy-tale canon in a genre that has always been one of multiplicity, multivocality, and polyphony (27).

This understanding of fairy tales as interconnected is central to my project here as well, and I, too, employ the metaphor of mapping and maps in my analysis of twenty-first-century fairy tales. Rather than map the genre or its history, I take a more literal approach to maps, examining mapping within the tales themselves and how certain metafictional narrative techniques transform the fairy-tale genre into a geographic landscape on a diegetic level. My fairy-tale map is many maps, not one, and each is created by the narrative strategies employed in creating the specific fairy-tale texts. Like those of Warner, Bacchilega, Rowe, and Haase, my analysis of fairy tales relies on the understanding of the genre as one of connections, and I explore how different texts in the twenty-first century envision these connections.

This project is a narrative analysis that employs and examines the metaphor of mapping in relation to contemporary popular and literary fairy tales that reconfigure well-known fairy tales—either by combining individual tales into a single storyworld or by self-referentially turning to fairy tales for guidance. The primary texts analyzed are the television shows *Once Upon a Time* (ABC) and *Secret Garden* (a Korean drama), *The Lunar Chronicles* young-adult novel series by Marissa Meyer, the *Indexing* serial novels by Seanan McGuire, and three experimental short works of fiction by Kelly Link. Some of these texts engage traditional fairy tales as maps, with characters using the well-known stories to plot their course; in other cases, I employ the metaphor of mapping to examine the narrative space created by these new tales as they combine traditional tales in inventive ways. All of the texts I study in this project have at their center a crisis about the relevance and sustainability of fairy tales, and I argue that they both engage the fairy tale as a relevant genre and remake it to create a new kind of fairy tale for audiences in the twenty-first century.

I approach fairy-tale maps from two angles, dividing the book into two sections. The first section analyzes fairy-tale texts that collapse multiple distinct fairy tales so that they inhabit the same storyworld, transforming the fairy-tale genre into a fictional geography. I use the metaphor of mapping to examine the complex narrative restructuring enabled by this form of pastiche, and I explore the translation of genre to physical location as a useful way of conceptualizing the process of reinventing traditional tales for new times and places. The second section analyzes the metaphoric use of fairy tales as maps, or guides, for lived experience. In these texts, characters use fairy tales both to navigate and to circumvent their own situations, but the tales are ineffectual maps until the characters chart different paths and endings for themselves, or reject the tales as maps altogether. These texts explore the complicated relationship between traditional fairy tales and modern life and the problems encountered when reproducing outmoded ideologies. My analysis focuses on how inventive narrative and visual storytelling techniques enable metafictional commentary on fairy tales in the texts themselves.

Warner returns to her mapping metaphor to end *Once Upon a Time*, this time relying on imagery from "Hansel and Gretel," a path in the forest once marked by bread crumbs now eaten by birds (180). Instead of bread crumbs, we are left with fairy tales to navigate by: "Fairy tales give us something to go on. . . . It is something to start with" (Warner 180). Warner's path leads readers to an understanding of fairy-tale history. In the texts analyzed here, fairy tales help the characters and audiences navigate the present. The tales become a way of thinking through problems and solutions, of understanding what no longer works in order to forge ahead. Like much of fantastic and speculative fiction, fairy tales are a way of imagining the real world otherwise. Jack Zipes has pointed out the utopian function of fairy tales and their promise of social mobility in a variety of works, including *Fairy Tales as Myth/ Myth as Fairy Tale*, and described the genre as a site of subversive discourse in several others, including *Fairy Tales and the Art of Subversion: The Classical Genre for Children and the Process of Civilization*, ultimately linking the two impulses in *The Irresistible Fairy Tale: The Cultural and Social History of a Genre*. Many other scholars like Lewis C. Seifert in *Fairy Tales, Sexuality, and Gender in France, 1690–1715: Nostalgic Utopias* and Anne E. Duggan in *Salonnières, Furies, and Fairies: The Politics of Gender and Cultural Change in Absolutist France*, have commented on the subversive function of fairy tales as political speech, critiquing dominant political systems from the protective guise of fantasy. Twenty-first century fairy tales continue this tradition, engaging real sociopolitical conflict from once upon a time.

Retelling fairy tales and adapting them for different audiences, times, and places has long been a part of the genre, and the end of the twentieth century in particular saw an explosion of feminist retellings. Writers like Anne Sexton, Angela Carter, and Jeanette Winterson transform popular fairy tales in ways that critique and reject their source tales' gender ideology, and at times offer alternative ways of being. Sexton's Snow White slides into the role of her stepmother, Carter's Little Red Riding Hood chooses to climb in bed with the wolf, and Winterson's twelve dancing princesses live happily ever after without their husbands. Broader ideological positions are dismantled by writers like Donald Barthelme and Robert Coover, whose fractured and fragmented fairy tales resist cohesion. Margaret Atwood, A. S. Byatt, Salmon Rushdie, Robin McKinley, Jane Yolen, and Tanith Lee are among the many, many, many others whose projects of retelling fairy tales reaffirm the genre's cultural importance while recognizing the shifting sociohistorical realities of the present day. The majority of these new and retold fairy tales engage fairy tales at the tale level, taking a specific version or singular tale type as their source. While there are exceptions to this generalization, the turn of the twenty-first century has seen a shift toward multiplicity: fragments from a variety of tales brought together, more than one fairy tale combined, other genres mixed with fairy tale, and serialization in print and on-screen. Fairy tales are not just fractured and fragmented but mixed up, mashed up, blended, and extended. These fairy-tale retellings that traffic in multiplicity engage not only individual tales or tale types but fairy tale as a genre. In examining the texts in this book through the metaphors of mapping, I explore how these critiques are narratively enacted and engage fairy tales metafictionally on the level of genre.

Make It New?

The 2011 American television season saw the premiere of two fairy-tale-themed dramas, *Grimm* on NBC and *Once Upon a Time* on ABC. Both shows promised viewers fairy tales with a twist. The opening of *Grimm*, a police procedural, claims that the fairy tales depicted on the show are "true," and the opening of *Once Upon a Time*, a melodrama, claims that its versions of fairy tales are "real" (*Grimm* 1.1, *Once Upon a Time* 1.1). Yet despite these truth claims, neither show traffics in fidelity to its sources, with both offering new twists on old tales. This focus on newness and twists is strange. There has been an explosion of fairy-tale texts in the last fifty years, with a variety of retellings across different mediums that re-envision the fairy tales of the past for our future needs. Feminist retellings in particular proliferated at the end of the twentieth century, and more recently there has been an expansion of retellings and adaptations that reflect a multitude of perspectives and identities. Basically, fairy tales are everywhere. And they all promise something new: new stories, new twists, new characters, new events, new angles, new tidbits, new. This is odd for a genre that is hundreds of years old. The earliest written version of "Cinderella" was recorded over one thousand years ago, and nearly every continent has produced multiple versions of the tale in a variety of languages and from a multitude of cultures.[1] It seems unlikely that there is anything "new" to do with this story. The same holds true for other fairy tales that can only boast hundreds of years of recorded history and not a thousand. Yet creator Edward Kitsis (with Adam Horowitz) claimed for *Once Upon a Time* that "I think this is the first time anyone's ever shown Snow White... swinging a sword—and she's pregnant!" (qtd. in Masters and Mitovich). However, fighting princesses have long been a staple of fairy-tale revisions, and strong female characters abound in traditional tales.[2]

Much of this concern with newness is actually new-to-you-ness, new to audiences raised on Disney films. The impetuous on newness is a logical one; that is, after all, how one sells books, television shows, and movies. Entertainment must dazzle audiences in a way never seen before, and academic work must add new contributions to the field to be funded. It makes sense that Kitsis would want to emphasize how his fairy tale differs from the norm, especially because *Once Upon a Time* invokes Disney films frequently and ABC is a subsidiary of the Disney Corporation. What is the point in telling a story everyone already knows? But the norm in this case is reflective of a construct, a myth about fairy tales instead of the reality of a multivalent genre comprised of many different variants of tales. The genre has always been about newness, variation, and retelling. The stories we think of as fairy tales have not been static for hundreds of years, but have always been changing to reflect their context. So with a genre this old and with hundreds if not thousands of versions of the different tales, how does one do anything new?

Once Upon a Time creator Adam Horowitz (with Edward Kitsis) described the premise behind the show: "The idea is to take these characters that we all know collectively and try to find things about them that we haven't explored before.... We are not generally retelling the exact same story as the fairy tale world" (qtd. in Keily). Kitsis and Horowitz address this problem of newness by retelling the genre as they retell specific tales. In taking on the entirety of the genre (at least as it is understood in American popular culture), Kitsis and Howard employ pastiche, or mash up, which is, of course, not a new technique and is a staple of the postmodern writer's toolbox. In promoting the show's premiere, Kitsis explained that "one of the things we are doing on the show is that we're sort of telling mash-ups.... So if you notice the pilot there's a war council with Grumpy and Geppetto and Pinocchio, so we're kind of presenting to the world a mash-up" (qtd. in Josie Campbell). Horowitz added that "one of the fun things for us coming up with these stories is thinking of ways these different characters can interact in ways they never have before" (qtd. in Josie Campbell). Horowitz also explained that "if you watch the pilot, we open after the happy ending.... We're interested in either telling the origin stories or the real character things. Like, why is Grumpy grumpy? Why is Geppetto so lonely he carves a little boy out of wood? Why is the Evil Queen evil? To us, that's much more interesting, exploring the missing pieces rather than retelling the story" (qtd. in Josie Campbell). This filling in and setting the stories after the happily ever after are also standard techniques in postmodern fairy tales, particularly in feminist retellings. But while these are not new techniques, nor techniques new to fairy tales, they are not the dominant mode of presenting fairy tales on television and in movies. The *Shrek* series, which engages both techniques, is an outlier in a media field dominated by Disney animated retellings and live-action retellings that often emphasize the adult themes of the source tales.

Fairy-Tale Pastiche

The term *fairy-tale pastiche* has been usefully employed by a few fairy-tale scholars to refer to fairy-tale texts that draw on a variety of fairy-tale sources, including different cultural traditions. While the primary definition of *pastiche* refers to an imitation of style, the secondary definition, which refers to a combination of elements from multiple sources, including style, is useful in a postmodern context. Similar to a *mash up* in music or *collage* and *assemblage* in art, a fairy-tale pastiche typically employs specific elements of fairy tales, such as characters, iconography, motifs, and other fragments, rather than plots or whole tales. While many of these elements of fairy tales are the standard motifs of folklore, like the Cruel Stepmother, and are generalized to the genre not to specific tales, others, like a glass slipper, are associated with specific tales and can be employed as either part of an adaptation of that tale or without the related "Cinderella" trappings. In her article, "Disrupting the Boundaries of Genre and Gender: Postmodernism and the Fairy Tale," Cathy Lynn Preston argues that "in postmodernity the 'stuff' of fairy tales exists as fragments (princess, frog, slipper commodity relations in a marriage market) in the nebulous realm that we might most simply identify as cultural knowledge" (210). Preston's use of *fragments* here is especially appealing as it encompasses both folklore motifs and elements of fairy tales that have been arrested from—fragmented from—specific fairy-tale sources for decontextualized use in retelling.[3] Karin Kukkonen explains in "Popular Cultural Memory: Comics, Communities and Context Knowledge" that "textual elements become generalised when they enter cultural memory. They are taken out of their immediate textual surroundings and original social contexts and turned into conventions, icons, character types and standard situations of popular media texts" (263), and I would add motifs to this list. Motifs and fragments conjure up ideas about their fairy-tale contexts without necessarily referencing a specific tale, so that a wicked stepmother character can appear in a text without belonging to a "Cinderella" or "Snow White" narrative. She still maintains the associations with that character, but a specific fairy-tale plot need not be invoked for the wicked stepmother to be understood in association with her genre context.

A fairy-tale pastiche necessarily relies on this process to engage multiple fairy tales simultaneously. The fragments invoked create a fairy-tale landscape, recognizable through "conventions, icons, character types and standard situations" that carry the genre mark of fairy tale even without the need to invoke specific texts to ensure audience familiarity. In *Critical and Creative Perspectives on Fairy Tales: An Intertextual Dialogue between Fairy-Tale Scholars and Postmodern Retellings*, Vanessa Joosen borrows the phrase "horizon of expectations" from Hans Robert Jauss to describe the set form and features of fairy tales that are disrupted in fairy-tale retellings.[4] In "Storyworlds/Narratology," Katharine Young likewise offers a list of "metaphysical constants" that define the fairy-tale storyworld, constructing a fairy-tale ontology that governs how readers construct fairy-tale storyworlds (216–17). These genre-specific metaphysical constants are shared across tales, and this is what allows the different tales to be set in the same place in a fairy-tale pastiche.

Preston's invocation of postmodernism is echoed by the fairy-tale scholars using the term *fairy-tale pastiche*. In "A Wave of the Magic Wand: Fairy Godmothers in Contemporary American Media," Jeana Jorgensen suggests the term "fairy-tale pastiche" to refer to texts that draw upon a variety of fairy-tale motifs and fragments rather than individual tales or fairy-tale plots, and she argues that these texts are "inspired by fairy tales but [are] not quite fairy tales themselves" (218). Her interest is in how these texts deploy fairy-tale material in the creation of a new text, and the multiplicity of tales invoked lends categorization more toward *pastiche* than *parody*. Adam Zolkover has also employed the term "fairy-tale pastiche" in "Corporealizing Fairy Tales: The Body, the Bawdy, and the Carnivalesque in the Comic Book *Fables*," an analysis of Bill Wilmington's graphic novel series *Fables*. Zolkover defines fairy-tale pastiche as "a postmodernist blending of elements from a variety of loci within fairy-tale discourse that serves at once as commentary, play, and a fairy tale in its own right" (41). While Zolkover's definition includes a turn toward criticism more associated with postmodern definitions of parody, his focus, like Jorgensen's, is on the combination of fairy-tale elements from different sources and different tales. An interesting distinction between the two definitions is that Jorgensen identifies the pastiche texts as "not quite fairy tales," while Zolkover identifies them as fairy tales. For my analysis, I consider the texts to be fairy tales though they may not resemble the traditional form associated with fairy tales.

Not every text with a fairy-tale allusion in it can be considered a fairy tale, but in the case of the pastiche texts under analysis here, fairy tales are the dominant genre employed, and the form of the traditional fairy tale is utilized within the larger context of the pastiche. Cristina Bacchilega and John Rieder, in "Mixing It Up: Generic Complexity and Gender Ideology in Early Twenty-First Century Fairy Tale Films," invoke Jorgensen's use of *fairy-tale pastiche* to discuss genre hybridity in fairy-tale film. The mixing of fairy tales with other genres relies on the fragmentation of fairy tales to supply the fairy-tale components of generically complex fairy-tale film (Bacchilega and Rieder 25–27). Bacchilega and Rieder refer to this gesturing to fairy tale as a genre, rather than to specific fairy tales, as invoking "the aura of the fairy tale" (40). Genre mixing is common in the texts studied by all of these scholars, as well as in the texts under study here. Generalizing fairy tales to their motifs and fragmenting elements of specific tales shifts focus from the level of plot to that of genre. I agree with both Jorgensen and Zolkover that more is in play in these texts than just the traditional fairy tale, but add that the "commentary [and] play" identified by Zolkover (41) and the "schizophrenic instrumentalization of fairy-tale matter" identified by Jorgensen (218) are indeed part of fairy-tale tradition despite their association with postmodernism.

Multiplicity is an important factor in the study of postmodern fairy tales;[5] however, in postmodern criticism and theory, *pastiche* has typically been employed as part of a pair of terms, *parody* and *pastiche*, in which it is not the privileged term. In "Hybridity, Hybridization," Lee Haring identifies *pastiche* as one of the "pejorative terms" used to "denigrate" hybrid folktales and fairy tales (470). Haring's discussion of hybridity centers on linguistics and narrative forms of hybridization rather than a blending of tale-types within a singular genre. Francisco Vaz da Silva refers to this latter form as "inter-plot hybridity" in "Hybridity" (188). The location of *pastiche* as a negative term here reflects the conception of *pastiche* as the nonprivileged term in the parody-pastiche binary. As a companion term to *parody*, *pastiche* refers to the imitation of a work or style which can include the intertextual use of multiple sources but does not have to. A typical distinction between *pastiche* and *parody*, put forth by Frederic Jameson in "Postmodernism and Consumer Society," is that pastiche is celebratory or at least neutral toward its source text(s) and parody is mocking. Jameson defines pastiche as "the imitation of a peculiar or unique style, the wearing of a stylistic mask, speech in a dead language: but it is a neutral practice of such mimicry, without parody's ulterior motive, without the satirical impulse, without laughter, without that still latent feeling that there exists something *normal* compared with which what is being imitated is rather comic. Pastiche is blank parody, parody that has lost its sense of humor" (Jameson 5).

Despite Jameson's claim that pastiche is "one of the most significant features or practices in postmodernism," it has not received the theoretical attention generated by its companion strategy of parody (4). Rather the impulse has been to defend postmodern works as critical, substantive, and complex; posit parody as a critical mode; and argue that maligned postmodern texts are not simply pastiche.[6] Linda Hutcheon, like many critics, takes issue with Jameson's depiction of parody as mocking, defining it rather as "repetition with critical distance that allows ironic signaling of difference at the very heart of similarity. . . . parody paradoxically enacts both change and cultural continuity" (*A Poetics of Postmodernism* 26). Hutcheon draws attention to the limits of Jameson's definition of parody, which only allows for "ridiculing imitation," but she does not go on to interrogate his definition of pastiche, focusing her attention here and in her later works on expanding understandings of parody as a critical mode (*A Poetics of Postmodernism* 26). Hutcheon does argue that "pastiche operates more by similarity and correspondence" and parody by difference, which follows Jameson's initial distinction between the two terms (*A Theory of Parody* 38).

Merja Makinen's excellent discussion of fairy tales and postmodernism in "Theorizing Fairy-Tale Fiction, Reading Jeanette Winterson" highlights the problems with the use of *parody* and *pastiche* as binary terms in which one is a critical mode and the other is not, and she connects the pairing to similar terminology in fairy-tale studies. Makinen aligns Jameson's *parody/pastiche* pairing with Jack Zipes's pairing of *revision/duplication* in *Fairy Tale as Myth/ Myth as Fairy Tale*. For Zipes, *revision* transforms the traditional tale and "alters" its traditional values, patterns, and images, and *duplication* reproduces and reinforces the ideology, patterns, and images of the traditional tale, creating a "look-alike" (9). *Duplication* here is like Jameson's *pastiche*, imitation without critique. Bacchilega complicates Zipes's pairing in *Postmodern Fairy Tales: Gender and Narrative Strategies* by arguing that retellings can both "transform" and "reproduce" the stories that they tell (10). She does not suggest that the two strategies of retelling are mutually exclusive, but rather that postmodern retellings do both simultaneously by reflecting, refracting, and framing their source tales (Bacchilega, *Postmodern Fairy Tales* 10). As recognized by Haring in general, pastiche here is the less desired term, and texts labeled as "pastiche" are perceived to lack critical engagement with their sources in order to reflect style.

Multiplicity has always been a part of the fairy-tale tradition, and the work of scholars like Elizabeth Wanning Harries has been instrumental in demonstrating the various narrative techniques employed in creating the intertextual web that is the fairy-tale genre. In *Twice Upon a Time: Women Writers and the History of the Fairy Tale*, Harries addresses Zipes's pairing by arguing that revision has always been a part of fairy-tale tradition and that "we need to develop a new word for procedures in retellings that go beyond simple revision" (15). Zipes, too, argues in *Fairy Tale as Myth/ Myth as Fairy Tale* that the tradition of the fairy tale is one of revision *and* duplication, and that the history of the genre must take into account this long-standing practice of repetition and repurposing. Harries argues that the distinction should not be what a twentieth- or twenty-first-century tale does to a traditional tale but the narrative strategy employed in the revision. Specifically, she offers the terms *compact* for traditional tales that employ "carefully constructed simplicity" and *complex* to describe old and new tales that are decidedly intertextual and "work to reveal the stories behind other stories" as alternatives (Harries 17). Harries is careful not to align *complex* tales with the postmodern *parody* or *revision* because she demonstrates that the narrative strategies of the complex tales predate the postmodern period. However, her division based on narrative strategies in which complex tales traffic in difference and intertextuality and compact tales are categorized by stylistic mimicry recalls the earlier pairings. Harries and Zipes, among others, insist that strategies such as revision and duplication are not postmodern techniques but are an essential part of the fairy-tale tradition. Makinen points out that retelling and imitation have always been a part of fairy-tale tradition, so that "postmodern fiction cannot really be said to rewrite the fairy tale as a previous, given, static text to be commented upon through parody. All it can do is re-engage contemporaneously with an already multilayered polyphony, adding a further critical layer to the plurality" (151).

Jameson's formulation of pastiche is one that is absent of critical attention to the source texts and instead invokes a sense of nostalgia through its imitation of style. Jameson uses the example of *Star Wars* as a pastiche of Buck Rogers–style television from the 1930s to the 1950s. He argues that parody of television serials in that style would be pointless, as "they are long extinct," but that *Star Wars*' imitation of the style is not pointless (8). Rather, it "satisfies a deep . . . longing to experience them again . . . to return to that older period and to live its strange old aesthetic artefacts through once again" (8). *Star Wars* as pastiche "reinvent[s] the feel and shape of characteristic art objects of an older period" (8). A more fitting example of the genre at hand would be *The Princess Bride*, the 1973 postmodern novel by William Goldman and its 1987 film adaption, also written by Goldman. The novel and film are works of fantasy, romance, and adventure, and have been referred to as fairy tale in promotional material and reviews. The book is more metafictionally complex, with a self-reflexive frame about its creation and the process of a fictionalized Goldman adapting a "real" book from his childhood. The interplay of truth and fiction raises questions about reality, memory, experience, and fiction that are on par with a great many postmodern works. The embedded story is likewise metafictional, drawing on a range of genre conventions with a jovial self-awareness. The film in particular is a nostalgic imitation of style that invokes popular romance, adventure, and fairy-tale conventions to create the particular feel of Errol Flynn–era swashbuckling films.

As pastiche, *The Princess Bride* reinvents the aesthetic of the Golden Age Hollywood film for a late-twentieth-century audience. But it also subtly critiques the conventions and aspects of that era that do not age well. Many of the jokes work because they call attention to the anachronism of a particular convention. For example, when faced with marriage to Prince Humperdinck (the villain), Princess Buttercup says that she would rather die than marry him (now that she knows her true love Westley is alive). His response, "please consider me an alternative to suicide," is funny because it calls attention to the ridiculous true-love-or-death dichotomy for women in the romance genre that is being invoked. These kinds of jokes proliferate in the film and book, and they critique the genre norms while maintaining a reverent respect for the genre. In doing so, the film and book do not just imitate the older styles; they update them to make them workable for a differently valued audience. They say, look, see, you can have a "classic" romance adventure without duplicating the unsavory bits.

While I, like Jorgensen and Zolkover, come to *pastiche* from its use in describing a text with multiple sources that draws from fragments rather than plots, I find that Jameson's formulation of pastiche as nostalgia is helpful in understanding the popularity of the fairy-tale genre and the centuries-old tradition of retelling tales. Jessica Tiffin, in *Marvelous Geometry: Narrative and Metafiction in Modern Fairy Tale*, recognizes that "the structures of fairy tale operate nostalgically" (4). Fairy-tale texts that use the trappings of fairy tales while updating ideological content employ a fairy-tale aesthetic that is familiar and comforting, and it satisfies for the audience a deep longing to experience fairy tales again even as we recognize the problems of stories in which a sleeping princess has no say over what happens to her body. While there are multiple ways I could parse the technique of bringing discordant tales together in a new text, *mash up* being a phrase commonly used outside of literary academia, *pastiche* brings together both the multiplicity of these new texts and the importance of maintaining a fairy-tale aesthetic even as the texts radically rework and at times reject their source tales. In the case of *Once Upon a Time*, pastiche as nostalgia is employed directly in the creation of the anachronistic yet timeless 1980s Storybrooke.

My use of *pastiche* to describe the texts in part 1 of this book is primarily based in the texts' use of multiple fairy-tale sources to construct the new text; however, I also draw on the celebratory definition of the term, recognizing that both definitions are at play in my analysis. Rather than employ *mash up* or other terms circulating in popular culture discourse, or create a new term, I find that in its dual definition, *pastiche* captures the multiplicity with which fairy tales are engaged at a genre level in the texts under study here. Jameson's connection of pastiche with nostalgia is particularly relevant to my discussion of *Once Upon a Time*, which evokes both familiarity and timelessness in its reproduction of a fairy-tale landscape and the static Storybrooke. But I diverge from the postmodern arguments that categorize pastiche as "blank parody" or "similarity and correspondence" without critical impetus, and instead align myself with critics like Angela McRobbie, who has argued in "Postmodernism and Popular Culture" that pastiche can be a "vibrant critique" that reflects the "wider conditions of present 'reality'" (21, 14). Like Makinen, I find the deployment of binary terms in the analysis of postmodern texts to be problematic. While categorization is certainly helpful in analysis, either/or pairings are inadequate to address the complicated and diverse ways in which postmodern and contemporary texts utilizing intertextuality engage their sources. In *Constructing Postmodernism* Brian McHale "proposes multiple, overlapping and intersecting inventories and multiple corpora; not *a* construction of postmodernism, but a plurality of constructions; constructions that, while not necessarily mutually contradictory, are not fully integrated, or perhaps integrable, either" (3). As Makinen, McHale, and others have pointed out, postmodernism is neither monolithic nor stable, and affixing static terms to texts that work to unsettle established narratives and recognize multiplicity would seem to go counter to the projects of postmodernism.

I would also argue that this is true of fairy-tale retellings, including those Zipes would argue are duplication. Like Bacchilega, I think that contemporary fairy-tale texts can both "transform" and "reproduce" their sources. I would not argue, for example, that Disney's live-action production of its animated *Cinderella* in 2015 is particularly complex. The film reproduces the animated classic's plot, iconography, and choreography. A shot-by-shot comparison of the two films reveals a great deal of similarity. But I would also not argue that this is a duplication of the 1950 film. Small deviations in the script, the scenery, the acting, and so on tell a slightly different tale, and the film reflects both its animated source and the plethora of Cinderellas produced between the two films. Cate Blanchett's performance as the stepmother recalls Angelica Houston's performance in *Ever After* in key moments through inflection and pacing, and whether intentional or not, the intertextual referencing extends motivation to Lady Tremaine in a way the animated film never did. The overall effect of the intertextual referencing is a subtle questioning of the absolute evilness of the stepmother. So while the film duplicates its 1950 source, it also includes revision with critical distance that challenges some of the assumptions in the source and reflects changing sociohistorical context.

I argue further that pastiche is a critical mode, much as parody is, and that by imitating style and quoting fragments, pastiche works on the level of genre and convention rather than the level of a specific text. Pastiche is both celebratory and critical, invoking both similarity and difference. The invocation of the fairy tale while critiquing it results in multivocality within the pastiche, where multiple discourses work with and against each other within the text. In "Feminist Fairy-Tale Scholarship," Donald Haase has described this multivocality as "simultaneously rejecting and embracing the fairy tale" (30). While plots may be retold, the interplay of fragments across narrative borders allows the pastiche to play with these elements in different ways, resignifying fragments in ways not possible in a single-source retelling. No story retold in conjunction with other tales can precisely duplicate its source. The introduction of multiple tales necessarily changes the stories being retold to logically account for the mash up of disparate material. The imitation of genre style in this context then houses elements not typically associated with traditional fairy tales while validating them *as* fairy tale. In texts that blur genres, this multivocality is also seen in how the multiple genres destabilize each other. The alteration to narrative genre conventions of fairy tales—the opening and closing formulas, external third-person narration, linear and sequential plot sequencing—can facilitate these plot-level ideological and cultural critiques. Rather than revising a specific tale with new features for a different ideological context, pastiche invokes similarity to authorize ideological and genre changes, demonstrating both the value of its sources (pastiche's celebratory function) and the need to transform them for different sociohistorical contexts (pastiche's critical function). Fairy-tale pastiche can celebrate its sources while critiquing their outdated ideology and transforming them into something new. Like parody, then, pastiche is also metafictional as it includes within itself commentary on its own place in a narrative tradition.

Metafictional Critique

The majority of texts in this project are metafictional, in that they are fiction about fiction and engage fictional texts as part of the plot. In the cases of *Once Upon a Time* and the *Indexing* novels, the characters are aware of their own fictionality; they know they are "living" stories. In *Secret Garden* and the short fiction by Kelly Link, some of the characters recognize that their lives are governed by fairy-tale scripts and actively engage those patterns.

These texts employ a variety of metafictional narrative strategies, strategies that draw attention to the constructedness of the text and remind readers that they are reading a work of fiction. Birgit Neumann and Ansgar Nünning ("Metanarration and Metafiction") define *metafiction* as the "capacity of fiction to reflect on its own status as fiction and thus [refer] to all self-reflexive utterances which thematize the fictionality (in the sense of imaginary reference and/or constructedness) of narrative" in *the living handbook of narratology*, a wiki maintained by narratologists (sec. 2). In *Narcissistic Narrative: The Metafictional Paradox*, Linda Hutcheon defines metafiction as "fiction about fiction—that is, fiction that includes within itself a commentary on its own narrative and/or linguistic identity" (1). Hutcheon divides contemporary metafiction into diegetically and linguistically self-conscious texts, and further divides those categories into "overt"—those that call attention to their own construction—and "covert"— those that refer to or discuss other texts within the text (*Narcissistic Narrative* 23).

Tiffin makes the point that the multiplicity and plurality of fairy tales as a genre results in a metafictional element to all fairy tales. Genre fictions, fairy tale included, "rely on their interaction with their generic traditions for the construction of meaning in any individual text. . . . narrative structure becomes a powerful tradition, a set of codes which is continually invoked, rediscovered, and recreated with the telling of every new version, and which thus relies on a self-consciousness about textuality which moves the narrative into the realm of the postmodern technique of metafiction" (3). Tiffin argues that for the fairy tale specifically, "self-consciousness of metafictional play rests on the foundation of a generic structure which is especially prone to self-conscious situation of its own texts within a highly structured tradition, even before contemporary writers begin their postmodern deconstructions" (3). Like Harries, Tiffin recognizes that many of the postmodern elements of contemporary fairy tales are part of a fairy-tale tradition that predates the twentieth century. The genre invites self-reflexivity through its multiplicity, variation, and awareness of tradition. Tiffin argues that "any fairy tale—classic or modern—positions itself intertextually within a complete discourse of fairy tale as cultural artifact, so that any tale becomes a necessary dialogue between its own specific instance, and the (unreal) textual expectations of fairy tales in general" (23).

A major intervention into the horizon of expectations in many retold fairy tales is that of the happily-ever-after ending, noted by Joosen under the category of "optimism" (14). The texts under study here are no exception, and most disrupt expectations of happily ever after through their serial structures. Serialization, whether in novels or on television, allows those who retell fairy tales to play with the genre's structure, and in doing so, subvert the ideological norms embedded in the happily-ever-after ending of a heterosexual marriage and rise in social class typical of the most popular fairy tales today. *Long-arc* and *short-arc* are terms that differentiate between plot arcs that continue over multiple episodes (long-arc serials) and those that are episode specific (short-arc series). In television serials, which have evolved from radio and print forms, and soap operas specifically, narratives are open-ended without definitive closure, and even when a plot closes, it usually reopens in some way. Episodes and seasons end with cliffhangers so that significant breaks in the broadcast of the show are marked by the climax of a plotline rather than its resolution, and multiple narratives run concurrently and interchangeably.

Jason Mittell, in *Complex TV: The Poetics of Contemporary Television Storytelling*, distinguishes between melodrama and other long-arc serials by focusing on melodrama's emphasis on relationships over plot. Mittell is interested in long-arc serials that emphasize plot and feature what he terms *narrative complexity*. Narrative complexity is a combination of series and serial structures, and Mittell defines it as the redefinition of "episodic forms under the influence of serial narration" (18). This combination allows for narrative complexity not possible in a traditional format in which the equilibrium of the storyworld must be reasserted with each episode so that every episode begins in the same place. The short-arc plotlines that span a single episode can be embedded within television serials that utilize soap-opera narrative structure. *Buffy the Vampire Slayer* is a prime example of this successful strategy of mixing both serial and series narrative structures, and its formula of a season-long plot arc featuring a Big Bad Villain encompassing episode-specific plots and minor villains is a very popular formula today. Mittell argues that this narrative complexity avoids episodic plot closure without employing the melodrama of soap operas (32). While he does not argue that soap operas lack narrative complexity, Mittell believes that soap operas' emphasis on relationships over plot makes them different from shows like *Buffy the Vampire Slayer*.

The fairy-tale expectation of a happily-ever-after ending, which usually means a royal wedding and accompanying rise in social and material status for the hero, cannot happen in serialization. Weddings are not endings on soap operas, and they are no promise of happiness. Jill Terry Rudy, in "Broadcast (Radio and Television)," notes that "there is a great deal of suspense associated with broadcast fairy-tale endings because fairy tale announces its metapoetics over distances of time and space and because so much is already known about characters and plots. This suspense involves not only how characters and situations may arrive at a happy ending but also the possibility that, this time, this story may end unhappily (as historically many tales do)" (372). Serialization creates an opportunity to both affirm and subvert the expected ending through delaying the end across episodes and seasons on the small screen and chapters and books in a novel series. In "Making 'Gay' and 'Lesbian' into Household Words: How Serial Form Works in Armistead Maupin's *Tales of the City*," Robyn R. Warhol explains that the "*serial form defies the dominant 'marriage plot' governing so much of popular fiction*. Due to its structurally mandated impulse to defer ending definitely, serialized domestic fiction has always tended to undermine the heterocentric marriage plot by unraveling instances of closure that turn out to be only provisional and temporary" (382). She emphasizes the *form* of serialized novels as able to "subvert dominant ideologies" embedded in texts, and she argues that serialization undermines the heteronormative sexuality explicitly tied to marriage as a mark of narrative closure (Warhol 383). Even when a series ends with a fairy-tale wedding, the deferral of that ending and the complication of the temporary endings that close episodes result in a focal shift away from the optimistic end.

For fairy-tale pastiche, this intertextual engagement with genre is direct because the combining of fragments from different sources reflects genre expectations *and* re-creates genre expectations by what is included and what is left out. In its dual celebratory and critical functions, pastiche functions metafictionally much as parody does. In *A Theory of Parody: The Teachings of Twentieth-Century Art Forms*, Hutcheon argues that parody is a type of metafiction that is "imitation characterized by ironic inversion, not always at the expense of the parodied text," and "repetition with critical distance, which marks difference rather than similarity" (6); thus parody is not mocking a text but imitating a text with ironic interventions. Pastiche, too, is "repetition with critical distance" but foregrounds similarity over difference as a way of authorizing its critical and transformative properties. The interventions in genre do not reject tradition so much as change it. Margaret Rose, in *Parody//meta-fiction: An Analysis of Parody as a Critical Mirror to the Writing and Reception of Fiction*, argues that parody is "the meta-fictional 'mirror' to the process of composing and receiving literary texts" (59). Metafictional parody raises questions about the production and reception of literature. Rose explains that parody requires that the parodist be "seen in the dual role of reader [of the parodied text] and writer [of the 'new' text]" (69), and the text be read as both itself and as a criticism, encompassing two positions at once. She also argues that parody as metafiction shows *what* is being represented as well as *how* it is being represented (Rose 90). Pastiche, too, depends on this duality of function. While neither Rose nor Hutcheon makes the same claims for pastiche, I would argue that metafictional pastiche functions in similar ways, and that the texts in this study employ parody as part of their metafictional repertoire.

Of Maps and Mapping

My analysis is divided into two sections, reflecting the two approaches to the geographic metaphor. Part 1 explores the concept of a shared narrative space created by the collapsing of narrative boundaries; this is the pastiche technique exhibited in text by different stories occurring in the same place. The shared storyworld reflects a reconfiguration of how we think about genre and individual stories as part of a larger landscape and as interconnected. The geographic metaphor of landscapes and maps is a figurative representation of the epistemological shift born of an increasingly interconnected world. Part 2 explores the concept of fiction, specifically fairy tales, as relevant to one's lived experience. These self-reflexive texts directly engage fairy-tale narratives as models for behavior and elucidate problems with this approach while validating the desire for the fairy tale as a personal map. Both sets of texts are metafictional, but metafictionality is the dominant mode in part 2. Serialization is an additional thread that runs throughout the chapters, with the first three chapters specifically focusing on serial texts in print and on television. Chapter 4 instead examines three short stories that resist the conventional endings in fairy-tale and literary fiction.

The texts selected are not unified by form or location, but by technique. *Once Upon a Time* (seven seasons) and *Secret Garden* (one season) are both television shows, and as such are produced in a different context than the print texts, with a mélange of creative contributors from writers and showrunners to directors and actors so that authorship on these shows is a constantly revolving collaboration that shifts between episodes and seasons. Marissa Meyer's *The Lunar Chronicles* series and Seanan McGuire's *Indexing* novels are both print series with single authors, but the structures of the novels and the context of their publication differ. *The Lunar Chronicles* contains four linked novels published traditionally, whereas *Indexing* is a two-novel series originally published electronically in serial form, one chapter at a time. Kelly Link's short stories offer a counterpoint to the longer fairy-tale novels. Like much of Link's short fiction, her work defies genre categorization and blends the fantastic with literary experimentation.

With the exception of *Secret Garden*, these are American texts, published and released in the United States by American creators. While they do have international appeal, they primarily engage fairy tales well-known in the United States and part of the European fairy-tale tradition that forms the American fairy-tale canon. *Secret Garden* is a Korean drama that draws upon the same Western tales as the other texts. It has been available to American audiences through streaming services like Netflix and Viki (formerly DramaFever) and is popular in South Korea, the United States, and internationally. I primarily examine American texts but do not believe that this metafictional mapping of fairy tales is solely an American phenomenon.

Introduction • 21

As my inclusion of *Secret Garden* demonstrates, contemporary fairy tales are not geographically restricted texts in our globalized and digitally connected world. They travel and migrate, as Warner and Bacchilega demonstrate in their respective works.

Part I: Mapping Fairy Tales

Chapter 1, "Genre and Geography: ABC's *Once Upon a Time* and the Mapping of a Fairy-Tale Land," establishes the mapping metaphor that frames this book and analyzes the pastiche technique prevalent in many contemporary fairy-tale series, both book and television, where fairy-tale characters inhabit the same fairy-tale realm and appear in each other's stories. The primary text discussed is ABC's television show *Once Upon a Time*, which is particularly interesting because of the extent to which villains and heroes in one tale act as different characters in others. This chapter argues that because these stories inhabit the same place, characters are able to fulfill multiple functions simultaneously, enabling the show to challenge the authoritative positioning of its sources. The show uses a variety of destabilizing narrative and visual techniques to disrupt traditional fairy-tale patterns as a means of recreating fairy tales for a post-Disney audience.

Chapter 2, "Genres Overlaid: Serialization and Hybridity in Marissa Meyer's *The Lunar Chronicles* and Seanan McGuire's *Indexing*," examines the pastiche technique discussed in chapter 1 as it plays out in serialized novels. There is a key difference between how the shared landscape functions in *Once Upon a Time* and how it functions in many novel series. In series such as those by Marissa Meyer and Seanan McGuire, the fairy tales are linked, so that each novel or chapter takes a separate fairy tale as its controlling structure even while other tales' characters appear as minor characters in the primary plot. In these series, genres are mixed: fairy tale and science fiction in Meyer's *The Lunar Chronicles* and fairy tale and crime drama in McGuire's *Indexing* series. This chapter argues that the series format works differently in novels than on television, and that the separation of the fairy tales created by the novels' structural boundaries reaffirms the traditional tales while the genre- and tale-blending content simultaneously challenges the classic fairy-tale form.

Part II: Fairy-Tale Maps

Chapter 3, "Asking for Directions: Metafiction and Metaphor in the Korean Drama *Secret Garden*," examines the use of Western fairy tales in the Korean television drama *Secret Garden*, which uses Hans Christian Andersen's fairy tale "The Little Mermaid." This chapter explores how the two main characters use the fairy tale to both navigate and circumvent their own situation, to communicate desire, and to bridge the gap between their different places in the world. The fairy tale serves as an ineffectual map until it is rewritten and the characters devise for themselves a different ending to the story. This chapter argues that the series reflects both the appeal of fairy tales as a map for lived experience and their limitations in providing actual guidance. The chapter explores the cross-cultural translation of Western tales, which depends on the audience's familiarity with the tale to allow them to see both its significance in the series and the ways in which it is transformed by the series.

Chapter 4, "Following Footsteps: Redrafting Fairy-Tale Maps in Kelly Link's Short Fiction," looks at three of Kelly Link's fairy tales that feature feet, shoes, and traveling as dominant symbols. "Travels with the Snow Queen," "Shoe and Marriage," and "The Girl Detective" were published in Link's short-story collection, *Stranger Things Happen*. This chapter examines how Link presents fairy tales and symbols of fairy tales as out-of-date instructions for lived experiences. Her characters turn to fairy-tale knowledge to solve problems and are led astray by that strategy. The nontraditional, destabilizing narrative techniques that characterize Link's work (such as lack of endings, nonlinear structure, and collage-style scenes) disorient readers and break fairy-tale narrative patterns, demonstrating in form what characters learn in theme: "fairy tales aren't easy on the feet" (Link, "Travels with the Snow Queen" 100).

The texts in both sections engage fairy tales with reverence, and I do not think it is unreasonable to say with love. At no point are fairy tales ridiculed in these texts. Mild fun may be poked, but the assumption that fairy tales are an important and worthwhile part of one's life is not questioned. The texts suggest shifts in how fairy tales can be viewed, but their vibrancy and vitality are applauded. For this reason, among the others outlined in this introduction, the concept of nostalgia and pastiche resonates with me for this project. These are not parodic critiques of fairy tales that challenge their value and place in our postmodern world. These are a reclaiming of fairy tales, another step in the long journey of a mightily adaptable genre. In remaking the fairy-tale genre for twenty-first-century audiences, these texts do not so much chart unexplored territory as they approach existing fairy-tale space from new directions, remapping the genre as our collective use of fairy tales changes.

I

Mapping Fairy Tales

1

Genre and Geography

ABC's *Once Upon a Time* and the Mapping of a Fairy-Tale Land

A COMMON WAY OF rewriting fairy tales for modern audiences is to mix up the stories: invert fairy-tale tropes, recast beloved characters, fill in backstory, imagine after happily ever after, blend genres, or literally mix up the tales. This literal mixing of stories results in a fairy-tale pastiche, wherein fairy-tale characters from different tales inhabit the same physical location and appear in each other's stories. Translating the genre of fairy tales into a geographic location where characters from a variety of different fairy tales mingle and intervene in each other's stories is not a new narrative trick for retellers. Several retellings have used this pastiche technique to keep contemporary audiences intrigued with traditional tales; for example, Stephen Sondheim's musical and Disney film *Into the Woods* (1986, 2014), NBC's miniseries *The 10th Kingdom* (2000), DreamWorks' *Shrek* film (2001) and its sequels, Bill Willingham's graphic novel series *Fables* (2002–15), Robert Coover's novel *Stepmother* (2004), and Michael Buckley's children's novel series *The Sisters Grimm* (2005–12), among others, all use this technique. ABC's *Once Upon a Time* (2011–18) is a recent, popular retelling that takes this approach. *Once Upon a Time* premiered as the highest rated nonsports show in its first season with almost thirteen million viewers, and the first few seasons consistently maintained high ratings before waning in the later seasons ("ABC's 'Once Upon a Time' Opens as the Season's #1 New Drama."). It was ABC's highest rated show in three years ("ABC's 'Once Upon a Time' Opens as the Season's #1 New Drama"). It was also met with positive reviews overall, though as the plots became more intricate in later seasons, critical reviews became more common (MetaCritic).

Geographic translations of fairy tales as a genre, such as *Once Upon a Time*, wherein the ambiguous settings of fairy tales become a fairy-tale world, typically mix tales from a variety of traditions, drawing on folklore from different (though primarily European) countries by multiple editors and authors. The Grimms' Märchen, however, have been the primary source for many of these retellings for the obvious reason of their versions being so well-known. *Once Upon a Time* is unique in that ABC's corporate ownership by Disney allows the writers of the show access to the Disney tradition to populate its Storybrooke without issues of copyright infringement.

Most of these retellings blur narrative boundaries to create a vast location in which multiple tales occur simultaneously, but the landscape is still that of the source tales—a dark forest or kingdom. However, *Once Upon a Time*'s Storybrooke, *Fables*' Fabletown, and *The Sisters Grimm*'s Ferryport Landing are isolated communities in Maine (*Once Upon a Time*) and New York (*Fables* and *Sisters Grimm*), separated from the "real world" but firmly placed in it. The communities are inhabited by fairy-tale characters who have been exiled from their fairy-tale worlds and are forced to integrate into American culture, with varying degrees of success. The characters' magic and timelessness necessitates separation from humans, but they are still forced to adapt to the outside world that threatens their very existence. These characters often struggle to sustain their fairy-tale culture in the face of a technologically advanced United States that does not need, and does not want, magic. In *Once Upon a Time*, the struggle between good and evil is often characterized in early seasons as between protecting (and restoring) the fairy-tale land and its people versus destroying it for vengeance and power. Using *Once Upon a Time* as a case study, this chapter will examine (1) the technique of translating genre into geography, including the narrative restructuring enabled by collapsing distinct fairy tales into a single world, and (2) how this metaphor of genre as physical location is a useful way of thinking about stories and the process of reinventing tales for new times and places.

Once Upon a Time has two main locations, Storybrooke, Maine, and the Enchanted Forest. Storybrooke is a small, quaint town stuck in 1983. That year, a curse worked by Regina Mills, the Evil Queen from "Snow White," and built by Rumplestiltskin swept up most of the fairy-tale characters living in the Enchanted Forest and transported them to our world, a land without magic. Separated from our world, but firmly located in it, Storybrooke is also without popular culture—1983 without MTV, Billy Idol, or The Go-Gos, truly "some place horrible," as described by Rumplestiltskin and Regina (1.1). The curse strips the fairy-tale folk of their magic, memories, and identities and replaces them with ordinary, stagnant, small-town lives. Time does not move during the curse, and it is not until the original curse begins to break that characters are able to progress, develop, and make their own choices.

The Storybrooke setting invokes nostalgia for a simpler time, the 1980s that would presumably reflect the childhood of the show's target adult audience. Demonstrating Frederic Jameson's notion of pastiche as nostalgia in "Postmodernism and Consumer Society," the Storybrooke setting primes adult audiences to associate the show and its content with their childhood. It is a distinctly white, middle-class American childhood, but one that is presented as normative throughout television's history. The association with a nostalgic Storybrooke, then, encourages audiences to make the same connection to fairy tales. Adult audiences will have encountered a variety of fairy-tale texts that challenge and retell the fairy tales of their childhoods, dominated in the United States by Disney animated films. In a promotional interview, cocreator Adam Horowitz stated that his and Edward Kitsis's interest in fairy tales comes from the genre's foundational impact on their storytelling: "The seed of it [*Once Upon a Time*] was that we were trying to figure out what it is about storytelling that we really love, and what we love is the mystery and excitement of exploring lots of different worlds. Fairy tales clicked with us because they were so much in the DNA of what made us storytellers, to begin with" (qtd. in Radish). But Horowitz also links the show's core tale specifically to his childhood experience of Disney fairy-tale film: "Snow White is ground zero for fairy tales. It was the first movie I saw, as a kid, and I remember being terrified, seeing the Evil Queen" (qtd. in Radish). Within the context of the nostalgic 1980s Storybrooke, audiences can more easily connect the fairy tales on the show to the "simpler" children's fairy tales of their past. Thus a specific mode of fairy tales, the one Elizabeth Wanning Harries refers to as "compact" in *Twice Upon a Time: Women Writers and the History of the Fairy Tale*, is invoked both stylistically on the show through repetition of fairy-tale patterns and by association with the nostalgic Storybrooke (17).

For the child audience of ABC's family show, Storybrooke is different enough from the reality of the show's airdates to be distinctly "the past" without recalling specific memories. The child protagonist of the show, Henry Mills, for example, is able to wander around town and the surrounding woods without adult supervision, and no one appears to have any concerns about crime or safety, experiences that the show's child audience likely cannot relate to. Though not invoking personal or cultural memory, the show still functions nostalgically for children by touting a simpler time before they were born. This connection also primes children to associate the fairy tales in the show with "simpler," older versions of fairy tales that may not reflect a twenty-first-century child's experience of fairy tales from parodies like the *Shrek* series or the *Hoodwinked!* films. In "Fairy Tales and Fairy Folk: Evolving Expectations of Contemporary Fairy Tales," Linda J. Lee has pointed out that because of the popularity of fairy-tale parodies at the turn of the twenty-first century, "American society is, perhaps, raising a generation of children whose experience with fairy tales is dependent upon fractured plots, inverted quests, and fuzzy boundaries between generic categories." Children can also be exposed to fairy-tale fragments before their sources tales. In explaining their choice of "Snow White" as the main tale for the series, Horowitz not only refers to his own experience, as cited above, but to that of his children:

> I've got twin daughters, who are 2½ years old, and I don't even remember showing them anything, but they know Snow White. It's amazing. When I was watching dailies for the pilot, they would see the stuff of Ginny in the coffin and start going, "Snow White is sleeping!" and I was like, "How do you know who she is already?" I think it's just something in our DNA. Because of that, everybody loves the character and loves that

story so much that it's going to continually be told, in new and different ways. (qtd. in Radish)

Children's first experiences with fairy tales could very well be with parodies rather than the source tales on which they are based, making the source tales referenced in *Once Upon a Time* less familiar than their contemporary incarnations.

The anachronistic Storybrooke serves an important narrative function through its nostalgic context that provides a frame of reference for how the genre of fairy tales is meant to be understood by the show's audience. For *Once Upon a Time* to "find things about [fairy tales] that we haven't explored before," as Horowitz claims it does, it must first establish an understanding of the genre to react against (qtd. in Keily). Invoking Disney, which the show does constantly, is one way to establish a fairy-tale tradition, but the repetition of stylistic features of classic tales within the context of a nostalgic past provides audiences with an ideal of fairy tales as a genre that is simple, straightforward, and quaint—old-fashioned. This is not a derisive implication, as nostalgia clearly implies fondness, and the show celebrates fairy tales as an important part of culture, but it does play into the myth of fairy tales as a simple genre, which does not reflect the reality of the complex genre.

The first episode of *Once Upon a Time* begins with a series of black screens and typed exposition: "There was an enchanted forest filled with all the classic characters we know. Or think we know. One day they found themselves trapped in a place where all their happy endings were stolen. Our world. This is how it happened . . ." (1.1). What makes "our world" horrible is the lack of happy endings, but also, I would add, the lack of magic and the loss of the fairy-tale narratives. Everything that makes the fairy-tale characters fairy tales is stripped away and replaced with the mundane troubles of a fairly stable small town stuck in the 1980s. The curse has been in place for twenty-eight years when the series begins, and time does not pass in Storybrooke, so that the characters may live, but they do not move forward (at least until Emma Swan, the curse-breaker, arrives).[1] The loss of magic, and with it, the loss of *wonder* and being part of a story greater than oneself, is what is horrible.

Genre and Geography • 31

There is no magic in Storybrooke until the curse is broken, thus our mundane world (which is also referred to as the Land Without Magic) is contrasted with the magical Enchanted Forest. Claudia Schwabe, in "Getting Real with Fairy Tales: Magic Realism in *Grimm* and *Once Upon a Time*," has commented on the division of magic by location in *Once Upon a Time*, positing it as a form of magical realism. Schwabe classifies *Once Upon a Time* as a "Reality Fairy Tale," a tale in which "magic crosses over into the real world," forming an overlapping "third reality" located in a specific place that blends the fantastic with the mundane (297). In this space, "real magic exists in today's world, which fuses the magical with the everyday—a literal magic realism" (295). For Schwabe, this magical realism is a vital part of the show's intervention into and challenging of its source tales. Referring to *Once Upon a Time* and *Grimm*, she argues, "Such stories suggest that the real world is nuanced with multiple layers of detail and meaning and with connections that are sometimes difficult to uncover given our limited perception" (299). Schwabe points out that the show's emphasis on villain motivation—showing backstory that depicts the villains before they were bad—demonstrates "nuance" along the good/evil divide, and she locates this nuance as possible because of the way magic and reality intersect on the show. She argues that "magic realist stories such as *Once Upon a Time* and *Grimm* indicate that the real world does not follow a black-and-white pattern reminiscent of the interior design in Regina's office. They rather urge the viewer to never stop questioning what might lie hidden beneath the façade of a certain object, person, or place" (314). The setting and initial world-building directly impacts the possibilities for character development and plot revision of the source tales.

Once the curse has been broken at the beginning of season two and the fairy-tale characters regain their magic and fairy-tale memories, those characters that were not swept up by the curse awaken in the fairy-tale world to a destroyed Enchanted Forest. They band together to try and restore what they can of their once-great kingdoms and to look for survivors. The secondary plot of season two is a battle for magic and enchantment between those who seek to preserve, restore, and return to the Enchanted Forest and those who want to destroy the Enchanted Forest and portals that allow travel to and fro. The second season of *Once Upon a Time* makes this threat against enchantment explicit with the presence of two non-fairy-tale outsiders—Greg Mendel and Tamara—who are literally trying to destroy all magic in the real world, including Storybrooke and its inhabitants. While active, the curse protects Storybrooke, keeping the fairy-tale characters trapped in town and non-fairy-tale outsiders outside the town limits. Once the curse is broken and magic returns, outsiders can cross the border.

As seasons progress, the season-long plot arcs take on different conflicts grounded in specific locations. Each season, starting with season three, typically has two major plots with distinct villains marked by a midseason winter hiatus. Season one features Regina and Rumplestiltskin as the primary villains, and they remain a constant presence on the show, shifting roles at multiple points, with breaking the curse as the primary conflict. Season two's conflict is centered on the inhabitants of Storybrooke protecting the town, their lives, and magic from Greg and Tamara. A second plot that is interwoven with the first for the entirety of the season features Snow White and Emma in the Enchanted Forest protecting those who escaped the curse from villains Cora (Regina's mother) and Captain Hook (whose role also shifts in later seasons). These two plots merge at the season's end.

Seasons three through six use the midseason hiatus to separate major story lines marked by new locations. Season three sees the main cast journeying to Neverland to save Henry from the villain Peter Pan (Rumplestiltskin's father) before Zelena, the Wicked Witch of the West (Regina's sister), becomes the primary villain and Oz is introduced as a new location. This plot also introduces Robin Hood, the second reoccurring secondary character based in legend and folk ballad after Mulan. Season four is split between the Snow Queen and the Queens of Darkness (Maleficent, Ursula the Sea Witch, and Cruella de Vil) as primary villains. The first half includes Arendelle as a location and Anna and Elsa from *Frozen*, and the second takes place largely in New York and introduces the Author as a major figure and explains the creation of the storybook that houses the fairy tales on the show. This second half is directly metafictional, with characters not only aware of their fictionality but explicitly trying to rewrite their stories. This is a progression from Zelena trying to relive her past and Regina trying to recreate the world in vengeance—the evil plots become explicitly more textual and self-reflexive as more stories are introduced and the show's geography expands. Season five is shared by King Arthur and Merlin in Camelot and Hades in the Underworld. Season six features the Land of Untold Stories and Mr. Hyde and the Evil Queen as the primary villains, progressing into a series wrap-up that brings together multiple plotlines and characters and reveals the origin of the dark magic that is the catalyst for the series' conflict. This season is a soft finale, with many major characters leaving the show.

Season seven, the final season, is a soft reboot featuring an adult Henry in much the same scenario as Emma in season one, tasked by his child—whom he does not know—to break a curse that has made all of the fairy-tale characters in a Seattle neighborhood forget their fairy-tale selves. It builds on previous seasons' lore and plots, and it culminates in a unification of the disparate story realms in a single location, creating genre and geographic unity and emphasizing Regina's role, making the whole series about her redemption.

Each episode of *Once Upon a Time* contains two story lines distinguished by location, and much of the tension in the show is created by the intertwining narrative threads. The "real world" of Storybrooke has a straightforward linear plot that is easy to follow, episode to episode, and

Map of Storybrooke, from *Once Upon a Time* season 2, episode 19, "Lacey"

adheres to a season-long plot arc, but the narratives set in the fairy-tale world are fragmented from an overarching season-long plot, instead organized by characters (providing origin stories that retell well-known tales) rather than time, meaning that *these* stories are not presented in chronological order. This fragmentation—moving the audience back and forth between episodes and presenting fragments of fairy-tale history out of order—keeps the audience unstable and confused, anticipating the twist on old tales, even though the reimaginings are fairly straightforward and Disneyesque in their plots. This basic formula becomes more complicated as the show progresses, so that the secondary plots of the fairy-tale world sometimes run concurrently or include backstory for characters in the real world—the non-fairy-tale characters introduced in the subsequent seasons, the fairy-tale characters that have been living on the outside because they traveled to the real world before the curse, and fictional characters from other narrative traditions.

Trying to explain the various connections between tales and the real and fairy-tale lands becomes difficult and time-consuming because the different narratives are so thoroughly entangled, and almost every character has at least two names. For ease, I refer to the fairy-tale kingdom as the Enchanted Forest and the real world town as Storybrooke. I also refer to characters primarily by their fairy-tale names or roles. For characters that are invented for the show, I use the dominant name used for the character in the show, as in the case of Emma Swan. Emma is the daughter of Snow White and Prince Charming and destined to break Regina's curse. The exception I make is for Regina, whose role as Evil Queen is eclipsed by her Storybrooke identity through her series-long redemption arc. Season six also sees an embodied version of Regina's alter ego the Evil Queen as a separate character, making it necessary to refer to the two identities as distinct characters.

In both Storybrooke and the Enchanted Forest, the characters from distinct fairy tales interact with each other across narrative borders. The stories the characters inhabit have been recorded in a book of fairy tales that belongs to Henry, Regina's adopted son. Henry is also the biological son of Emma Swan, the prophesied curse-breaker/savior and daughter of Snow White and Prince Charming (Henry's father is Neal Cassidy/Balefire, son of Rumplestiltskin). While the tales are separated within the covers of the

The Book of Fairy Tales, from *Once Upon a Time* season 1, episode 15, "Red-Handed"

book, the scenes that depict the stories in flashback clearly show the interplay across tales, with Regina apprenticing under Maleficent or Little Red Riding Hood aiding Snow White, for example. In commenting on the blending of tales within a single episode, Cristina Bacchilega argues in *Fairy Tales Transformed? Twenty-First-Century Adaptations & the Politics of Wonder* that "this episode of *Once Upon a Time* [1.11] transports the Genie as a narrative prop into the storyworld of the 'Snow White' fairy-tale adaptation and capitalizes, in its visual and thematic tropes, on the generalized familiarity its target audience has with an *Arabian Nights* phenomenon that, over centuries, has transformed *Alf layla wa-layla* or *The Thousand and One Nights* into the globalized *visual* production of an exoticized magic that embodies both eroticism and deviousness" (149). Bacchilega's critique of the use of *Arabian Nights*, specifically Disney's version, *Aladdin*, as a "narrative prop" for the primary tale of "Snow White" could be made for a great many of the intertextual references in *Once Upon a Time*, particularly for the first season.

While I stand by my argument of pastiche, the early episodes are focused on how the variety of fairy-tale characters intersect with and intervene in the "Snow White" story. It is only as the series expands into additional seasons that other tales take the primary role for more than one episode. However,

Regina still stands at the center of this fairy-tale landscape, and most everyone connects back to her eventually. The point of Bacchilega's narrative prop is an important one because it emphasizes a narrative hierarchy that, once established in the first season, is complicated with the introduction of more villains. Once Regina begins her redemption arc, this is no longer a "Snow White" story, despite the central presence of Snow White and Prince Charming in the narrative. But the inverse is also true: elements from "Snow White" become narrative props in the other fairy tales presented, such as when Snow White takes on the role of hunter/companion in the recounting of Ruby's story of "Little Red Riding Hood"—where Ruby is both girl and wolf, and Snow White helps her on her journey through the woods. Once the curse is broken at the beginning of season two, the main characters band together to face new problems and move forward, beyond the pages of this storybook. Subsequent seasons bring new villains and new lands as the main characters travel to Neverland, Wonderland, and Oz, among other places.

In *Once Upon a Time*, characters travel between worlds, and each world is associated with a book, such as *Frankenstein*, *Alice in Wonderland*, *The Wonderful Wizard of Oz*, and *Peter Pan*, and the *Alice* books were featured in a one-season spin-off, *Once Upon a Time in Wonderland* (2013–14). Season three has the main characters leaving Storybrooke (by magic pirate ship and magic bean travel) for Neverland on a rescue mission. This book-equals-world configuration suggests that the individual fairy tales are able to merge into one world because they are stories in a collection of fairy tales—one book to rule them all. The book-world logic works out quite well and is a strong metafictional metaphor to which storytellers keep returning. While texts like *The Neverending Story* (1979 book/1984 film) make this journey explicit, the idea that reading a book is like traveling to a new world and that every book contains an adventure is fairly standard rhetoric for literacy campaigns in libraries and public schools. That the fairy tales exist concurrently in collections, and therefore in the same storyworld, is fairly logical and mirrors the intertextual understanding that tales influence each other and cross cultural and geographic divisions.

Once Upon a Time draws primarily on fairy-tale traditions for characters, motifs, and episode-specific plots, though in later seasons the source material broadens to include legends, myths, children's novels, and gothic fiction. The literary source material seems to mostly congregate around nineteenth-century fiction—*Frankenstein, Dr. Jekyll and Mr. Hyde*—or Euro-American children's fairy-tale novels—*Alice's Adventures in Wonderland, The Wonderful Wizard of Oz, Peter Pan*—but the folk narrative sources do have a broader cultural range, including *Beowulf*, Greek mythology, Native American mythology, Middle Eastern folktales, and Chinese legends. Other notable texts include the romances of King Arthur and the ballad of Robin Hood. *Once Upon a Time*'s entry into many of these texts is through the Disney versions, and the visual referencing of the Disney films saturates the show's design, but the show does not draw exclusively on the Disney corpus, nor does it use only Disney material when doing so. The show's dark portrayal of Peter Pan, for example, is far more similar to Barrie's novel than to Disney's films.

When characters on the show speak of different worlds or lands, they are referring to different storyworlds and narrative landscapes. The show does not use the words "world" and "land" haphazardly; they serve to differentiate characters from different traditions and books. For example, while Mulan is a Disney princess, she is not a fairy-tale character, and the show acknowledges this by having her clearly state that she is from a different "land" than Sleeping Beauty and Prince Phillip (2.1). She is, however, a character that originates in folk narrative, and her land is linked to fairy tales generically. Even in the first episode, a cursed Snow White explains that "they [fairy tales] are a way for us to deal with our world" (1.1). Snow White does not yet realize that she is a fairy-tale character, but the audience clearly does and learns that the collection of fairy tales she refers to is in fact a history of her world, the Enchanted Forest.

The Enchanted Forest is a part of the Fairy Tale Land, so named by the *Once Upon a Time Wiki*, and includes adjoining kingdoms of fairy tales. Snow White, Sleeping Beauty, Beauty, Cinderella, and the Little Mermaid live in kingdoms that share borders, and the characters interact with each other. Prince Charming is able to rescue Rapunzel because he walks through the forest where her tower stands. There are shared ports and trade cities; roads run from one fairy-tale location to another. The tales located in the

Enchanted Forest are from European fairy-tale traditions and most closely recall the classic tales of the fairy-tale trinity of Charles Perrault, the Brothers Grimm, and Hans Christian Andersen. The Disney influence is unmistakable as characters are able to walk from one animated Disney film location to another. This makes the show distinctly American in its use of fairy tales. Classic tales are invoked, but as American versions, they draw on Disney films and their literary sources. Other non-Disney tales are also present, such as "Rumpelstiltskin" and "Little Red Riding Hood."[2]

The Fairy Tale Land contains geographic locations besides the Enchanted Forest, and these are realms of folk narrative—legends, myths, and folktale—or at least tales that have been told in the style of folk narratives by Disney. Sherwood Forest can be reached on foot. Camelot is a few days' ride. Mulan's home, the Empire, can also be reached on horseback but is much farther away. Agrabah is across a desert. Both Arendelle and DunBroch can be reached by boat. Drawing upon stories that have roots in legend and folktale, the Fairy Tale Land offers a fictional world that invokes oral tradition in ways that the other worlds based on novels do not. All of the folk narratives are part of the Fairy Tale Land. But as the user maps from the *Once Upon a Time Wiki* demonstrate ("Once Upon a Time Wiki: Map Making Contest"), the show is careful to make geographic

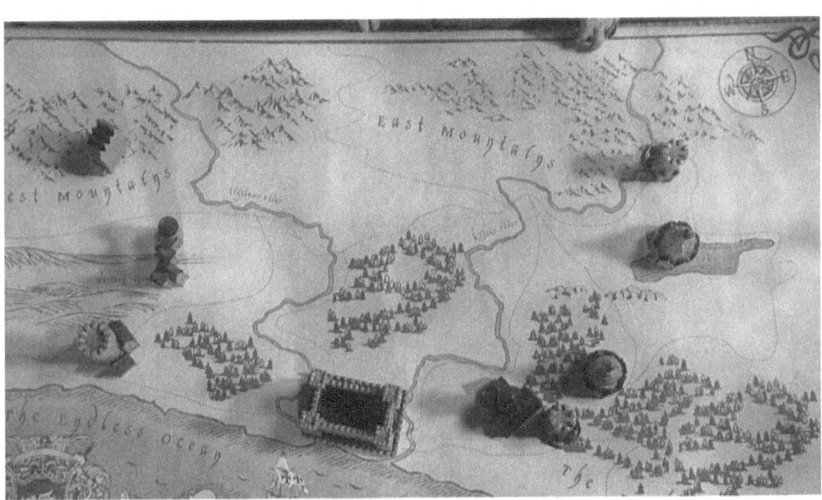

Map of the Enchanted Forest, from *Once Upon a Time* season 1, episode 12, "Skin Deep"

Genre and Geography • 39

distinctions between tales from different traditions and acknowledges that not all folk narratives are fairy tales by distinguishing between the Enchanted Forest—where the fairy tales live—and its surrounding areas—where legends and myths reside. It is important to note here that "The Fairy Tale Land" is not a name used in the show. It is the name used by fans, media, and the *Once Upon a Time Wiki* for convenience when discussing these linked areas ("Fairy Tale Land"). The Land of Folk Narratives or even the Land of Wonder Tales would be more accurate.

Though the specific tales referenced all have very well known, multiple film and literary versions, they also exist in cultural memory and carry the marks of folk narrative tradition. As such, the characters and places are greater than individual sources. The characters and the locations of their stories are linked both by genre and by their existence in this "nebulous realm," to borrow a phrase from Cathy Lynn Preston (210), that audiences recognize as belonging to a folk tradition that predates their own experience of the texts.

DunBroch is an interesting example, as it is the only one not based on a folk narrative source. The other Fairy Tale Land locations have a Disney incarnation and literary sources, and multiple source texts are used in creating *Once Upon a Time*'s version. DunBroch is straight from Pixar, now owned by Disney, and is a part of a legendary Scotland. Pixar's film *Brave* is not based on a traditional folk narrative, though it uses a variety of folktale motifs and is structured in a classic fairy-tale order. Though it may be a modern fairy tale, it does, nevertheless, draw upon folklore, such as will-o'-the-wisps, and falls into the realm of what Michael Dylan Foster and Jeffrey A. Tolbert term the "folkloresque" in *The Folkloresque: Reframing Folklore in a Popular Culture World*. It would be easy, then, to argue that the Fairy Tale Land is really Disney Land due to the abundance of Disney properties that make it to the show and share this geographic landscape. However, I would argue that is not Disney precisely, but an American Fairy Tale Land that features Disney predominantly because Disney has had great commercial success as progenitor of American fairy tales. An American Fairy Tale Land would account for the non-Disney tales that do feature, at times prominently, on the show.

This Fairy Tale Land can be traversed by normal means—by foot, horseback, carriage, boat, or magic colored smoke. To travel to another world, a magic portal is necessary. The Evil Queen or Rumplestiltskin can disappear in a puff of purple or red smoke and reappear where they wish within the Fairy Tale Land, but their magic is limited. This means that there are parallel worlds, and these worlds are based on works of fiction or, as in the case of the Land Without Color—Dr. Frankenstein's home—film. In the episode "The Doctor," Rumplestiltskin explains the limits of his power. Rumplestiltskin has asked the Mad Hatter to bring him Dorothy Gale's ruby slippers, which will allow him to travel across worlds. The Mad Hatter is unsuccessful but offers to transport Rumplestiltskin in his magic hat, but Rumplestiltskin replies, "No, no. Your hat only transports between magical realms. I need to get to a land without magic" (2.5). This scene marks the Land Without Color as a Magic Realm, and the show establishes boundaries between realistic and fictional worlds. Our world, in which Storybrooke is meant to be located, is referred to as the Land *Without* Magic. Rumplestiltskin cannot get to our world to find his son who traveled here through a magic portal. He is seeking magic slippers from Oz that have enabled characters to cross the fantasy-realism boundary. So while fictionalized versions of our world exist on the show as separate from ours, they are also classified as lands *with* magic. The introduction of *Frankenstein*—before any of the characters travel to magical worlds like Oz or Neverland—sets up rules for differentiating between worlds and how to traverse their boundaries.

The physicality of this retelling, the transformation of shared genre into shared geography, is a powerful narrative technique with a lot of potential. But it also serves as a metaphor for the changing nature of fairy tales and the crisis of relevance and sustainability as fairy tales are transformed for new times and places. Once the curse is broken at the end of season one, the characters immediately want to find a way back to the Enchanted Forest, but they cannot. It was destroyed as part of the curse, and no one knows if anything is left. Season two allows Emma and Snow White to travel to the Enchanted Forest by means of a one-way magic portal between worlds. There they discover that while most of the Enchanted Forest was destroyed and is now overrun by fairy-tale monsters, a small corner of the land has been preserved. The landscape is one of destruction—trees uprooted and castles in ruin.

Before the curse, the Enchanted Forest was a network of kingdoms in a shared geographic location. Kingdoms interacted for trade, marriage, and the occasional epic quest, but individual fairy-tale narratives were not completely mixed together like they are in Storybrooke. The exceptions are Snow White, whose journey through other kingdoms to escape from Regina allows her to encounter multiple characters outside of her story, and Rumplestiltskin, who embodies the role of magical helper in multiple tales. There are also trade centers and port towns. But for the most part, scenes from the precurse Enchanted Forest show only a couple of tales overlapping at a time.

The postcurse Enchanted Forest is different. Mulan explains that one small corner of the Enchanted Forest was protected from the curse. Those living in that area were spared, and all of the survivors have flocked to that area, where the land is still viable. More like a refugee camp than a kingdom, this area requires the mixing of narratives in similar ways to Storybrooke. The borders of the former kingdoms, and for that matter books or folk narrative genres, no longer exist, and everyone must live and work together, freely mixing into each other's narratives. Lancelot from Arthurian legend, for example, is leading the survivors. So even if the Storybrooke folk find a way back to the Enchanted Forest, which is one of the plot arcs for season two, it is no longer their home. Part of their desire to leave Storybrooke is to go back to the ways things were before the curse, when things were simpler and everyone had a story to follow that, while it might overlap or merge with another's story for a while in interesting ways, was still their *own* story following an expected narrative pattern.

In Storybrooke, their identities are in question. Not only have the characters been thrown together with others from different tales but they have been uprooted and put into an entirely new and strange world where their existing plots no longer work. Regina, for example, wants redemption in the second season and tries to earn the love of her adopted son. The Storybrooke folk do not know how to deal with that. She is the Evil Queen, and they want to treat her like one, mobbing her house to kill her once the curse is broken. Even after Snow White intervenes and saves her (because good people do not kill—a truism that Snow White herself violates later in the season), the townspeople still shun her and occasionally try to kill her. They have good reason, of course, as she irrevocably changed their lives and destroyed their home, but the problem is also one of narrative. Storybrooke is full of new stories, new narrative paths that force the characters out of the roles they are used to and into new situations. In fact, the series overall tells the story of Regina's redemption and her journey from Evil Queen to Good Queen. Adjusting to the mixing of narrative threads means that characters must inhabit different roles and recognize that other characters can also inhabit different roles.

While the different fairy tales did mingle in the Enchanted Forest, the curse has made it impossible for the tales to separate. The fairy tales cannot go back to the way they were because the world they are from no longer exists in that state. To survive in the Enchanted Forest and Storybrooke, these characters—these fairy tales—have to change. The series finale reinforces this as Regina unites all story realms together, creating a geographic space grounded in narrative unity. The stories cannot be separate, and characters are enabled to create new lives for themselves that are not bound by the dictates of their original narratives. In this way, *Once Upon a Time* metaphorically explores how creators and retellers of fairy tales must make the tales do something new to survive twenty-first-century American audiences. The recent spate of dark and "edgy" fairy-tale films and television and the frequent online and cosplay adaptations of Disney princesses speak to the current desire for new fairy tales. We like our princess stories, but the Disney model no longer works, at least not as is. Fairy tales are a strong genre and mightily adaptable; they aren't going anywhere. But they are changing, and *Once Upon a Time* offers a metafictional glimpse of the struggle of making new narrative paths when all the old rules and divisions are gone.

Critiquing Disney

While *Once Upon a Time* primarily uses Disney films as its starting place, it would be a mistake to say these are simply live-action Disney characters. *Once Upon a Time* is in a unique position to critique and crack the Disney model of fairy tales by means of its greater access to the Disney sources. Jack Zipes, among others, has discussed the lengths Disney goes to protect its intellectual property, and in *Relentless Progress: The Reconfiguration of Children's Literature, Fairy Tales, and Storytelling*, he explains that Disney has licensed Tinker Bell's name despite her being a creation of J. M. Barrie (36). One does not use Disney property without risking the ire of their legal department. But ABC, which produces and airs *Once Upon a Time*, is owned by the Disney corporation, meaning that *Once Upon a Time* is already a part of the Disney corporate family. The episode that introduces the "Beauty and the Beast" story and provides backstory for Beauty, named Belle, and Rumplestiltskin as the Beast, contains a pointed critique of the Disney fairy-tale model. When asked by Rumplestiltskin why she agrees to be his prisoner, Belle says, "there aren't a lot of opportunities in this land for women to show what they can do, to see the world, *to be heroes*" (emphasis added, 1.12). Rumplestiltskin gives her a chance to step into the hero role and save her village and her family. In using "land" here, Belle is referring to her home, the Enchanted Forest. For viewers, "land" also refers to the Disney canon. The tale-blending geographic setting of the precurse Enchanted Forest draws extensively on Disney fairy-tale films, and Belle's scenes in particular are saturated with visual references. This line of dialogue from the show is a metafictional moment that relies on the genre/geography metaphor to establish a critique of source material that places *Once Upon a Time* adjacent to rather than wholly encompassed by the Disney corpus. So while the show extends Disney's hold on American fairy tales, it also opens up those same Disney tales to be critiqued and reconfigured.[3]

This is only one small moment, but for an audience that names Disney as its childhood source of fairy tales and does not know about all of the brave women that already exist in fairy tales, it is quite an important moment. *Once Upon a Time* authorizes the audience to recognize the flaw in Disney—the lack of women heroes. And the show provides an array of women heroes and villains who enact heroism is varying ways. For Disney, it is still a "safe" challenge because it reinforces the Disney tradition, but small punctures like this still open up the tales for bolder retellings.

In what I would argue is a very targeted and deliberate critique of Disney adaptations of fairy tales, that was nonetheless viewed as Disney-pandering by online critics,[4] season four brings Elsa and Anna from Disney's *Frozen* to Storybrooke and pits them against the Snow Queen, creating a plot that is an ice battle between two different versions of Hans Christian Andersen's tale "The Snow Queen." Elsa is first presented as a potential villain, causing chaos in Storybrooke with her magic powers, and then is revealed to be a victim in need of aid. The "true" villain of this plot is the Snow Queen, Elsa's aunt in the Fairy Tale Land and Emma's former foster mother in our world. Both women are cursed by the same ice powers, and both have been stripped of family because of it. While Elsa is able to bond with her sister, the Snow Queen was entombed by hers. Eventually family bonds and love prevail—a consistent theme with the show—and the women are reconciled with each other and Emma, who shares some of their power. The Snow Queen is redeemed from her villainous role, and in an act of selfless love, she sacrifices herself to save the other women and the town, an act that recalls both Disney's film and Andersen's fairy-tale oeuvre.

While some fans of the Disney film were notably excited about this addition of the newest princesses to the show, others found the inclusion to be too soon, too trite, and too financially motivated. Liz Medendorp, for example, claims, "In what appears to be more of a publicity stunt to capitalize on the immense popularity of this recent animated hit [*Frozen*], Storybrooke is looking more like Disneyworld than a classic fairytale world." I would argue that by presenting a new retelling of "The Snow Queen" and literally pitting the title character against Disney's princess, *Once Upon a Time* is saying, "No, this is how you do that story." Elsa and Anna are not depicted kindly on *Once Upon a Time*, with Anna's clumsiness and Elsa's lack of ability and control exaggerated to the point of ridicule at times. The Snow Queen, in contrast, is shown with grace and poise and is given complex motivation and characterization, which reveals the conflict between Elsa and Anna to be petty and their characters flat. *Once Upon a Time* most definitely capitalizes on *Frozen*'s success for this season, and the centrality of Anna and Elsa for eleven episodes most assuredly benefited Disney by keeping their product present in the minds of viewers. I do not argue against those critiques of this plot, but I do think that the show also critiques the Disney film and its model of fairy-tale adaptation that flattens complex stories to fit them into the Disney fairy-tale film formula. By showing an alternative to the Disney version immediately after it was released, the show emphasizes that it is just one version of the tale and disrupts the primacy of Disney's film. The multiplicity presented, not just by creating a competing Snow Queen but by also extending her powers to Emma and creating a secondary story, emphasizes the plurality of fairy tales. While Andersen is not directly referenced, the use of his title in referring to the Snow Queen makes it possible for viewers to look up and find his story. The *Once Upon a Time Wiki* also recognizes Andersen as a source and points users to the story ("The Snow Queen").

Medendorp's critique uses the geographic metaphor of worlds, contrasting Disney with classic fairy tales, but the show's plurality of Snow Queens living in a shared space makes Disney a part of the "classic fairytale world." The show's critique of *Frozen* is enabled by the shared location and the blurring of narrative divisions. *Once Upon a Time*'s setup of fairy tales inhabiting a shared space allows multiple versions of the same tale-type to play out simultaneously and against one another, creating a third version of "The Snow Queen" from the interplay. *Once Upon a Time* critiques Disney in multiple ways, but its formulation of worlds and realms adds a level of critique beyond rewriting and pointed metafictional comments. The interplay between stories in a shared location opens up those stories in new ways at the points of intersections.

In a dramatic divergence from its source material, Disney's Snow White never murdered anyone, but the Snow White in *Once Upon a Time* does. In a complicated and multiepisode plan, Snow White decides to kill Cora, Regina's mother and a primary villain of season two. She curses Cora's heart and manipulates Regina into returning Cora's heart to her body, resulting in Cora's death. She not only took a life but caused Regina the trauma of being responsible for her own mother's death in the process. In contrast,

Disney's Evil Queen was simply evil and without complex motivation, but *Once Upon a Time*'s Regina is motivated by multiple factors, including an abusive mother who killed her fiancé. Making the villain a victim of abuse is its own cliché by now, but it allows the show to break down some of the good/evil constructions of the Disney films.

The mixing of fairy-tale narratives often punctures the values of the source tales. The introduction of Mulan into the story of "Sleeping Beauty," for example, undermines the Disney film's focus on one true love. Mulan helps Prince Phillip find his Sleeping Beauty in the Enchanted Forest and protects her once he has presumably been killed, but in doing so, a love triangle is created where it is suggested that Phillip and Mulan could have easily lived happily ever after had he not been able to wake the sleeping princess. While a romance between Phillip and Mulan is not confirmed on-screen, it is certainly implied as Beauty accuses Mulan of loving him, which Mulan denies. But in Phillip's death scene, he tells Mulan that he is sacrificing himself to save her, then includes Beauty as an afterthought. His final words, "I love you," are directed at both women as he looks between them, not at either one. Phillip has *two* loves, and duty has led him back to the first (2.1). Mulan defends Sleeping Beauty out of loyalty to her prince, and in subsequent episodes the two women bond over their mutual love. Their relationship is enabled by disregarding the Disney film's emphasis on "true love." They do eventually find a way to restore Phillip's soul, and the love story becomes even more complicated.

The insertion of Mulan into the Sleeping Beauty story offers a potential queering of the tale. Mulan essentially replaces the prince in the Sleeping Beauty story, going so far as to rescue her princess when needed. Their growing friendship and mutual admiration (as Mulan also begins to see in Beauty what Phillip does) can be read romantically as well as platonically. Though the show does not introduce a lesbian love story with these characters, the very fact that Mulan fulfills the role of Beauty's prince invites that reading and creates space for audiences to further reimagine these stories. Building on the implications here, season five sees Mulan playing advisor and traveling companion to Little Red Riding Hood. While mutual attraction is hinted at, Mulan advises Red to pursue a romantic relationship with

Dorothy Gale, saying, "Don't make the same mistake I did. Don't wait until it's too late to tell someone how you feel" (which is still left open; Mulan could be referring to either Phillip or Sleeping Beauty in her speech [5.18]). However, the repetition of motifs present in "Sleeping Beauty"—Red kissing Dorothy awake from a sleeping curse—encourages audiences to connect the present same-sex romantic relationship to the potential one in the past, and the *Once Upon a Time Wiki* does that in its character description of Mulan ("Mulan").

As Mulan and Sleeping Beauty travel together in season two, however, Beauty admires Mulan's ability to fight and to protect herself, and she quickly realizes that her inability to protect herself puts them in danger. In a way, this Sleeping Beauty bridges the gap between one of Disney's oldest princesses and one of their more recent. While Disney still has a long way to go in creating complex fairy-tale princesses, *Once Upon a Time* presents several models of multifaceted women whose strengths are varied, and it does not only equate *strong* with the ability to kick ass, though they do that too. More importantly, the women are clever and brave and face difficult emotional and moral situations throughout the series, showing that female strength is not simply an issue of killing bad guys. They are also weak and make wrong decisions with damaging consequences.

Though any one fairy tale could be retold to include these same character changes, and many of the wonderful retellings that exist today work so well because of complex characterizations that reflect modern struggles, the mixing of the different tales together allows the writers of the show to move flat, stock characters into complexity with little dialogue by relying on audiences to see how the differing stories conflict when forced to occupy the same space. Shared geography is in many ways the cornerstone of the show, creating opportunities for divergence from sources, which is the newness that interests its creators. The interplay across stories as narrative borders collapse reconfigures not only character traits and plots but also the tropes and motifs expected for the fairy-tale genre. In conceptualizing the genre of fairy tales as a geographic location, *Once Upon a Time* broadens this horizon of expectations, to return to Vanessa Joosen's phrasing, and plays with the unexpected. In particular, Disney's Mulan and

Sleeping Beauty *cannot* exist in the same world without something changing immediately. While Sleeping Beauty is not made over to be a warrior princess, she is no longer the Disney princess invoked in the first scene in which she appears.

The full series interrogates hero and villain roles with its complex characterization of many of the villains (often providing backstory) and its metafictional critique of the fixity of hero and villain as stable narrative roles. The show introduces issues of perspective and relationality by connecting heroes and villains specifically to actions and not plot (recalling Vladímir Propp's configuration of fairy-tale functions). Regina's series-long character arc is the focus of this troubling of roles, but other characters (Rumplestiltskin, Emma, Captain Hook, Snow White, Zelena, Elsa, the Snow Queen, etc.) also exhibit fluidity in their hero or villain status.

Villains and Heroes

On *Once Upon a Time*, villains can be the victims or the heroes of their own story. One of the truly fantastic aspects of this show is how it utilizes (unintentionally, I would argue) Vladímir Propp's functions outlined in *Morphology of the Folktale* to show that the role a character plays in a tale is not equivalent to that character. A single character can be both hero and villain, or a magical helper, depending on which story is being told. By having all of these stories inhabit the same place, characters are able to fulfill multiple functions simultaneously, and the show is able to challenge some of the authoritative positioning of its sources.

While pastiche is a common technique in postmodern and contemporary retellings of fairy tales, many of these texts rely on intertextual referencing and allusion—citation, or, to borrow a musical term, sampling. Fragments of fairy tales are decontextualized and reassembled in new ways, into new texts. Other texts like *Once Upon a Time* weave together different narrative threads so that a fairy-tale element is fragmented from one story line and recast in another. Fairy-tale characters appear as main characters in their primary narrative and as supporting characters in secondary plots.

Once Upon a Time is a particularly interesting example because of the extent to which villains and heroes in one tale act in different roles or functions in others. For example, fan-favorite Rumplestiltskin is the villain in his tale, the cursed hero from "Beauty and the Beast," the crocodile from *Peter Pan*, and a magical helper in almost every other tale present. Characters can be both villain and hero, main and supporting character, and their dominant roles at any one time are dependent upon which classic fairy tale lends the organizing plot structure. Characters are able to fulfill the plot functions from multiple tales simultaneously because all of these stories inhabit the same shared landscape enabled by the pastiche. Rumplestiltskin is both villain and hero or Regina is both villain and princess in a single episode. The multiplicity of character functions on *Once Upon a Time* challenges the authoritative positioning of its sources, including Disney, and reimagines fairy tales for the twenty-first century.

In the second half of season four of *Once Upon a Time*, this challenge to fairy-tale tradition becomes explicit as the villains set out to make themselves the heroes of their own stories. The show offers two paths to rewriting one's story: the easy way, reversing the roles so that villains become heroes; and the hard way, villains changing their behavior to act as heroes would. The Evil Queen, Regina, whose character development has been a central focus of the show since episode one, chooses to change her behavior, whereas Rumplestiltskin and the Queens of Darkness (Maleficent, Cruella de Vil, and Ursula the Sea Witch) decide to change the rules by finding the author of their storybook and making him rewrite it. In searching for the author of their tales, villains in Storybrooke are seeking to enact the narrative technique of role reversal and to flip character roles without otherwise changing the plot. They fail where the Evil Queen succeeds. In this way, *Once Upon a Time* engages in metafictional commentary that addresses how fairy tales can be remade for the twenty-first century and critiques narrative trends in retelling fairy tales. The shared geography enabled by the pastiche technique is a productive way of conceptualizing the process of reinventing traditional tales for new times and places.

The primary plot of season four to find the author of the book of fairy tales and make him rewrite it so that villains can have happy endings is actually a plan of Regina's and Henry's, and it develops after Regina turns to the light side and decides to become a hero. Regina begins searching for the author in order to change her story, and she is doing so because her efforts to be good, to be a hero, are not being recognized. This plot builds on the implication that these fairy tales inhabit the same land because they live between the covers of the same book, as neighbors.

In season four's first episode, Regina explains, "This book is why I'm suffering.... Every story in it has one thing in common. The villains never get the happy ending, and it's always been right. I thought not being the villain would change things, but this book, these stories, only see me one way" (4.1). Season three ends with Regina not only deciding to be a hero but being recognized as one by Henry and one of that season's main villains, Zelena, the Wicked Witch from Oz. She takes on a hero's mantle and moral code, fighting bad guys but not killing them, doing what is right even when it is hard, and putting others before herself. She fights the temptation to do evil, but instead of being rewarded for this good behavior as she expected, she finds her happy ending thwarted and loses her true love. In addition, the supporting characters on the show do not trust this new Regina. The dwarves still hate her, and people in town still see her as a murderous evil queen, which makes sense because she killed people as if it were her job. And as villain, it was. Despite this, she chooses to sacrifice her happiness and comfort to do the right thing and starts putting herself in harm's way to protect everyone else. Even Rumplestiltskin lumps her in with the heroes. But every time she comes close to a happy ending, it is snatched from her. So she claims that she is fated to be a villain no matter what her actions are and locates this rule that "villains don't get happy endings" with the author (4.8).

Because she is the villain in the storybook, none of her good actions carry any weight. Her ending is still determined by her primary role as a villain in the story of "Snow White." Regina's plan is to "Find the writer. We must find out who wrote this cursed tome and then force them to give me what I deserve. It's time to change the book. It's time for villains to get their happy endings" (4.1). This plan is a villainous one, as it involves dubious actions, but it also shows that, despite her intentions, Regina still sees herself inhabiting the role of villain even when she has decided to overcome it. Regina is trapped by her role as Evil Queen and is struggling with the problem that good behavior cannot overwrite one's function in a story.

This is a problem of character versus plot-function. A structuralist approach to narrative, such as Propp's foundational analysis of fairy tales, identifies characters by how they move the plot forward. Regina is there to cause obstacles to the heroes Snow White, Prince Charming, and Emma Swan. Thus, she is a villain. In Regina's own backstory, she would be Propp's victim-hero, or perhaps an innocent persecuted heroine (princess), who faces obstacles in the plot, but her hero is killed. Regina's mother is the villain in her story, and her mother is the one who creates the obstacles that prevent Regina's happiness. Because that plot does not successfully follow a traditional fairy-tale pattern that ends in a happily ever after, Regina's happy ending is not possible. Her fairy tale ends abruptly as it collides with Snow White's, and Regina fulfills the function of villain in Snow White's story when she seeks revenge for being wronged by the child Snow White.

Propp explains that the functions of characters are "stable, constant elements in a tale, independent of how and by whom they are fulfilled" (21). Functions are also "spheres of action," and characters can inhabit multiple spheres simultaneously (80). So a witch character can be both a villain and a donor—someone who gives magical objects to the hero. Propp explains that "the will of the personages, their intentions, cannot be considered as an essential motif for their definition. The important thing is not what they want to do, nor how they feel, but their deeds as such, evaluated and defined from the viewpoint of their meaning for the hero and for the course of the action" (81). Propp's examples show unintentional and reluctant helpers and donors, but inadvertence works both ways. Characters who want to help but get in the way of the hero clearly set obstacles in the hero's path despite their good intentions.

This is Regina's problem. Narrative structure makes her a villain, but her development as a character has her doing things that villains do not do. She *intentionally* fulfills the roles of helper and donor on a regular basis, but she still fulfills the function of villain as long as she struggles with the heroes. She is able to do this because the stories that need helpers are taking place in the same area. Much of this later struggle is a matter of disagreement over methods. For example, when going undercover to spy on the Queens of Darkness, Regina not only aids the villains in order to keep her cover but she refuses help from Emma Swan and Snow White, changes the plan when she disagrees with it, and makes it difficult for the heroes to intervene. The functions may be stable, but as a character Regina is not, because she participates in multiple and conflicting spheres of actions. Regina's story expands beyond the limits of traditional fairy-tale patterns when character development and character function clash. This expansion is enabled by the collision of different tales in the shared setting. Regina is able to be Regina and not the Evil Queen because there are other stories that need helpers and heroes. Unlike in the storybook, where the boundaries of single tales are clearly demarcated, the show dissolves the boundaries and mixes tales, allowing for complexity to develop.

Regina's development as a character is contrasted with Rumplestiltskin's lack of development. Earlier in the season, Rumplestiltskin decides to take his happy ending by pretending to be a good guy, still lying and manipulating people in private, but publically being seen doing good deeds and saying the right things. But the rule that says that villains lose and heroes win is still in effect. Rumplestiltskin cannot take a happy ending because he is still enacting the role of villain while acting the role of hero. He is still working within the narrative system of the storybook and within the villain's sphere of action. The show makes much of his failure out to be weakness, but he is the embodiment of the darkest magic in existence and really does not stand a chance until the darkness is stripped from him in the final moments of season four. But even then, he continues to be the series' primary villain—a constant presence until the final episode.

Regina, on the other hand, is not just trying to be good to get a happy ending but trying to be a better person for the people she cares about. She is trying to *earn* a happy ending. These two villains-turned-heroes demonstrate two distinct paths to a happy ending: Regina's, changing the character to fit the rules, and Rumplestiltskin's, changing the rules to fit the character's desire. While both say that they want the author to rewrite the ending, they are actually asking for two different modes of retelling. Regina is asking that characters be able to move between functions based on their actions *and* intentions—so a villain can earn the role of hero. But Rumplestiltskin is asking that the functions be reversed. Regina wants to open up the structure and make it flexible, Rumplestiltskin wants to keep the structure and move characters around. Importantly, both characters realize that the author of the storybook has the power to make these changes, suggesting that fairy tales are not necessarily fixed forms.

Eventually, Rumplestiltskin and the Queens of Darkness find the author, Isaac, and make him write a new book, one in which the villains win. To do so, Isaac flips the good/evil alignment of the characters: the heroes are now villains, and the villains are now heroes. It is a basic role-reversal technique, but there is very little inventiveness to his new story. Snow White and the Evil Queen are simply switched and placed into each other's roles. The stories have not changed, just the names.

When Isaac gives a speech at a press conference for his book in the real world, he says:

> I wrote it [*Heroes and Villains*] because I believe folks are sick of heroes getting everything in these classic fairy tales. Hence the radically different endings for Snow White, Prince Charming, and all the rest. Something different for a modern audience. What happens when villains win the day? (4.22)

What Isaac fails to realize is that reversing the roles of the characters is not the radical act he thinks it is, which is why it is so easily undone with a simple sentence. Season four ends with Henry, the new author, writing in the book with his magic pen, "Thanks to the hero Regina's sacrifice, Isaac's villainous work was undone" (4.23). Henry is able to change Isaac's book using the story's own structure. Regina is, after all, the hero now. Isaac's attempt to rewrite the storybook fails for the same reason Rumplestiltskin's attempt to take a happy ending fails. Reversing the rules reinforces the rules. Role reversals like this require fidelity to the original structure in order to work. By flipping the characters so that they inhabit opposing hero/villain roles, the stability of hero- and villain-functions is secured. The villains cannot envision a narrative structure that is not centered on a hero at odds with a villain where only one can be victorious. And they certainly cannot envision another plot structure that is not centered on competition. So when Rumplestiltskin makes Isaac switch everything around, he dooms himself to failure by his own binary thinking. If the characters can be switched once, they can easily be switched again using the same logic and the same rules.

Isaac's evil act that resulted in him being banished into his own book is actually a much more radical retelling. There, the binary of good and evil is broken down and muddied. He enters the Fairy Tale Land and convinces the heroes—Snow White and Prince Charming—to do something evil, and in the process they *knowingly* hurt an innocent child by kidnapping Maleficent's daughter (who is in fetal form in a dragon's egg) and magically transferring all of the potential darkness from Emma (who is in utero) to her (4.16). Ironically, it is their desire to keep good and evil separate, instead of accepting that everyone, their daughter included, has the potential for both good and evil, that motivates the heroes to act unwisely. Eventually Snow White realizes that "[Regina is] not all evil, and [Snow White is] not all good. Things are not that simple" (4.9). But the desire for a binary understanding of morality, which is exemplified by the opposing character functions of hero and villain, is shown to be problematic even while Isaac's act is vilified. It is important to note here that Isaac's more radical action is dependent upon the shared landscape of the stories and an intentional mixing of the narratives in a single location. The straightforward role reversal leaves the narratives intact: Regina and Snow White stay within the borders of the "Snow White" plot. The options for the characters are limited by the functions of the single story. Isaac's interaction and intervention in Snow White's tale crosses the border between her story and Maleficent's. As the stories merge in the forest and Snow White takes the road to Maleficent's castle instead of her own, the options for the characters suddenly expand. There are more functions that need to be fulfilled as multiple stores begin to unfold in the same place and along the same road.

Isaac's manipulation is clearly marked as evil by the show. However, his *method* of creating ambiguity is lauded when enacted by Regina, whose choices are shown to be morally sound. Regina's method of rewriting meets with approval because she gets what she wants and becomes the hero the characters need, whereas Rumplestiltskin's easy switch results in failure. The boundaries between villain and hero are able to be collapsed in large part because the fairy-tale pastiche allows multiple fairy tales to occur at the same time. As characters from one story fulfill roles in other stories, they are able to inhabit multiple narrative functions simultaneously. And because the individual fairy tales are not separated on the show, these functions can conflict, creating contradictions that allow for character development, as in the case of Regina.

One difficulty with the show is that while it does push characters into new roles and reconfigure stories, blurring lines between good and evil and questioning the values of the source tales, it often responds to these punctures by doubling down on the good/evil binary and returning characters to their "original" states as part of its open-ended serial format. Regina's struggle to love someone other than herself and to act selflessly is a compelling plot arc, but every episode that complicates her character is followed by one that reasserts her evilness. At least, in the first few seasons. By seasons five and six, she is mostly redeemed, and by season seven she is elected Good Queen.

Snow White's logical choice to kill Cora, and not so logical choice to use Regina to do so, makes for a complex episode that shows Snow White's growth as a character as she recognizes situations in which killing is an appropriate choice and her willingness to do something morally objectionable to save her people. She is faced with a choice that is not as simple as good versus evil and responds as such. But then several episodes follow in which she is practically catatonic because she is so overwhelmed with grief. What she did was wrong, and the show reinforces a firm line between good and evil with her guilt. What keeps this plot from totally reverting into the simplistic good/evil worldview though is that when Snow White goes to Regina to ask Regina to kill her, Regina starts to comply, taking Snow White's heart, but then stops because she realizes that Snow White is asking for death primarily to end her own guilt. While Snow White does believe that what she did was wrong and does feel sorry for what she did to Regina, her motivation in wanting to die does not stem from her views of a moral right and wrong, her desire for justice, or the belief in punishment. While Snow White does hold those views (based on her earlier speeches and encounters), she wants to end her own suffering and not have to deal with the fact that she—not only a good person but a symbol for goodness and purity—killed someone, in a premeditated way and by cruel methods that hurt others. She becomes quite good in her actions after this, but the character of Snow White has been thrown into question. Narratively, this is possible because of the mixing of fairy tales enabled by the shared physical space. Cora—the Miller's daughter—is present to give Regina backstory and to bring the tales of Snow White and Rumplestiltskin together. In addition to the pastiche technique utilized in the show, many of the more complicated changes are enabled by the show's length. As a seven-year television series, writers can revisit characters and plots multiple times and create complex stories not possible in a shorter format like film.

Serial Fairy Tales and Metafiction

Once Upon a Time is a long-arc serial drama that utilizes specific narrative strategies to build suspense over multiple episodes, and it combines series and serial structures in what Jason Mittell terms narrative complexity. Episodes contain short-arc plots that resolve in that episode while simultaneously contributing to long-arc plots that feature a primary villain who spans the season. *Once Upon a Time* typically features two major villains per season separated by a winter hiatus; the closure of one plotline is accompanied by the introduction of the next, presented frequently as a cliffhanger. Once characters can leave Storybrooke, the main villains are generally identified by a new location, so that the show must journey to Neverland or Oz and characters must interact with fantastic characters from closely related lands and genres. Individual episodes show the heroes solving specific problems usually, but not always, connected to the main plot, and frequently focused on a specific fairy tale. Episodes have narrative resolution for the short arc, typically by both solving the immediate problem and retelling a short fairy tale, and are open-ended for the long arc. *Once Upon a Time* also utilizes soap opera conventions with its open-ended narratives and multiple, interwoven plotlines. Episodes typically contain two major plots, separated by setting (magical or mundane) and/or time (current or past); however, there are usually additional plotlines featuring the supporting characters so that a single episode may follow multiple narrative lines. Then there is the melodrama. *Once Upon a Time*'s focus on relationships between characters and how their happily ever afters are ripped away is firmly in the territory of soap operas. *Once Upon a Time* blends character- and plot-driven story lines so that both feature prominently, and the emphasis shifts within and across episodes.

Serialization is a key feature of *Once Upon a Time* that cannot be overvalued. While the fairy-tale horizon of expectations includes an optimistic end, in a series, no marriage can be a happily ever after, as the union of Snow White and Prince Charming on *Once Upon a Time* demonstrates. Their wedding and Snow White's pregnancy is what prompts Regina to curse everyone into oblivion in the very first episode of the show. Robin Warhol argues that this negation of the expected end is a feature of serial publication. Serialization undermines the domestic marriage plot in print serials by suspending closure and "unraveling instances of closure that turn out to only be provisional and temporary" ("Making" 382). Serialization opens up narratives to allow for non-normative configurations, and while *Once Upon a Time* has retold and created a variety of interesting fairy tales, it is the *structure* that opens up these fairy-tale texts in complex and inventive ways.

Rebecca Hay and Christa Baxter, in "Happily Never After: The Commodification and Critique of Fairy Tale in ABC's *Once Upon a Time*," point to the delay of closure as a defining feature of *Once Upon a Time* and its main divergence from the Disney fairy-tale formula: "it delays the conventional happy ending by transplanting fairy-tale characters to contemporary Maine, where they struggle with their love lives, family relationships, and making ends meet" (316). Like Schwabe, Hay and Baxter locate the difference in narrative structure from conventional tales to the show's blend of fantasy and reality. Hay and Baxter's description alludes to a blend in genre as well, which Schwabe names as "fairy tale and drama" (304) and Bacchilega connects to soap opera (*Fairy Tales Transformed?* 121). In addition to the blend of fantasy and reality, Hay and Baxter also point to the serial structure of *Once Upon a Time* as a television program for allowing the creation of complex plots and characters and ensuring audience interest (317).

Serialization works in conjunction with the pastiche technique and translations of genre to geography. The interplay among different fairy-tale narratives occurring in the same place creates complexity that extends narrative lines across episodes and seasons. The introduction of new fairy tales enables short-arc plots that provide background and character development for the main ensemble cast: What would happen if Prince Charming happened upon Rapunzel's tower? What if the little mermaid saves Snow White from drowning? These interactions create relationships among characters that can be tapped into in developing the short-arc plots. The location-based narrative interplay supports the serialization structure.

For fairy-tale melodramas like *Once Upon a Time* this episodic delay of closure suspends the expected happily-ever-after ending, and audiences are left waiting to see in what new ways happiness can be ripped from our beloved heroes, and how our most hated villains can narrowly escape their just punishments. Serialization here functions metafictionally, as it calls attention to the genre norms subverted by the transformation from one form (short work of fiction) to another (multiseason television serial). Combined with pastiche, the serialization creates a heavily metafictional context for the show's self-referentiality and its interrogation of itself as a work of fiction.

Season four is the most overtly metafictional season, as the characters not only demonstrate their continued self-awareness that they are living storybook characters but they actively try to rewrite the stories they are living. As season four unfolds, the extent of the author's power is revealed, and *Once Upon a Time* explicitly maps out its fairy-tale tradition. August, one of the helper and donor characters—who is also Pinocchio—explains that,

> There have been many authors throughout time. It's a job, not a person. And the one trapped in here was just the last tasked with the great responsibility. [Emma: Which is?] To record, to witness the greatest stories of all time and record them for posterity. The job has gone back eons. From the man who

watched shadows dance across cave walls and developed an entire philosophy, to playwrights who tell tales of poetry, to a man named Walt. Many have had this sacred job, great women and men who took on the responsibility with the gravity that it deserved until this last one. He started to manipulate rather than record. He did something, I don't know exactly what, but something that pushed them over the edge. (4.17)

August makes a truth claim, that fairy tales are history, real events from magical lands that have been recorded in the storybook that frames the show. They are the greatest stories of all time, which means that they need to be documented so they can be shared. This is the job of the author. To record, not create, not rewrite. The irony that this genre truth comes from a character known for lying is glossed over.

Important here is who inhabits the role of author. This is a book, and yet the history of fairy tales given is a visual one, from shadows to plays to films. It is oddly devoid of actual folklorists and fairy-tale authors. Plato, presumably Shakespeare, and Walt Disney are invoked, but well-known writers of fairy tales like Charles Perrault and the Brothers Grimm are not. And it completely ignores the long list of female authors of fairy tales, despite including the word *women* in the speech. While in some ways it makes sense to single out Walt Disney—this is, after all, ABC which is owned by the Disney company, and the show trades on the recognizability of Disney versions of most of its tales—the show clearly retells fairy tales and fantasy from other writers, including Perrault, the Brothers Grimm, Hans Christian Andersen, J. M. Barrie, Frank L. Baum, and Lewis Carroll, among others. So to ignore the other fairy-tale creators, especially ones obviously invoked by the show, and replace them with men not known for fairy tales is clearly dishonest and fairly insulting to both fairy-tale fans and authors. What this history of authorship does is elevate fairy tales from the nursery and into Western canonical literature and philosophy. This genealogy claims that Disney's films and *Once Upon a Time*, and, by extension, the stories on which they are based, are as important as Plato's work and Shakespeare's plays. The show first makes this argument with Mary Shelley's novel *Frankenstein* and its film legacy, and it does so by introducing a very different world that establishes genres as location to be traversed.

Frankenstein is clearly a work of the fantastic and a work of great literature. The use of *Frankenstein*, as well as the many other non-fairy-tale texts such as Robert Lewis Stevenson's *The Strange Case of Dr. Jekyll and Mr. Hyde*, places the show and fairy tales alongside these classic fantasy and science fiction works.[5] Allusion and intertextual referencing can serve many purposes, but an important one is forcing a connection between the current text and the invoked one. Connecting *Once Upon a Time* to non-fairy-tale literary and cinematic classics also legitimizes fairy tales as equivalent stories. The show makes this claim explicitly in Isaac's speech. This works in different ways and is problematic in many others, but one productive function is to legitimize fairy tales as literature. The world-crossing magic of *Once Upon a Time* equalizes this comparison by showing that they are all just a quick magic portal away. The divisions and connections among worlds—and the revelation that some worlds are linked more closely than others—are also divisions and connections among genres, and fairy tales are presented as a subset of folk narratives, which are part of the wider genre of the fantastic. By using *Frankenstein*, the show reasserts its understanding of what is and is not a fairy tale.

As a text that is genre fiction, canonical Western literature, and cinema classic, *Frankenstein* shows that stories we enjoy can also be important cultural works, can pose ethical and philosophical dilemmas, and can be worthy of adult consideration. These are the claims *Once Upon a Time* makes about fairy tales. They are not just stories from our childhood; they are complex stories that can intrigue adults and tackle serious issues via the fantastic. By connecting *Once Upon a Time* to non-fairy-tale literary and cinematic classics, this metafictional genre mapping legitimizes fairy tales as suitable, popular entertainment for adult audiences in twenty-first-century America. Fairy tales have a place in our adult cultural imagination, alongside *Frankenstein* and other classic works of literature. To quote Snow White in the show, fairy tales "are a way for us to deal with our world" (1.1).

In addition to its claims about the history and value of fairy tales, Isaac's speech about fairy-tale authors also makes an argument about what constitutes a bad fairy-tale author. This author, Isaac, took over in 1966 when Walt Disney died, which emphasizes Disney as the last true author of fairy tales (4.22). Isaac's crime is also Walt Disney's crime, and that of almost every writer who retells fairy tales. He changes the stories. Isaac starts revising the stories to make them more interesting. His unforgivable offense is that he enters into the storyworld and becomes a part of it, then manipulates Snow White and Prince Charming into stealing Maleficent's daughter so that they can take all of the potential evil out of their own daughter and put it in Maleficent's and banish the bad egg to our horrible 1983. He dooms an innocent child to a life of evil, separates her from her loving mother, and sends her to a horrible world without magic. All because "it [made] for a better story" (4.17). And in many ways it does.

Complicating the established narratives and introducing moral ambiguity brings new life to tales audiences "think we know," to refer back to the show's opening lines, and reinvents them for different cultural moments. This is precisely what many fans of contemporary fairy tales love, and it is an established part of the long tradition of the genre. The metafictional narrative of *Once Upon a Time* conflates this act of writing with real life, positioning the fictional characters as living people in the storyworld who have to live with the consequences of their actions after the action of the fairy-tale plot has been resolved. One might wish a fictional villain dead (or even an annoying coworker), but still live a nonviolent life in reality. The characters on the show are presented as inhabiting both states of being simultaneously, fictional character and real person. So while fans may root for the violence and evil acts because they are exciting and make for engaging television drama, we also are expected to engage with the emotional turmoil and mental anguish of moral characters who suffer after committing immoral acts, which makes for engaging television melodrama. All of the villains, new and old, in Storybrooke and the Enchanted Forest want to find this author because he has the power to change their stories on a whim. In this way, *Once Upon a Time* metafictionally explores how creators and retellers of fairy tales must make the stories do something new to survive twenty-first-century American audiences, and it explores the ramifications of some of these decisions. The old patterns are no longer adequate, and trying to play with the old rulebook is not going to work anymore. Transporting characters from different fairy tales to the same place and seeing what might happen creates opportunities to show the limitations of older versions of tales. The stories "we think we know" will unfold differently in new times and places. *Once Upon a Time* explicitly addresses this concept as it brings pastiche, serialization, and metafictional awareness together in a way that maps genre to geography to create a Fairy Tale Land or a true Wonder Land.

2

Genres Overlaid

Serialization and Hybridity in Marissa Meyer's *The Lunar Chronicles* and Seanan McGuire's *Indexing*

Anchoring a fairy-tale land to a specific place can be achieved in multiple ways. *Once Upon a Time*'s slippage between genre and geography creates a place—both figuratively and literally in the storyworld—to theorize fairy tales as a genre and examine the interconnectedness of tale types and the variation of fairy-tale fragments possible when tales collide. As Jessica Tiffin argues in *Marvelous Geometry*, the genre of fairy tale is inherently metafictional because of tales' self-conscious attention to tradition, form, and style. A feature of the genre, this self-consciousness is a notable site of reinvention for fairy tales in print as well as on-screen. Pastiche, serialization, and metafiction come together differently in different texts and media, but the survivability and adaptability of fairy tales in the twenty-first century features prominently in works that employ these techniques. The fairy-tale novel proliferated at the end of the twentieth century, and the twenty-first century has seen an expansion of the fairy-tale novel series as readers choose to spend more time in fairy-tale lands.[1]

Like television series, novel series provide expanded space for telling stories. More pages (or more episodes) equal more opportunities for character development, psychological depth, and plot complexity. In the case of retelling fairy tales, this expansion provides space for a great deal of added context that can open up old tales for new meanings, and the popularity of the fairy-tale novel is a testament to the success of this technique. Novel series have added room for expansion that can, like television series, last for many installments. Novel series occur in different forms. Perhaps the most common is that of a longer story broken up into episodes that continue for several books, culminating in a final novel that wraps up the series' plot. Typically this kind of series follows the same band of characters for each novel, like J. K. Rowling's Harry Potter series or Jim C. Hines's Princess series. Others may switch character perspectives with each novel, such as Marissa Meyer's *The Lunar Chronicles*, so that each novel brings a new perspective even as it continues moving the main plot forward. Still other series take an expanded universe approach, as in Terry Pratchett's *Discworld* series, where all books are connected by a shared setting but all do not follow the same characters or a primary plot. In cases like this, each novel usually has a contained plot and does not continue from a previous novel. Though the *Discworld* series can be read chronologically, it can also be read out of order or by groupings by character that function as miniseries (such as reading all of the witch-based books, of which *Witches Abroad* is a noteworthy example for its use of fairy-tale pastiche).[2] Many longer series following the same set of characters take a similar approach of each novel telling a separate adventure or groupings of two or three books telling an adventure. Seanan McGuire's *Indexing* series is a two-book series, telling two separate but related stories with the same group of protagonists; however, McGuire's series differs from the other types of series described here in its release format. *Indexing* was first published as a serial, with chapters released periodically, rather than as a completed novel.

There are many fairy-tale novel series that employ pastiche by bringing together characters from different fairy tales in the same location.[3] Meyer's young-adult science-fiction fairy-tale series *The Lunar Chronicles* and McGuire's government agency/ police procedural fairy-tale serial *Indexing* offer two examples of the varying ways fairy tales can be employed in the series format. *Indexing* is similar to *Once Upon a Time* in its use of overlapping tales, while *The Lunar Chronicles* preserves narrative divisions across the series with each book focusing on an individual tale. The two approaches to blending fairy tales within a novel series produce differing effects and allow for different narrative possibilities in retelling. *Indexing*'s engagement with fairy-tale scholarship as an additional intertext provides another layer of metafictional critique in its engagement with genre expectations. I begin this chapter by looking at *The Lunar Chronicles*, which preserves narrative boundaries while nonetheless utilizing pastiche to bring in characters from different tales, before turning to *Indexing*, which offers some integration of tale plots through its use of pastiche, though not to the extent seen in *Once Upon a Time*. The main distinction between these two approaches to pastiche is a geographic one: *The Lunar Chronicles* contains fairy-tale plots in individual geographic locations in the series, while *Indexing* presents a shared geographic space in a single location. The location of the fairy tales in the novels' landscapes helps to articulate the relationships of the included fairy tales to each other. Whether the linked tales are overlapping or adjacent, the novels' use of geography reflects the structural choices that characterize the relationships among the tales in the fairy-tale genre.

Both series employ multiple genres in retelling fairy tales so that the fairy-tale pastiche is also a blending of genres. In drawing upon tropes and stylistic features from multiple genres, the two series employ fairy tales to different effect. In *The Lunar Chronicles*, the fairy-tale plot and motifs provide a narrative path, a familiar structure that orients readers as they traverse the unfamiliar science-fiction terrain. In *Indexing*, the opposite is true. The police procedural genre provides orienting structure and stable methodology for navigating the unfamiliar and mixed-up fairy-tale landscape. In both cases, the mixing of genres builds upon the mixing of fairy tales in fixed locations. The genre blending, series structure, and fairy-tale pastiche intersect in different ways in each series, but the result in each case is a conceptualization of the interconnectedness of fairy tales grounded in geographic metaphor.

The Lunar Chronicles

Marissa Meyer's series *The Lunar Chronicles* dabbles in issues of disability, race and ethnicity, racism, globalization, scarcity and precarity, transgender identity, body dysmorphia, slavery, captivity, war, and medical ethics in regard to experimentation, among other themes. Like many young-adult books, the themes are heavy. Many of these themes are tangled, and while some clear ideas are presented (slavery is wrong), the complexity of others is represented in the difficulties of the series' main protagonist's struggle with her multiple and conflicting identities. The character embodies multiple positions simultaneously, and the fairy tale provides a map to navigate these complex issues by providing a narrative path, a trail of bread crumbs. The focus on the Cinderella character's foot/shoe and its symbolism, like in Kelly Link's stories in chapter 4, keeps in the forefront the ideas of traveling and movement. Cinder cannot stay where she is, and her foot is both a literal means of transport and a touchstone to the fairy tale that guides the plot of the first novel and the overarching plot of the series.

Before bringing multiple tales together, the first novel in the series establishes hybridity as a core concept for the series as a whole. *Cinder* begins with the protagonist—Cinder—removing her mechanical foot in a market booth dotted with grime, grease, and lug nuts. This foot is Cinderella's shoe, and Cinder's careful placement of the "too-small" foot on the table, despite calling it a "piece of junk," sets up reader expectation for how this Cinderella story is going to work (Meyer, *Cinder* 3). Shoe to foot is an easy transition: this is a Cinderella story with robots and wires, and our heroine will lose part of her body, not its adornment. But Cinder's attitude toward the foot also suggests the novel's relationship to the fairy tale and how the reader can expect the tale to unfold.

Rather than a dainty foot seen through the prince's eyes as something to be valued, this too-small foot is a problem. Cinder is a cyborg: a human with mechanical parts in place of body parts she lost in an accident that should have claimed her life. Cyborgs, on this future Earth, are little more than servants and are test subjects for biological experiments. They are feared by the community as "mutant[s]" and "outcast[s]" and not considered fully human, let alone equal (178). They are property, not people. Rather than pass as royalty, this Cinderella must pass as human (which is later complicated when readers learn that she is also a Lunar, which is a mutant from the moon). The tiny foot does not symbolize beauty but Otherness. Cinder, as a biological creature, has outgrown the foot given to her as a child. Her stepmother, who sees her as a burden, has not invested in upgrading her mechanical parts. So the too-small foot becomes an object of revulsion as it signifies Cinder's *not*-humanness. It is the life Cinder wants to leave and is trying to escape, not the one to which she is running. But this too-small foot is also the fairy tale. Readers, too, have outgrown the small foot. I am tempted to say child's foot here, as that is literally what it is—a young woman is wearing a child's foot—but fairy tales are not only children's stories, so the adjective feels wrong even though the misconception that fairy tales are for children is still widespread and informs this retelling. Nonetheless, the Cinderella stories from Walt Disney and Charles Perrault, among others, do not quite fit our current lifestyle, where we carry computers in our pockets for watching videos of an astronaut playing his guitar on a space station. Glass slippers are unbelievable (despite fairy godmother Helena Bonham Carter's insistence that they are comfortable in the 2015 Disney live-action *Cinderella* film), but mechanical prosthetic limbs actually exist.

Cinder's dislike of her foot makes narrative sense—she has outgrown it and it marks her as an outcast—but her need to respect it also makes sense. When Cinder places the foot on the table, she "set[s] it up like a shrine amid the wrenches and lug nuts" (6). She may not want to go back to the too-small foot, but it is still a part of her and has supported her and carried her along the path that has led her here, moments before she meets the prince and embarks on a new journey. Her relationship to the foot is also a guide for the reader, telling her how the fairy tale will be evoked. It is a beacon to which the novel will return, but it is not the plot that will push the story forward. It is part of the novel, but the novel is also more than the fairy tale on which it is based.

The foot is also the giveaway. It is the foot that reveals Cinder for who she is—a cyborg, not a human; a mechanic, not a princess (or so she thinks). This initial scene also sets up the horizon of expectations for characters and plots: Cinderellas need small feet; Cinderellas need wicked stepmothers and wicked stepsisters; Cinderellas need fairy godmothers and magic; they need princes, and balls, and big orange pumpkins to ride around in. Cinderellas need to be abused and humiliated; Cinderellas need to be secret princesses. This list of expectations is a catalog of the fragments associated with Cinderella stories, and many of these elements exist in popular culture memory without ties to a specific version of the fairy tale. These expected characters and plot points become the frame of the novel *Cinder*, and more broadly the series. The science-fiction elements may flesh out the story and move it around, but the fairy tale is the skeleton that keeps the story upright, even if it may be too small.

The invocation of multiple fairy tales in the series and multiple versions of Cinderella in the novel—though Disney is clearly a primary source—builds on the series' interest in hybridity. Cinder's own hybridity and multiple levels of identity—mechanic, girl, Lunar, human, cyborg, princess—work as a metaphor for the hybridity of genres as well. While the plot revolves around issues of hybridity and how one is defined as human, the novels themselves are generic hybrids, bringing together tropes and motifs from both fairy-tale and science-fiction genres. Echoes of fairy-tale narratives appear in a variety of popular stories, from classic novels such as *Jane Eyre* to tales spun by sportscasters about the latest Cinderella quarterback. Plots and fragments of fairy tales are often used by writers as a base story line because they both offer a structure for the narrative and allow readers to quickly decode the story being read. Given the widespread use of fairy-tale narratives, it is not surprising that genre blending is a common technique among contemporary writers of fairy tales. Nor is it surprising that science fiction and fairy tales are becoming a popular combination in the twenty-first century.

As Amelia Rutledge argues in "Science Fiction and Fairy Tales," in science fiction, fairy tales have two functions: "a structural formula . . . of quest and initiation" and "compensatory fantasies" (452). This reliance on quest structure and wish fulfillment is, as Rutledge explains, "strategic" because well-known fairy-tale conventions "make arcane content more accessible to its readers" (454). The *familiar* frame of the fairy tale allows readers to focus on the *inventive* science-fiction aspects of the novel—such as dangerous Others, devastating plagues, and the politics of invasion—instead of the structure. The quest structure—find the princess, save the world—is routine, and stopping the global-scale invasion is a science-fiction standard.

The usefulness of familiar ground when processing new information is explicitly stated in the novel. When faced with the fact that the prince-in-disguise is at her booth asking for help, the narrator explains, "[Cinder] was glad to have routine tasks for her hands and routine questions for her mouth" (Meyer, *Cinder* 9). Like the fairy tale's role in the novel, the routine tasks make it easy to process the new and difficult information, giving Cinder "something to focus on so she wouldn't get flustered and lose control of her brain's net connection again" (9). The fairy-tale structure can be returned to, to keep readers moving through the plot. The politics of the novel are fairly straightforward once everything has been revealed (and subsequent novels do bring in new information, complicating the reader's understanding of the storyworld), but the reader learns about Lunars and the past as Cinder does. When Cinder becomes overwhelmed and flustered, she returns to her work, and the novel returns to the fairy tale, giving readers time to process the new information before the novel introduces something else.

This structure can be seen when Cinder first learns that she is *not* human. A doctor conducting experiments on cyborgs tells Cinder that she is Lunar. Cyborgs are test subjects for a vaccine for the plague, and Cinder has been "volunteered"—basically sold—as a test subject by her stepmother. Upon examining her, the doctor learns that she is immune to the plague because she is Lunar. Lunars are humans with mutated genes that allow them to manipulate what others perceive—a trait called *glamour*—and they live on the moon in a separate political state (43). They are manipulative mutant mesmers from the moon. The doctor here also functions as an authority—his scientific authority creates narrative authority as he is able to explain to Cinder who she is, and he provides a great deal of exposition that is presented as objective and trustworthy because of his role in the narrative and his genre alignment to science fiction, despite Cinder having just met him and him experimenting on her. He is later revealed to be a Lunar fugitive living under an assumed name and is the scientist responsible for the Lunar super soldiers who are mutated to be part wolf, as well as being the father of the Rapunzel figure introduced in the third novel.

Lunars are feared and reviled on Earth, and Cinder's own response when learning that she is Lunar is to recall the "cruel, savage[ry]" of the

Lunars and try to distance herself from the stories of their immorality (178). She immediately recognizes that if her new identity is known, her life will become that much more complicated and that she will experience a new level of oppression. But she also struggles with the schism between what she knows about Lunars from rumor and what she knows about herself. *She* is not a monster even though others, like her stepmother, see her as one. In addition, the doctor explains that she is a shell—a Lunar without glamour—which would make her not only a mutant outcast on Luna but also extremely vulnerable should anyone learn who she is. The Lunar queen has shell children killed because they are immune to glamour in addition to not being able to produce it.[4] Shells are Lunars without the mutated gene, making them basically humans who cannot be controlled. This scene of revelation comes at the end of a chapter, and Cinder is barely registering what the doctor tells her. The next chapter transfers the focalization from Cinder to the prince, and readers are given a break from Cinder's point of view as Prince Kai greets the Lunar queen as she arrives on Earth, and readers are shown how glamour works. When Cinder becomes the focalizer again in the following chapter, she is working and thinking about the prince's ball and its implications for her identity.

Cinder's processing of her new identity is couched in the familiar. She begins repairing the prince's android and thinking about dancing and balls while registering the new reasons why she should not accept the prince's invitation to the ball—the grease and grime of a mechanic, the metal skin of a cyborg, and now the genes of a Lunar. Plus, she is a fugitive; all Lunars on Earth are. As Cinder counts the cards stacked against her, the narrative returns to fairy-tale themes: the ball and fairy godmother. Iko, the family's android and Cinder's closest friend, shares the role of magical helper in the story (Cinder is the other magical helper figure in this novel, in that her ability to glamour is actually just blocked by her cyborg components and is unblocked just before the ball). Iko is an androgynous android who identifies as female and so occupies herself with fantasies about makeup, clothing, and boys; shoes are her weakness (193). She saves the materials—including the too-small foot—that Cinder later uses to dress herself for the ball (323, 324). Iko's presence also opens up space for transgender representation in the series. While Iko does not transition in *Cinder*, she does gain a female body in *Cress* after having been a spaceship in *Scarlet*, and with each of her nonhuman, nonfemale bodies, Iko expresses body dysmorphia that resolves when her body matches her identity. Iko's entrance at this point serves as a distraction for Cinder and helps to resituate the reader by emphasizing the romance plot of "Cinderella." Iko's fantasies of dancing with the prince and her teasing Cinder into admitting that she really does have feelings for the prince reorient the reader to the familiar fairy tale and reaffirm the direction of the plot. Despite the Lunar revelation, the political turmoil, and the plague that has now claimed Cinder's younger—and kind—stepsister, Cinder will go to the ball. Her stepmother has her arrested, steals her foot, and dismantles Iko first, but there will be dancing.

Because she is a cyborg, Cinder's hybridity is clearly on display for readers even as she hides it from the prince. The cyborg body—a body that is both human and not human—is a powerful metaphor, and to quote Donna Haraway in "A Cyborg Manifesto: Science, Technology, and Socialist-Feminism in the Late Twentieth Century," "cyborg imagery can suggest a way out of the maze of dualisms in which we have explained our bodies and our tools to ourselves" (181). Cinder's hybridity has been discussed in terms of racial identity by Sierra Hale in "Soldering Together Young Adult Science Fiction: The Cyborg and Implicit and Explicit Racial Spaces in Marissa Meyer's *Cinder*," though, as Hale points out, the series fails to connect this metaphor to the historical racial oppression on which it is mapped. *Cinder* takes place in a future China, and each of the other novels has a different geographic location. Cinder is of mixed race, whereas her family is Chinese.[5] The physical descriptions of background characters suggest a racially mixed location, but the dominant ethnicity is Chinese. As subsequent novels move to different continents, the ethnic makeup of the characters shifts to reflect the dominance patterns of their contemporary real-world counterparts. The novel has also been discussed as a site of queer possibilities by Jennifer Mitchell in "'A girl. A machine. A freak': A Consideration of Contemporary Queer Composites," where she argues that Cinder's "status as [a] conglomerate" is a "fundamentally queer composite" (57).

While not all cyborgs in science fiction are treated as second-class citizens, the oppression of cyborgs in *The Lunar Chronicles* is clear. But the cyborg body in *Cinder* obscures the mutant body at times. It is the identity by which others recognize her, and it is Cinder's legal identity. Cinder's stepmother says to her, "You are *not* human, Cinder. It's about time you realized that" (Meyer, *Cinder* 280). In response Cinder recognizes that, legally, "she had no rights, no belongings. She was nothing but a cyborg" (281). Cinder leaves this argument to find Iko's dismantled body. The dismantling of Iko is an act of power on the stepmother's part showing Cinder that her stepmother owns everything, including Cinder's friends, but it also reinforces the precarious state of cyborgs. They have no legal rights, and the vaccine testing that usually results in a cyborg's death demonstrates the same lack of bodily autonomy that allowed Iko to be dismantled on a whim. As with many works of the fantastic, the fictional Other of the cyborg metaphorically references the real-world injustice of racism, slavery, and identity-based oppression. *Cinder* specifically, but the series as a whole, invites readings through a disability lens because the representation of Cinder as disabled (first as a cyborg and later as a Lunar shell) and her varying attitudes toward her identities engage disability tropes.[6] Iko's android body is another on which Otherness can be mapped, and her gendering of herself makes her a particularly useful character for those interested in metaphors of transgender experience.

Cinder's mutant body and her Lunar physiology are both a benefit and a curse, as they act as a magic wand, granting Cinder the ability to wish for people to behave in certain ways and make it happen. But unlike the fairy godmothers of classic tales, Cinder questions this power and does not want to use it. She has seen the corruption and desolation caused by wielding glamour for selfish aims, and she struggles with differentiating her own use of glamour from that of the Lunar queen. There is also the issue of Cinder's nonhuman status, meaning that she has experienced lack of autonomy and has been forced to act against her will, as a slave. There is a parallel between the oppression via mind control, which is fantastic and fictional, and the oppression via laws, which has a basis in a reality that can be found on both Cinder's Earth and the reader's. The queen glamours others for political and personal gain; Cinder does so to save her herself and others. But the act of imposing one's will on another and removing that other's ability to choose is the same, regardless of intent. Cinder struggles with that, and her own personal quest—one not resolved in the novel and continued throughout the series—is to accept who she is while not abusing her newfound ability. Cinder is the missing Lunar princess, so Cinder differentiating herself from the Lunar queen has far-reaching ramifications for the rest of society.

The novel ends with Cinder escaping from prison with the knowledge that she is a princess. She goes to the ball in rags and dances with her prince on her too-small foot. (Her stepmother took the new, fitted foot when she dismantled Iko to reinforce Cinder's own status as property.) Going to the ball is a great risk to Cinder's own life, but she wants to warn the prince and reveal the Lunar queen's duplicity. Once there, she is revealed to be a cyborg and a Lunar. When she flees, she loses her too-small foot on the palace steps, "wires [tearing] loose" as it is wrenched from her body (365). The prince has her arrested at the insistence of the Lunar queen. As a Lunar in hiding, Cinder is, after all, a fugitive. Imprisoned, alone, and deprived of her cybernetic limbs, she is gifted a new hand and foot by the same doctor who revealed her true identity. He does so again, telling her she is the missing princess and the only one who can defeat the evil queen. She has to escape and save humanity, including her own. The novel ends with the story of "Cinderella" open, and while the next three novels focus on political turmoil and show Cinder gathering the aid she needs to overthrow the queen, "Cinderella" is left without a prince and without an ending. Readers expect an ending, and a happily-ever-after one at that. This is, after all, a *fairy-tale* science-fiction novel. The final novel in the quartet returns to the "Cinderella" fairy tale. In doing so, Meyer reconciles the love story and political alliance between Earth and Luna and the larger issues about hybridity and oppression of those demarcated as Not-Human. Cinder is successful, becomes queen of Luna, and enters into a relationship with Kai, reuniting the two empires and forcing her people—from both worlds—to reevaluate how they view each other. But Cinder's own struggles with her identity *and* her recognition that her power is just as dangerous as the current Lunar queen's and her stepmother's suggests that Cinderella marrying her prince will not solve the world's problems.

Cinder uses the fairy-tale structure of "Cinderella" as a narrative map for its dystopian examinations of the body—the cyborg body, the disabled body, the diseased body, the alien body—and physical hybridity. While the action of Cinder's plot hinges on a devastating plague and the threat of an alien invasion, the novel uses Cinderella-in-disguise as a frame for the cyborg and mutant protagonist passing as human in a world that fears and loathes the nonhuman Other.

While Cinder is a retelling of primarily one fairy tale, The Lunar Chronicles series uses multiple tales, and each novel takes a separate fairy tale as its controlling structure. Cinder uses "Cinderella," Scarlet "Little Red Riding Hood," Cress "Rapunzel," and Winter "Snow White." There is an allusion to "The Snow Queen" with the character of Prince Kai who is lured away and controlled by the Lunar queen and her glamour, but there is no structure from "The Snow Queen" lent to the novels. There are also short stories and a shorter prequel novel set in this storyworld that provide background and expand minor points in the series, but only one, "The Little Android" introduces a new fairy-tale frame from "The Little Mermaid." Building upon the multiple hybridity metaphors of the first novel, subsequent novels link different fairy tales together, creating an expanding pastiche that reaches peak complexity in the final novel. The fairy tales in the series stack, so that the first novel has one fairy-tale intertext, the second has two, and the third three, so that the last novel combines elements from the largest number of tales and closes the Cinderella narrative begun in the first novel. While Cinder ends before the prince finds his Cinderella-in-disguise, Scarlet's plot follows "Little Red Riding Hood" so that the wolf has been faced and defeated by the novel's conclusion. Cress, too, resolves the major plot points of "Rapunzel," including the blinded prince having his sight restored, but the romantic happily ever after is left open so that Cress/Rapunzel and her "prince" are not a couple until the end of the final novel. This ending also sees Scarlet/Little Red Riding Hood paired with the wolf and Winter/Snow White paired with the huntsman character before closing on Cinder/Cinderella and Kai/Prince Charming/Kay. The first fairy tale frames the series, but the other three fairy-tale plots are each contained in a single novel even while those tales' characters run around in the other fairy-tale plots.

The covers of the different novels separate the source fairy tales, keeping them discrete retellings until the very end of the fourth novel. Each novel is set in a different location, anchoring each tale to a geographic space (*Cinder*/Cinderella in China, *Scarlet*/Little Red Riding Hood in France, *Cress*/Rapunzel in Northern Africa and a satellite, and *Winter*/Snow White on Luna). While Cinder is a character in the subsequent novels, her actions do not follow the plot of the "Cinderella" fairy tale. In *Scarlet* she breaks out of prison, releasing another prisoner, Thorne, who joins her, takes off in a stolen spaceship, and investigates her childhood in France. The last action is when she merges with the "Little Red Riding Hood" plot and rescues Red/Scarlet, whom she believes is about to be eaten by a wolf, actually a mutated wolf-hybrid Lunar super soldier. Scarlet and Wolf (who is a reformed villain after falling in love with Scarlet) join Cinder's team and aid her in ending the Lunar queen's tyranny. In *Cress* Cinder rescues Cress/Rapunzel from a spy satellite with the help of her crew, travels to Africa to find a doctor who can help her (while separated from Cress and Thorne, who crashed into the Sahara), and kidnaps Prince Kai as part of a plan to overthrow Luna's queen.

In these sequels, Cinder's actions are not driven by the Cinderella plot, and neither is the structure of the novels. Instead, the structure of the novels derives from the fairy tales of the titular characters, and Cinder's plot is the subplot. It continues the series but does not drive the novel, and it unfolds in the background. This is accomplished with alternating point-of-view chapters. The majority of the chapters are focalized through the titular character, and these are interspersed with chapters that follow the other characters. This is a continuation of the pattern begun in *Cinder*, where the chapters alternate between Cinder's and Kai's viewpoints, but this pattern becomes more complex with the addition of each new character, which also introduces a new narrative thread and point-of-view to follow, so that the final novel contains the most diversity in terms of focalization. But the primary chapters of the three sequels are focused on the "Little Red Riding Hood," "Rapunzel," and "Snow White" plots.

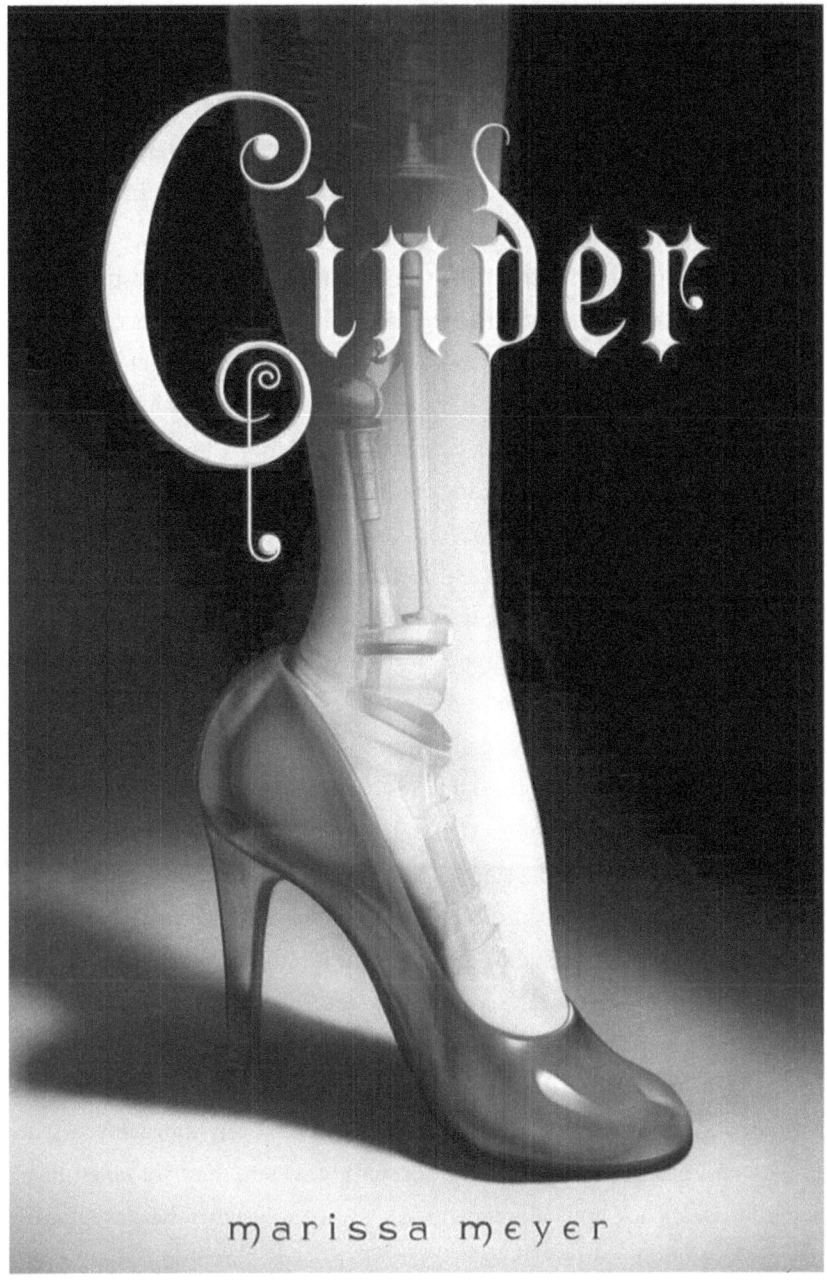

Cinder by Marissa Meyer, 2012, cover image by Michael O based on artwork by Klaudia Jakubowska, designer Rich Deas.

Scarlet's grandmother is missing, taken by the wolf pack, and she must journey across France's forests to find her. She is accompanied by Wolf, who is charming if rough. They find her grandmother, who has been held prisoner by Wolf's unit, and Wolf betrays Scarlet so that she, too, is imprisoned. He, however, breaks her out because he has fallen in love with her, and Scarlet and Wolf are rescued by Cinder, who shares the role of huntsman with Wolf. Cress was taken from her parents as an infant by the Lunar queen's second in command, a powerful user of glamour, and imprisoned in a satellite. She is denied all contact with other people and is dependent upon her guardian for necessities and affection; she also has long, unruly hair. She begins helping Cinder, and Cinder decides to rescue her. Thorne, Cinder's companion and an escaped convict, takes on the role of prince. The rescue is discovered, and Cress's guardian causes the satellite to crash to earth with Cress and Thorne inside. Thorne is blinded in the accident, and the two wander the dessert until they are separated, Cress is kidnapped, and they are reunited at the home of the doctor Cinder has gone to find. He creates eyedrops to restore Thorne's sight, and Cress administers them. In both cases, the major plot points of the fairy tale are resolved, though Cress and Thorne do not declare their love for each other until the final novel.

In *Winter*, Winter is the stepdaughter to the Lunar queen and strikingly beautiful without the use of glamour. In fact, not using her glamour has caused her to suffer from hallucinations and mental instability, but she has chosen to avoid glamour for moral reasons. The jealous queen, who was horribly disfigured in her childhood and uses glamour to appear achingly beautiful, orders the guard in love with Winter, Jacin, to kill her. He fakes her murder and sends Winter off with Scarlet (who has been imprisoned by the Lunars and is an exhibit in a zoo) into hiding, where they are taken in by a soldier wolf pack and a lumber-producing community. The deception is discovered, and the queen tricks Winter into eating a candy apple that is poisoned with the plague. She falls ill and is placed into stasis until Jacin is able to return to her with the antidote and save her, at which point they are reunited.

It is at this point that all of the fairy-tale plots are resolved (except for the closing happily ever afters) and all of the characters are reunited to initiate their plan of overtaking the Lunar capital and disrupting the queen's coronation as an Empress of Earth. There is a bloody battle in which every fairy-tale character is injured and most are separated from each other. Cinder and her companions are successful, and after a final shoot-out with the queen, Cinder, who is the missing Lunar princess, is declared the rightful ruler of Luna with plans to eventually convert the government to a republic with elected officials. In the resolution, the fairy-tale couples are all given happily ever afters; none marry, but all are situated in long-term relationships with the promise of a future. The final scene is of Emperor Kai presenting Queen Cinder with her child-size android foot lost at the ball, and Cinder tossing it out of the palace and into the lake below, ridding herself of the "constant reminder that she was worthless, she was unimportant, she was nothing but a cyborg" (Meyer, *Winter* 823).

Each novel is also separated into "books" that are denoted by lines from the organizing fairy tales, providing readers with guidance as to what will occur in each section of the novel. Book 1 of *Cinder* begins with "While her sisters were given beautiful dresses and fine slippers, Cinderella had only a filthy smock and wooden shoes," and this section establishes Cinder's character, status, and the familial relationships (1). Book 4, which contains the ball scene, is introduced with "The prince had the stairway smeared with pitch, and when Cinderella tried to run away, her left slipper got stuck" (Meyer, *Cinder* 283). The pattern is maintained throughout the series; for example, Book 5 of *Winter* contains the scene in which Winter eats the poisoned apple candy and begins with "The mirror answered: 'You, my queen, are fair; it's true. But the young queen is far more fair than you'" (655). "Fair" here is referring to Winter's beauty, kindness, and moral superiority, but not her complexion (Winter has dark skin). These opening lines from the fairy tales serve as orienting passages that reorient readers to the fairy-tale plot that provides structure as the science-fiction plot of revolution becomes more complex and distanced from the source tales. Like the opening and closing gestures of classic fairy tales, these lines bring readers back into the fairy-tale space from which the novel's plot may have pulled them, and the fairy-tale space offers the young-adult audience stability and security about what will happen next.

Indexing

The shared geography of *Indexing* facilitates a questioning of genre formation by asking by whose authority these narrative lines have been drawn and why they were drawn in these places. The Aarne-Thompson (AT) index, *Types of the Folktale*, is a central feature of the series, and it is present as a resource for both reader and characters. The AT index serves as a tale map, noting where stories share narrative boundaries and landmarks, but it also reveals how constructed the tale-type categories are by the difficulties characters face in mapping stories onto the index. The geographic pastiche of *Indexing* is built upon a collapse of the AT index in the novel. The index catalogues stories in a conceptual space, making narrative divisions and metaphorically mapping the genre to demarcate discrete areas and assign specific stories to these areas. When the conceptual mapping of indexing (referring to the act itself and the series) is brought into the real world of the series' storyworld, the constructedness and artificiality of the index is revealed. The geographically bound pastiche creates a space to visualize for readers and actualize for characters the series' conceptual argument about the fluid nature of stories in general and in fairy tales in particular. The stability of the fairy tales is brought into question and revealed to be transient. Rather than orient readers to the story as in *The Lunar Chronicles*, the flexible narratives of the fairy tales raises questions about genre formation and the authority by which genre decisions are made.

The shared fairy-tale landscape of Seanan McGuire's *Indexing* series is more similar to the configuration used in *Once Upon a Time* than it is *The Lunar Chronicles*. Like *Once Upon a Time*, *Indexing* and its sequel take place in a modern American city and various fairy-tale characters live in the same location. The protagonists are agents of the Aarne-Thompson Index (ATI) Management Bureau, and their job is to stop fairy-tale incursions before they affect reality. Their motto is "defending happily ever after," and in the second volume of the series, the Bureau is described as "an organization dedicated to keeping stories from eating the world" (McGuire, *Indexing* 3; *Reflections* 4). A memetic incursion is when people and events begin to conform to fairy-tale narrative patterns, and incursions are triggered by a person strongly resembling a fairy-tale motif. The fairy-tale-aligned people are referred to as being on the "ATI Spectrum," being "story touched," or being "cursed," with ATI Spectrum as the preferred, neutral term of the Bureau (*Reflections* 17). Because fairy tales are frequently violent, they pose a very real danger to both the fairy-tale characters and any bystanders. Agents of the Bureau try to end the active tales with as little damage and death as possible. For example, during an incursion of "Goldilocks and the Three Bears," it becomes clear to the characters that they cannot stop the Goldilocks story, so the agents assume the roles of the three bears to convince Goldilocks to apologize, pushing the narrative to a variant that does not end in Goldilocks's death (*Indexing* 92–93).

While not a fully open-borders configuration of pastiche like in *Once Upon a Time*, the *Indexing* series contains greater opportunities for narrative pastiche than *The Lunar Chronicles*. Fairy tales mingle in a shared geographic space even as chapter divisions provide orienting structure for readers. Individual tales, noted by their tale type, are identified at the beginning of each chapter, directing readers to the fairy-tale narrative that will unfold in the ensuing pages.

Indexing and its sequel, *Indexing: Reflections*, were first published as part of the Amazon Kindle Serials program (began in 2012 and since discontinued). Subscribers could purchase the ebook and receive episodes periodically as they were released by the author. After the book was completed, readers could purchase the collected episodes as an ebook or printed book. This serial publishing mirrors the serial publishing of novels that has long been a part of literary history, and it shares several rhetorical elements with serial television.

McGuire's two-book series contains the hallmarks of serial publication and serial television, such as plot and character recaps within each episode designed to reacquaint readers who have not visited this fictional world in a few weeks. These marks of serialization were not edited out in the novel version, preserving the serial format for readers even as they binge episodes (i.e., read the book as one would any novel, multiple chapters at a time). The move to novel form also preserved the episodic structure of the text. The episodes, now chapters in the book, are not numbered or referred to as chapters but are marked by a title and status update that identifies the fairy-tale plot that anchors the episode. (I reference the printed version.)

Structurally, each episode is typically dominated by one fairy-tale plot and the non-fairy-tale plotline of the government agency for whom the protagonists work. The setting is an unnamed American city, and in each episode, the physical space is changed in minor or major ways to facilitate the unfolding narrative, from the appearance of an anachronistic rickety wooden bridge over a creek to a fully formed gingerbread house that sprung up overnight in a forest. In instances where the location remains the city, other factors take on fairy-tale shape, such as the H1N1 flu virus merging with a sleeping sickness and affecting anyone in proximity to the Sleeping Beauty character. The differing episodes are enframed by the Snow White story, which is the fairy tale to which the narrator belongs. It is a constant touchstone to the novel, and the main plot eventually brings in "Snow White" fragments, though not structure. Each episode is anchored by a different fairy tale, one that the protagonists are investigating. The episodic structure takes on a monster-of-the-week format, and the characters are later able to link several of the memetic incursions and recognize that they are connected to the main mystery of the novels, which is not revealed until several episodes in. In many ways, the novels read like television episodes, and the serial, as opposed to series, structure is the main reason for this.

Each episode in the novel begins with a tale type that drives the plot of that episode forward. When episodes feature more than one anchoring tale type, the switch in organizing tale is denoted with a subhead that follows the format of the episode headers:

Memetic incursion in progress: estimated tale type 709 ("Snow White")
Status: ACTIVE (Indexing 1)

The narrative is organized around tale type, and McGuire uses the real Aarne-Thompson index numbers for the majority of the tales referenced

(I refer to McGuire's numbers with an ATI designation to recognize the fictional Aarne-Thompson Index and follow up with the Aarne-Thompson-Uther [ATU] numbers if the fictional tale type differs from the scholarly ATU index numbers or titles). The anchoring tale type is usually the type of the fairy-tale incursion that the protagonists are investigating rather than the tale type of the main characters. The exceptions are when the protagonists' stories are affected by a case.

Four of the five main protagonists are on the ATI spectrum, and one agent is a regular human, not affected by the stories. These characters can interact with other fairy tales, including taking on roles or functions in those narratives, as in the "Goldilocks and the Three Bears" (ATI 171/no ATU) example. If their story is too close in type to the tale type being investigated, they have to limit exposure. For example, Henrietta (Henry) Marchen, the narrator and primary protagonist, is a Snow White, and once she is fully activated as a story, she has to be careful around princes or risk falling into her narrative and being completely taken over by it: "You're a fairy-tale princess, Henry. You get too close to a sleeping prince and you're not going to have a choice" (*Indexing* 323). When compatible narratives are in close proximity, the force of narrative closure will use the people available to bring the story to an end.

In instances where the characters and plots from different fairy tales interact, the characters talk about the interactions in the story but the text does not mark the interactions with headers. The novel structure implies separate, distinct tales even as the novel's overall plot shows stories mixing and morphing at a more complex level, such as when a "Beauty and the Beast" story morphs into "The Little Mermaid" type. This is, in part, due to the style/format of the subheads that mimic the kind of government paperwork the characters complain about doing. The paperwork and the fictional AT index (as well as the real one) imply discrete order, whereas the "lived" experience of the characters demonstrates far more fluidity than the structuralist approach allows. In order to be cataloged and filed, the different events must be described and labeled to fit the filing system of the Bureau. The disconnect between the characters' field experience, where they experience and discuss overlapping and mingled tales, and the reporting system, which requires incursions to be isolated and typed, is a subtle reminder that the organizing structure of the index is external to the stories.

Played for humor in the text, Henry complains about doing her paperwork on multiple occasions, as do several of her team, including human Agent Andy Robinson and Junior Agent Demi Santos (ATI 280 The Pied Piper/ ATU 570* The Rat-Catcher), who complain but do their paperwork (*Indexing* 48, 80). Agent Sloane Winters (ATI 315 The Treacherous Sister/ ATU 315 The Faithless Sister) does not complete her paperwork, true to the Wicked Stepsister character she is, and Agent Jeffrey Davis (ATI 503 The Shoemaker and the Elves/ATU 503 The Gifts of the Little People) happily does the paperwork of others, true to his supernatural helper type (*Indexing* 124, 48). While it seems like a standard complaint about bureaucracy, Henry's explanation about the tediousness of paperwork is an important element of foreshadowing; she explains,

> There are a lot of things in the Index that can only be documented the old-fashioned way, with paper and specially prepared typewriter ribbons. Even those don't work as well as doing it by hand. . . . Enter a report into a computer, where no eyes can see where it goes, and sometimes it will change. Those changes are never good, especially not if someone reads that modified story and takes it for the original. That's how variants are born. (*Indexing* 34–35)

The documentation implies stability, but as the stories change—deviate, mutate, and create new variations; morph into related types; or combine in ways that create new stories—it is clear that the stability is a product of the documentation of narrative structures, not the stories themselves. The stories are adaptable, they are flexible, and some are uncategorizable. Because the fairy tales are alive, and narrative is presented as a force of nature, all of this structural play occurs in both narrative and geographic space. The changing of the stories is not happening in the pages of the AT index, but in the geography of the storyworld.

Indexing: Reflections includes more background of the character of Sloane Winters, a Wicked Stepsister whose story is "frozen" or "unresolved/averted" (*Indexing* 59, 95). Sloane's background reveals the artificiality of the AT index and demonstrates a problem with the index categories and how the Bureau uses them, a problem that has existed since the index's inception. As a young woman Sloane recognized that reality was being reshaped around her—she, her mother, and her sister began mistreating her stepsister—and she recognized the shape of the Cinderella story. Rather than submit her family to the cruelty of the story, Sloane left, rendering the story averted: "she broke a Cinderella in formation by *walking away*" (*Reflections* 206). Found and used by agents of the Council of Librarians and the then-nascent ATI Bureau, Sloane survived for hundreds of years as a Wicked Stepsister *in potentia* by controlling her murderous desires. The early agents who found her kept her under close watch and used her powerful ability to detect stories to aid in their work, and as an agent of the Bureau Sloane continued that work and became a field agent fighting against memetic incursions. Sloane's methods are often violent and unusual, but effective. In *Indexing*, when faced with a difficult Rapunzel scenario (ATI 310 Rapunzel/ ATU 310 The Maiden in the Tower), "Sloane just yelled at the story until it went away" (119). She shows abilities that others on the ATI Spectrum do not share, and she seems to have outlived most other story-touched individuals.

Marked as dangerous by the Council and then the Bureau because of her averted role of villain, Sloane is also not able to be categorized. There is no tale type in the fictional ATI that centers on Cinderella's Wicked Stepsister. When given the choice between imprisonment and joining the Bureau as a field agent, Sloane consents to be miscategorized so that she is considered eligible for duty. To be a part of the Bureau, she must be able to be identified by Aarne's *Verzeichnis der Märchentypen*, the first version of the AT index, even if that means misrepresenting a story to fit the parameters of the types described in the index. Sloane explains to a man of authority in the Bureau who makes this offer, "none of these stories are mine. . . . I am not Cinderella. You cannot hang my sister's story on my shoulders" (*Reflections* 213). His response shows how the classification system can be used to contain stories rather than describe them:

> "Ah, but you see, we've found the story for you!" The man sounded smugly pleased with himself. "Number three-fifteen, 'The Treacherous Sister.'"
>
> Sloane frowned. "Sir, I've read every book of fairy tale and folklore I could find, from all around the world. I have sponsored translations. The story you reference has nothing to do with me. It's about sisters who are untrue to their brothers, usually through the crime of falling in love inappropriately. I want to poison people. I want to feel murder on my fingertips. You can't give me a label that doesn't fit. It serves no true warning."
>
> "The stories will be what we say they are," said the man. "That's the point of this exercise. We'll remake them in the image that suits us best. Accept your designation and become an agent in our new bureau, or submit to imprisonment."
> (*Reflections* 213–14)

Sloane accepts but makes the point that this misdesignation is a lie. Her story is not in the index. Rather than create a new entry, her story is twisted to fit what already exists in order to preserve the authority of the index and the Bureau.

The reporting system of the Bureau is mimicked by the headings that identify tale types, which reinforces for the reader the artificiality of the system. The italicized headings serve as an entry point for readers of the serialized form, reacquainting them with the narrative type in play and bringing readers quickly into the serialized novel after a break from the narrative. But headers used within episodes pull readers out of the story being told by creating a jarring break in the narrative from the authorial insertion and by creating gaps between sections of text that compel readers to make a connection. The novel suggests that structure is not internal to stories; rather, stories are mapped onto existing, external structures, as opposed to structure being uncovered within the stories.

The acknowledgments section of both volumes includes a note about the index:

> The Aarne-Thompson Index to Motifs in Folk Literature is a real thing, and is used by folklore and fairy-tale scholars the world over. My copy weighs about twenty pounds, and can be used to squash spiders of any size. If you're interested in learning about more, I highly recommend checking the folklore section of your local library. There's so much to learn about the stories that we have created, and which have created us in turn. (*Indexing* 405)

The note mixes up the titles of Antti Aarne and Stith Thompson's *Types of the Folktale: A Classification and Bibliography* and Thompson's *Motif-Index of Folk-Literature*, but it is clear McGuire is referencing the former because she uses tale type numbers that mostly align with the AT index and not motif numbers. For example, the Wicked Stepsister motif in *Indexing* is identified with tale type 510A (Cinderella), not motif S34 (Cruel Stepsister). The second book replaces the sentence about spider squashing above with one more serious in tone, but the passage is otherwise identical: "My copy previously belonged to the state folklorist of Minnesota, and is one of my most prized possessions" (*Reflections* 326). This addition, which removes the lighthearted description of the tome, changes the tone of the note to be more serious and respectful of its content. It also offers a truth claim of authenticity by tracing the genealogy of the book to a folklorist and a value claim by calling it a "prized possession." This claim of authenticity is particularly important and interesting because of McGuire's occasionally inconsistent use of the text.

In most cases, the references to the tale type numbers in the index are accurate: 709 for Snow White, 410 for Sleeping Beauty, and 510A for Cinderella, for example. In other cases, the numbers are accurate but the type names used are the ones associated with the most popular versions of the tales: for example, 503 is identified as The Shoemaker and the Elves, not The Gifts of the Little People, and 315 is named The Treacherous Sister, as opposed to The Faithless Sister. Sometimes numbers are mentioned, but with so few details it is difficult to confirm tale type: 305 is mentioned in context with blue-white flowers; 511 is mentioned in context with murderous stepfamily (which seems to align with ATU 511, One-Eye, Two-Eyes, Three-Eyes) (*Indexing* 3, 6). In other instances, the number referenced is not the correct number: 280 is used for the Pied Piper, but that number is for The Ant Carries a Load as Large as Himself in the AT index, and the Pied Piper story is identified as 570*, The Rat-Catcher, in the ATU edition.[7] McGuire uses 171 for "Goldilocks and the Three Bears," but there is no 171 in the AT index, nor the ATU revision. The Story of the Three Bears is identified in several places online as type AT or ATU 171, including the Multilingual Folk Tale Database and SurLaLuneFairyTales.com, but this is not consistent with the AT/ATU numbering.[8] McGuire's use of the AT index is *mostly* accurate and occasionally inventive.

The inconsistencies in McGuire's use of the fictional ATI echoes for readers familiar with the real ATU index its limitations. Torborg Lundell has argued of the real AT index in "Gender-Related Biases in the Type and Motif Indexes of Aarne and Thompson" that "though folklorists may know of the limitations of the Indexes, potential researchers from fields outside of folklore may regard these works as definitive, not realizing their particular weakness in terms of gender attributions" (150).[9] For the majority of the readers of the series, McGuire's truth claims in the acknowledgments section combined with the predominance of accurate references reinforces the authority of the AT index even as the fictional version in the series is shown to be problematic.

For the most part, when McGuire references a tale that does not have a tale-type number, it is a literary work that is not included in the AT index. Novels like *Alice's Adventures in Wonderland*, *The Wonderful Wizard of Oz*, and *Peter Pan* are children's fantasy novels frequently studied by fairy-tale scholars and marketed as fairy tales. These literary fairy tales are described in *Indexing* as too new to have been indexed, along with many of the fairy tales by Hans Christian Andersen. The narrator, Henry, explains,

> Little Mermaids are a relatively recent addition to the Index: technically, they're not listed in the ATI, since the version used by mundane scholars only looks at true folktales and motifs, not stories whose authors have been identified and listed in the

public record. Maybe we shouldn't list the voiceless girls and boys either, but our job is hard enough without splitting our best defense into multiple rulebooks. Everything goes into our official Index. (*Indexing* 304)

Here Henry offers a divergence between the real ATU index and the fictional one. Interestingly, one of the examples Henry gives in the next line as not being in the mundane index, Thumbelina, could be cataloged as AT 700 Tom Thumb/ATU 700 Thumbling with a female protagonist. The main tale referenced in the passage, Andersen's "The Little Mermaid," is a focus of this episode and identified in the opening header as type 138.1 (*Indexing* 294). It is the one clear instance where McGuire has made up a tale type number that reflects the AT system, and the number is one that is not in use in either the AT or the ATU editions of the index.

The use of a new number with the narrative explanation above that explains its newness is a careful navigation of the fictional versus the real AT index. This passage is an important explanation because it accounts for the differences between the fictional ATI and the real AT numbers, both identifying where McGuire's artistic license is in use in fictionalizing the index by documenting the addition and validating the other numbers in use in the text as real. The Pied Piper and Goldilocks exceptions, then, stand out as being deviations that are not accounted for by the careful explanation. This passage also provides rationale for expanding the fictional ATI to include tales and literary works that are recognized as fairy tales today but are not the folktales under study in the AT index, and it opens up the possibility of new tale types being added to the fictional index. There is at least one instance of a made-up tale type, the Girl Who Runs, that is mentioned in passing as a hypothetical new type (*Reflections* 131). The ability to augment the index also opens up the scope of the ATI Management Bureau to include legends and other genres of folk narrative. *Indexing*'s mapping of the folk narrative genre recalls that of *Once Upon a Time*, where similarities among genres are given precedence over differences.

The first book in the series raises the issue of adding urban legends to the index because they are "a new form of memetic incursion that's been getting more codified with every repetition" (*Indexing* 181). The fictional ATI can be updated to reflect popular use of the tales. Though the emphasis is still fairy tales, the second book in particular references a wider range of folk narrative characters: stock characters like a Storyteller or Evil Queen, urban legends such as Bloody Mary, myths such as the minotaur in the labyrinth, and legendary women from a variety of sources ranging from Maid Marian and the Lady of Shalott to Sweet Polly Oliver and Anne Bonny the Pirate Queen. The inclusion of nonfolktale material makes the use of ATI numbers impossible and introduces questions about definition and genre, such as what the difference is between a fairy tale and an urban legend, a myth and a ballad. At least as far as the characters in the novels are concerned, they are all powerful narratives that live in a shared cultural space—beyond written texts—and can shape reality. The inclusion of nonfolktale material also raises issues of an evolving index. As the ATI expands to include other folk narratives and literary tales that appear as memetic incursions, then it can also expand to include new stories as they are written or told, dispersed, and repeated. Repetition is presented as a key element of what makes some tales more dangerous than others, and McGuire's discussion of these additions recalls Karin Kukkonen's explanation of how elements of stories exist in popular culture memory in her article "Popular Cultural Memory: Comics, Communities and Context Knowledge." Repetition is a key feature of this process (Kukkonen 265). But underlying all of this potential for change to the ATI is the possibility for change to the existing stories and new stories.

Change comes in many forms, and blending stories and genres is one method explored in the novels. Like novel series that use stacking formulas, *Indexing* and *Reflections* are also genre-blending novels. Fairy tales are mixed with detective fiction centered on government agencies, and the *Men in Black* film series launched in 1997 is referenced in regard to Henry's favored work attire (*Indexing* 4, 72). While the *Men in Black* reference is clothing-based, it is also a genre reference, letting readers know that this is not a typical government agency. There is a bit of the procedural subgenre about the books, as the focus is frequently on the methodology used to stop an incursion and the minutia and regulations of bureaucracy, though the mix of mystery and fantasy lends itself to the urban fantasy genre. As with

The Lunar Chronicles, the blend of genres allows for a familiar structure on which twists and complicated material can be built. Where *The Lunar Chronicles* uses the fairy tale to guide readers through science-fiction complexities, *Indexing* uses the crime format as a stable background for the variation and multiplicity of the fairy tales invoked and to complicate readers' understanding of fairy tales as a genre. It is actually a good introduction to how the AT index works for someone who has never encountered a tale index before.

As with *Once Upon a Time*, in *Indexing* different tales overlap and engage with each other as characters are able to enact roles in each other's stories. They step in to fulfill a narrative function, so that a princess can step into the role of a prince-rescuer to kiss a princess awake, as when Henry kisses a comatose Jeff in *Indexing* and a sleeping Sloane in *Reflections*. Points of similarity in plot and function are used as entry points into another story. This is utilized strategically by the team to stop memetic incursions on multiple occasions. The presence of a Pied Piper on the team, for example, creates several nonviolent opportunities for interference. Demi is able to use her music to affect multiple kinds of animals, not just rats, and that allows for the team to remove animals and people from dangerous situations or use them as weapons or tools simply by finding the right music. As the team archivist, Jeff researches variants and tale types. If he is able to identify a tale type where a piper can affect nonanimal substances, then Demi can use that connection to affect a seemingly unrelated tale. This is a major plot point in *Reflections*, where Jeff's knowledge of a little-known variant of a piper affecting liquid is used to enable Demi to pipe explosive, transformative glass out of the area of danger, allowing agents to enter the area (*Reflections* 50). In this instance, the glass slipper from a Cinderella story has been weaponized to transmute anyone who touches it into glass, and the newly transformed matter has the same properties even when broken into shards. The reliance on variation for interaction across tales is quite interesting. Conceptual connections noted in the index create opportunities for interactions among tales in the physical world.

The series assumes multiplicity that is often absent in retellings. While there are postmodern retellings, like Robert Coover's *Briar Rose*, that utilize multiple variants of the source tales, many retellings of fairy tales take a specific version as a source or work from a well-known outline of the tale (the tale type parameters). The variation in the retelling is from the new text, not its sources, and the focus is on what the writer is doing differently from what readers expect, frequently based on a widely popular version such as those of Disney, Grimm, Perrault, and Andersen. When novels retell lesser-known stories, the connection can be missed by readers whose experience of fairy tales is popular-culture based, even when the tale is named in the title, as with Holly Black's *The White Cat* (which uses Madame D'Aulnoy's "The White Cat"). In many retellings, the fairy-tale text retells a specific version, not necessarily a tale type, and in doing so creates a new version of the type. McGuire accounts for this in Henry's explanation of where variants come from. But *Indexing* takes a wider scope, retelling not single versions but engaging tale types and the fairy-tale genre as a whole. While specific versions are referenced, and have to be for the literary texts like the Alice and Oz books for which there are clear canonical origin texts, the agents enter into the mimetic incursions not knowing what kind of variant they will encounter. Every Sleeping Beauty incursion is different, but they all share certain elements in common, and those shared elements, cataloged in the ATI, serve as reference points for redirecting the narratives and for making changes.

The primary setting of the novels is an American city and its surrounding areas, and as incursions occur, they do so in the shared location of the city. Other ATI offices exist in other locations, but the novels focus on this location. Typically, incursions occur singularly so that the team is only fighting one fairy tale at a time, but as the climax rises in the first novel, multiple incursions happen simultaneously to the point that not only are multiple teams deployed but teams are split up and agents move from one incursion to the next with no break—the stories begin overlapping. Fairy tales can reshape the real world, not only by making people behave in ways that are out of character for them (but in character for the fairy tale in question) but by reshaping the environment. In an encounter with ATI 2035 The House that Jack Built, for example, the team is on cleanup duty, corralling and collecting the various elements in Jack's building chain (*Reflections* 30). In another example, woods grow up around a school and a gingerbread house appears out of nowhere (*Reflections* 70). It is literally a case of narrative shaping geography to better fit the story.

While this is a pastiche technique like in *Once Upon a Time* where the characters from different tales live in the same storyworld and interact in each other's stories, the stories do not overlap and mix together in the same way. In *Once Upon a Time* the stories converge as main characters in one story take on typically minor roles in others (with some notable exceptions), and the stories frequently run concurrently, so that Snow White is helping Little Red Riding Hood even as she is hiding from her Wicked Stepmother. Most of this occurs in the past of the Enchanted Forest or in other magical locations, and the narratives depicted are recognizable as fairy tales retold. In the modern day Storybrooke, the narratives that drive the seasons' plot may be inflected with fairy tales, but they are not typically specific tales being retold, such as breaking the curse and restoring magic to Storybrooke in the first season or villains trying to make the author of their stories change the endings in season four. The retelling of the fairy tales and the telling of new stories with the fairy-tale characters are separated by magical and mundane locations, even as both types of stories play out in storyworlds defined by genre, not specific tale.

In *Indexing* the fairy-tale retellings are separated from the main plot of the book in a similar structure, but the overlapping and mixing of tales differs. In a moment of intertextual referencing, *Reflections* acknowledges this same-but-different parallel in the two texts. Sloane says to Jeffrey, "Uh, does this look like an enchanted forest to you? Have you been watching that show on ABC again? Just because she's [Henry] a fairy-tale princess, that doesn't mean the laws of reality don't apply to her" (*Reflections* 110). The main difference that Sloane points out is the lack of magic in the *Indexing* series' storyworld. Fairy-tale narratives unfold in ways that conform to the laws of physics even if their very presence could be described as magical; there must be logic to the way the narrative unfolds so that, in this case, Henry needs to be on life support to survive her coma even if the coma itself was caused by eating an apple, a narrative if not magical event. The mundane world of reality, which is a world like the reader's, is invaded on a regular basis by fairy-tale narratives that reshape the people and landscape into fairy-tale characters and plots. The agents of the Bureau, many of whom are fairy-tale characters themselves, are able to interact with the stories, taking on roles within the narrative or using (for lack of a better term) fairy-tale superpowers granted to them by their story to affect the narrative of the invading story.

Fairy-tale plots are typically isolated from each other, happening in discrete locations in the real world even as fairy-tale characters move around that world without restriction. In the few instances where specific fairy-tale narratives exist in the same space, this is presented as a mislabeling of the incursion or a transformation of the narrative. In one instance, the team is called to an ATI 709 Snow White in process, only to discover that it is really an ATI 410 Sleeping Beauty, and later it is revealed that this kind of mistake has happened before (*Indexing* 16, 54). In another, the team realizes that the ATI 181.1* The Little Mermaid that they are investigating was meant to be a Beauty and the Beast. The narrative targeted a girl who lost the ability to walk in an accident as a potential mermaid, but because she was well-adjusted and accepting of her situation, it focused on her brother, a potential Beast, and transformed him into a Mermaid (*Indexing* 311). This leap is possible because "Beasts and Mermaids are both defined by how much they long to be human" (*Indexing* 311). The mix in narratives creates unexpected deviations from The Little Mermaid tale type, which makes the case difficult to investigate. The characters explain to each other that stories don't "normally mix like this" and that "if he [the Mermaid] was meant to be a Beast, which is a very active role, but became a Mermaid, which is more reactive, he could have unconsciously combined aspects of the two stories" (*Indexing* 313). In either case, only one tale type is actually present in any given moment, even if that tale type changes from one to another. In the examples provided above, these mix-ups are a direct result of narrative interference from the novel's villain, Birdie Hubbard, a storyteller whose goal is to obtain the original AT index so that she can further change and control stories to meet her desires.

The narrative landscape of the storyworld, then, is one organized by tale type. Fairy-tale characters are able to engage other stories only if they are able to leave their own, which for characters in active stories means only if they are able to keep their stories' narratives at bay. They are changed by their stories to better conform to the tale type if the story is fully active, but their narrative paths can be avoided if they do not engage with motifs or plot points: Henry avoids apples and princes, Jeffrey avoids shoes, and Sloane does not poison people. This requires a conscious awareness of their role in a fiction on the part of the characters. The self-awareness of their own fictionality and that they are not "real" people marks the primary difference between the fairy-tale characters that work for the Bureau and those that do not. Agents know their role in a fiction, but victims of the fairy-tale incursions do not. Henry even postulates that she is part of a bigger fiction, which is both a moment of foreshadowing for the reveal in the conclusion of *Indexing* that reality is also a tale type and recognition that *Indexing* itself is a work of fiction (13). Metafictional awareness is a key component to McGuire's storyworld, and it is enabled by her use of the tale-type index.

The use of the tale-type index is not new, nor is the reliance on type rather than a specific version of a tale. McGuire is not the first to do this, but it is not common to refer to multiple variants as variants. The metafictional approach here is unique in that the fairy-tale characters are not only self-aware of their fictionality but also aware of the academic scholarship and popular discourse about their fictionality. Only some of the characters are aware of their existence in a fiction, and those are the fairy-tale characters, the ones twice removed from reality, as it were—doubly fictional. The *Indexing* series is not just metafictional, but metacritical. These characters then use that scholarship within the fiction even as they point out its flaws.

Part of this metacritical discourse in the novel is the use of the concept of the monomyth as a way of connecting multiple variants to an ur tale. While the idea of an "original" version of most fairy- and folktales, such as "Snow White," is not sought after by contemporary fairy-tale scholars, the concept of originality is part of popular discourse on fairy tales, with discussion board posts and magazine articles referring to "original" versions of popular tales and adaptations (such as Disney's), typically meaning "older." Scholarship within fairy-tale studies is more interested in variation and multiplicity of tales or of specific versions of tales or traditions than in tracing the very first version of a story. Even many of the original literary tales of Andersen, such as "The Little Mermaid," clearly draw on folklore and other literary material, even if Andersen was the first to combine the various motifs in a particular way. The *Indexing* novels do not elevate an original or suggest its superiority so much as assume that there must have been a first version from which the others evolved. The concept of simultaneous development across multiple cultures is not present. The novels do not suggest that the original is better, just that there is one.

The novels also feature a mythic landscape, a collective unconscious manifested as a physical geographic location that unites tales within specific types even as it separates those types from others. Each tale has its own space, and the one featured in the novels belongs to the Snow White story, the Whiteout Wood. The inhabitants of the Whiteout Wood are all Snow Whites that have died or are in a coma. Henry enters it first through a coma and through dreaming, and it is a major location in both novels. Henry is able to speak with these other Snow Whites and learn about her story and its variants. She also learns about how narratives behave and have desire, and in the second book she speaks with the origin of her story. Here, too, she (and readers) is introduced to the concept of the monomyth. The "hero's journey" is quickly dismissed as "too simplistic" to describe what a monomyth is, and the Snow Whites explain it as "the tale type that took over longest ago" (*Indexing* 372). This tale type is the reality that the fairy-tale narratives are trying to reshape, and it resembles the reader's reality.

When educating Henry about her tale type, the other Snow Whites in the Whiteout Wood define the monomyth as the "basic pattern at the heart of all the other stories. . . . Some people say it's the hero's journey, but that's too simplistic" (*Indexing* 372). Another Snow White adds, "It's too complicated, too. . . . The monomyth is the story that's managed to win" (*Indexing* 372). A monomyth is presented as the dominant tale type, and it can change. The memetic incursions are instances where one tale type distorts reality, effectively becoming the monomyth for that short period. Henry uses this knowledge when confronting the villain in the first book to shape reality around her to the Snow White tale type to ensure her success (*Indexing* 400–402), a tactic she repeats in the sequel. *Monomyth* in the novels refers both to a dominant tale type and the template for a tale type (its required motifs and components) more so than a hero's journey specifically.

The use of the Whiteout Wood and the shared unconscious space of the story touched, organized by tale type, also indicate the influence of Jungian concepts of archetypes and the collective unconscious, both of which underlie Joseph Campbell's work with monomyth even if the novel rejects his formulation of the hero's journey.

At the climax of the novel, when facing the novel's villain, Henry realizes that "Snow White began as its own monomyth, with dead girls in a whiteout wood, and with blood to stain the snow" (*Indexing* 399–400). Here *monomyth* is synonymous with the core elements of a tale type, which for Snow White is a girl's blood on the snow. Stories that share these core elements constitute a tale type and exist in a shared mythic space that is realized in the novels as a geographic space outside of reality. The fairy-tale characters belonging to that story, in this case Snow Whites, are doorways between the shared place of the tale type and the reality in which many tales interact as they try to reshape the dominant tale type that configures the landscape. A living Snow White whose consciousness is in the Whiteout Wood can be a doorway for another Snow White to enter into reality because the Snow Whites, as fairy-tale stock characters, are interchangeable. The Snow White narrative does not care about the individuality of specific Snow Whites; it cares about the shape of the story, that it follows a path that leads it to the story's end.

The tale-type spaces share borders that can be crossed, but they do not overlap. This border-sharing is explored through the transformation of Henry from the Snow White of Snow White and Rose Red (ATI 426/ ATU 426 The Two Girls, the Bear, and the Dwarf) to the Snow White of ATI 709, Snow White. It is also another example of how stories can be changed from one type to another. Born as the Snow White twin of a pair of girls, Henry is switched to a different tale type when her sibling Geraldine realizes as a child that he is a boy. The narrative recognizes Gerry's gender identity, which makes the story of two sisters impossible, and the narrative snaps back on Henry, who is claimed by a different tale type. The same narrative switch happens to Henry's aunt and villain of *Reflections*, Adrianne, who becomes an ATI 709 Snow White after her Rose Red sister reshapes her story to that of Sleeping Beauty (ATI 410). Henry's switch is presented

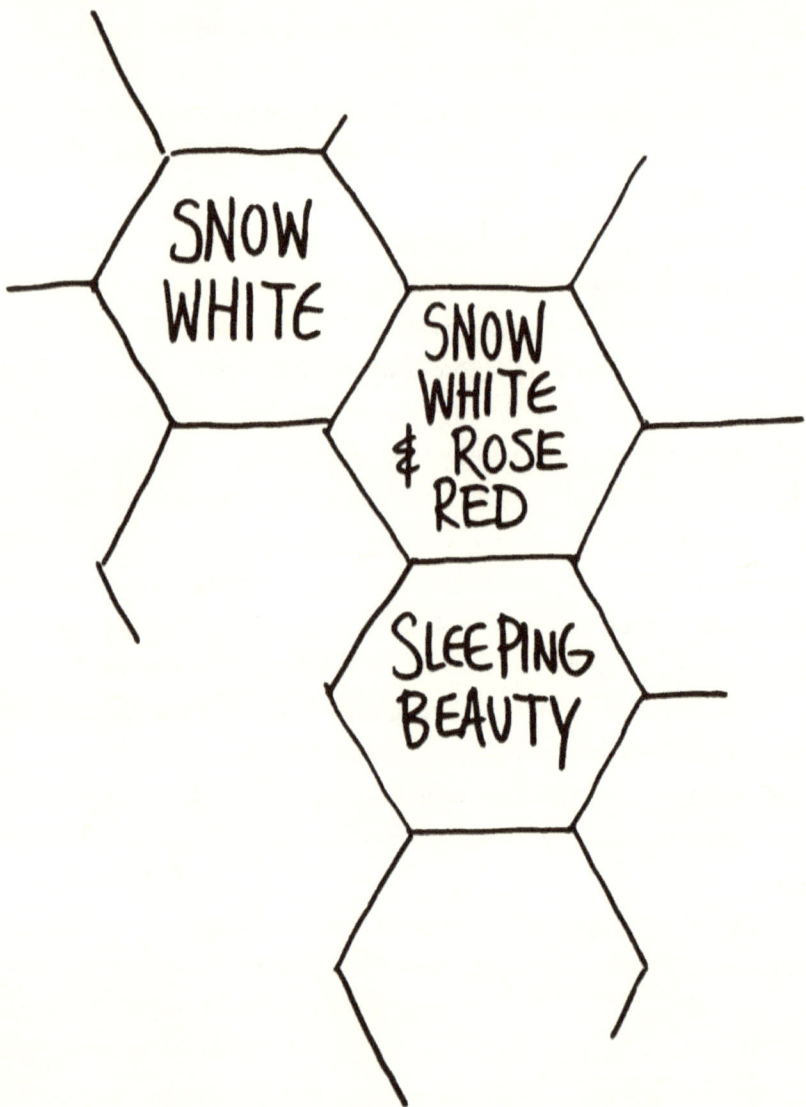

Tale types share narrative borders in a collective unconscious space in *Indexing* and *Reflections*.

as a natural occurrence—the narrative's response to the reality of Gerry's gender—whereas Adrienne's switch is presented as unnatural—one person actively changing her behavior to force the narrative to change.

The unnaturalness of Adrianne's situation—the trauma of being rejected by her sister and her narrative—turns Adrienne into a villain. While Henry is depicted as troubled by the rejection of her birth narrative, she also supports her brother's transition, resulting in her acceptance of the narrative switch. This attitude toward the narrative changes, and its reflection of seeing narratives as static or adaptable, plays a major role in how villainy is understood in the series. The villains in both books are villainous because they want to change the stories to achieve their desires, which is precisely what Henry and her team do to thwart their plans. The crimes seem not to be changing the narratives so much as the motivation behind it—selfish desire or to protect the greater good. Furthermore, Henry and her team's recognition that narratives naturally change is at odds with both the villains' and the Bureau's attempts to contain narratives in specific forms. As the villains try to force the stories into specific forms, they also attempt to fix them in that form, and the entire apparatus of the Bureau is to contain and stabilize narratives. The novels pose a difference between controlling narratives and reshaping them that is born out of whether or not one understands narrative as a semiautonomous force of nature.

Narrative is talked about by the characters as a force of nature that has desire or wants. At first, it is described as a force of nature with the story taking the path of least resistance to reach its conclusion, like water flowing downhill in response to the force of gravity. As the novel's plot progresses, the narrative energy is described in more animal terms—"hunting" the characters (*Indexing* 212). Still a natural force, but one with desire, whether instinctual or conscious, the narrative is described as being alive and active. The novel suggests that this shift in description is accompanied by the narratives being "weaponiz[ed]," manipulated by a storyteller to reach the most catastrophic and destructive endings (*Indexing* 326). The narrative is not hunting in this case, but the storyteller is and is using the narrative's force to do so. But the stories are presented as wanting to end, and the drive of the story is always for an ending. The shared geography of *Indexing* functions as a backdrop for the series' exploration of tale similarity and the development and evolution of stories. The shared location of the city presents a space where the artificiality of the AT index categories are revealed: tale types are confused for each other, mingle and interfere with others, or morph from one into another. The Whiteout Wood presents a location defined by tale type where variants of a single type are connected and present in one place. Both configurations rely on a geographic metaphor to anchor the pastiche technique. The serial, episodic structure delays narrative closure even as individual cases are solved, and the AT index is the metafictional and metacritical center to the series' contemplation of the nature of stories.

Stacking Narratives

The stacking of narratives, where each novel brings in a new fairy tale, provides organization for the pastiche technique that brings disparate fairy tales together. It is not a free-for-all like in works like *Once Upon a Time*, *Fables*, or *The Sisters Grimm*, where the potential for intermixing is vast. Stacking limits which fairy tales can interact and across which narrative borders. Even when one tale lends the organizing structure to an episode of *Once Upon a Time*, the potential for intermixing is unlimited. An episode focusing on "Sleeping Beauty" can feature Snow White and Mulan, or Captain Hook can show up without any previous indication that the stories converge. The open geographic space that the tales inhabit on *Once Upon a Time* removes narrative borders that separate tales. Any story that is at home in the Enchanted Forest of *Once Upon a Time* is a potential intertext at any given time. As the series expands to other lands, so does the possibility for intermixing because the magic portals that connect the Enchanted Forest to Oz, for example, can also connect to other lands. The barriers are harder to transverse, but they are still, for all intents and purposes, open borders. Will Scarlet of the *Robin Hood* ballads can just as easily travel from Sherwood Forest in the Enchanted Forest to Oz or Wonderland, making his appearance in an Oz-centric episode perfectly logical for the storyworld, despite the difference in lands.

For novels that stack, like *The Lunar Chronicles*, that potential is limited. The shared landscape is not an open space; it is a space with narrative and geographic borders, so that the Cinderella character can move from the Cinderella story of the Eastern Commonwealth to the Little Red Riding Hood space of France, but the narrative of Cinderella does not traverse that geographic boundary. Characters can move around, but stories are fixed to specific locations: "Cinderella" in the Eastern Commonwealth, "Little Red Riding Hood" in France, "Rapunzel" in space and the Sahara desert, and "Snow White" on Luna. Even though specific characters may play crucial roles in another character's story, their narratives cannot follow them. So, for example, even though Scarlet plays a crucial role in *Winter* by negotiating with a soldier wolf pack and using her status as Wolf's mate, she is acting as a helper figure, taking on the role of the dwarves in "Snow White" by protecting Winter from the queen and keeping her hidden. She does not act as Little Red Riding Hood in *Winter*, despite encountering wolves for a second time and being more savvy and less trusting in her dealings with them (an allusion to the Grimms' version of the story in which there is a second wolf encounter). The two narratives do not unfold simultaneously for the reader, and the characters from other tales appear as cameos and almost exclusively in helper roles or non-fairy-tale-function background roles. Fairy tales in *Once Upon a Time* comingle across narrative borders and sometimes unfold simultaneously for the viewers, whereas in *The Lunar Chronicles*, the fairy-tale plots are separated by the series structure, one plot per book. The separation of fairy tales across novels creates narrative barriers that are reflected in the geographic locations of where the individual fairy tales play out. This is not unique to *The Lunar Chronicles*; Jim C. Hines's Princess series uses a similar structure with each novel featuring a different fairy-tale protagonist and her accompanying fairy tale and each novel using a different location even though the princesses work together as a team in each novel.

This kind of structuring offers both stability and clear rules about what can happen in a given retelling, but it also limits the ways the tales can be retold. Cinder cannot be broken out of the "Cinderella" narrative despite the potential of the science-fiction genre because the novel derives its narrative stability from a specific fairy tale. In contrast, in *Once Upon a Time* Rumplestiltskin can be both baby-stealing villain and romantic hero in the same episode because of the interplay between the "Rumplestiltskin" and "Beauty and the Beast" tales. Both forms of pastiche/ fairy-tale mixing make firm symbolic connections between genre and geography.

Connecting plot to place provides clear cues to the reader about what can happen in any given space. This allows reader attention to be pulled to the other "new" things an author or text may be doing. Because readers know that *Scarlet* is a "Little Red Riding Hood" retelling, the reader can focus on the inventiveness of the genetically engineered werewolf or the characterization of Scarlet as tough and independent rather than on how the "Cinderella" story from the first novel unfolds. The shift in geographic location and signaling of the source tale through the title and the book section epigraphs tells readers that they can set aside the "Cinderella" narrative and not have to worry about how it will progress. The ending of the series—that Cinder will have a happily ever after—is all but assured by the successful resolution to the "Little Red Riding Hood" plot and the invocation of fairy-tale narrative space through the epigraphs. This structure tells readers that they can focus on only one fairy tale at time even though the fairy-tale characters transition from one book to the next. The stability of the fairy-tale plot—one tale per book—is an important part of the genre mixing that relies on science-fiction tropes for its complicated plots. In series like *Indexing*, in which the ways the fairy tales are configured is the new, inventive aspect, the other genre provides the stable background, using the tropes of agency-based crime drama but not reinventing them. The difference in geographic structuring signals to the reader which genre is the author's background and which is the playground. The geographic restriction placed on the narrative structure limits one kind of narrative play, but it opens up another.

Indexing and *Reflections*, published as both serials and a two-book series, follow the serial structure of television shows more than the stacking of *The Lunar Chronicles*. However, the ways in which the fairy-tale plots are kept separate even as the fairy-tale characters share a storyworld is similar to the stacking of the novel series. The stacking happens on an episode basis rather than a novel basis. The main difference here is how McGuire uses tale types to organize and differentiate between the fairy tales as they appear in the novel. The scholarly organizational system is applied to the fictional storyworld so that even as fairy tales coexist in the same geographic place, they are separated by narrative type. Deviation from this order, which is presented as unstable and artificial at times, is a problem to be solved by the series' protagonists.

The use of the AT index in the series brings to attention how similar different tale types are, and how many motifs are shared. They are not interchangeable, but the points of similarity are necessary for the interaction across narrative borders. The connections between some stories, like many of the princess tales, are pretty clear in the text, but the ways that the Pied Piper and the Shoemaker and the Elves are worked in are more nontraditional, yet the connections are still there. The use of the index allows for the fairy tales to be combined in interesting ways that are not possible without the cataloguing of similarities and differences. The AT index is an important source text, more so than the stories themselves, but of course the novel relies on reader familiarity with those stories. *Indexing*'s pastiche is about more than characters appearing in other stories or trying to retell those stories. It is about understanding what makes the stories different.

More so than any other text I study in this book, *Indexing* and *Indexing: Reflections* use and showcase the academic study of fairy tales. There is a seriousness to the series' approach to fairy tales that recognizes the primacy of fairy tales in everyday lives—which I would argue all of the texts do—but it also recognizes the importance of understanding a fuller history of the genre and its depth, breadth, and variation in a way that other twenty-first-century texts do not. In all of the texts under study here, fairy tales are important and they shape how we engage with the world. Fairy tales are valued, and in reshaping them, writers are criticizing fairy tales not so much as inappropriate but as needing to be updated to reflect current social standards. This is part of a long tradition of fairy tales being shaped and reshaped to reflect specific sociohistorical moments and engage in cultural debates. But the *Indexing* series also demonstrates the need to know the actual history of the genre and not just the Disney versions plus a handful of other stories. McGuire's series brings in the importance of understanding that history itself—not so much because she engages the history but because she emphasizes how much fairy tales "naturally" change.

I do not want to argue that one method of geographic pastiche is superior to the other, even as I do argue that the open-borders approach is more

Genres Overlaid • 103

generically complex for the fairy-tale genre. Instead the two methods serve very different purposes and offer two different types of fairy-tale retellings or usage. The two different approaches to narrative geography produce two different kinds of retellings: retelling a specific tale (closed borders) or a genre (open borders). I would argue that both methods highlight the fairy tale in the retelling. *Cinder* is not less of a fairy tale because the fairy tale supports the science-fiction imagination. The novel's structure and tone is generically fairy tale, and one cannot describe the novel without the fairy-tale genre. It might even make more sense to call it a science-fiction fairy tale, making *science-fiction* the adjective. The fairy tale is a main focus, but it is not the only focus.

In both of these novel series, narratives are tied to place, and the mapping of the storyworld and the world building that occurs draws on reader assumptions about genre. How the text posits the connections between the source fairy tales is an explicit part of that world building. The structure of the narrative is reflected in the world building and vice versa. Mapping the geographic space of the storyworld can reveal how the fairy tales will interact. I am sure it is possible to have a text that is a hybrid between these two models of linked and stacking narratives, though I struggle to imagine a retelling in which tales are divided by narrative physical location but the plots of those tales are not. These two types of pastiche are just the beginning of mapping the ways fairy tales are used, and I hope that an exploration of other texts not discussed here will reveal other ways that genre and geography are linked in contemporary fairy tales.

II

Fairy-Tale Maps

3

Asking for Directions

Metafiction and Metaphor in the Korean Drama *Secret Garden*

THE 2010–11 KOREAN DRAMA *Secret Garden* uses Hans Christian Andersen's "The Little Mermaid" to anchor a cross-class love story in contemporary South Korea. Kim Joo-Won, a wealthy businessman from a powerful family, becomes obsessed with stuntwoman Gil Ra-Im but sees no future with her due to their class differences. He proposes that she be his mermaid—stay by his side and then disappear like a bubble when the relationship ends—and she refuses. As with many contemporary Korean dramas, *Secret Garden*'s conflict hinges on the difficulty of a younger generation transgressing social boundaries when a more powerful, older generation wants to enforce social norms, but the emphasis on Andersen's story offers a metafictional model of turning to fairy tales in times of crisis. Joo-Won tries to enact fairy-tale plots when faced with social obligations that conflict with his personal desires, and the show depicts him and Ra-Im enacting, rejecting, and rewriting "The Little Mermaid" as they navigate their difficult path.

Joo-Won uses "The Little Mermaid" as a map to try to navigate the unfamiliar and difficult romance, only to find that the story of repeated sacrifices on the part of the mermaid, which ends in her death, is not adequate for their relationship. He is mystified by Ra-Im's rejection, and the series depicts the two negotiating social pressures that demand their separation, as happens in Andersen's tale, and their own developing love and commitment to each other, which is facilitated through a magical soul swap that forces the two to experience one another's family, social, and gender expectations; to develop an unparalleled intimacy; and to depend upon each other for their own survival. Ultimately Joo-Won rewrites the mermaid's story as a way to articulate his own desire to break his social obligations, drafting a new fairy-tale map that better reflects the options available to star-crossed lovers in the twenty-first century.

Secret Garden both depicts and performs how fairy tales can be used to work through personal and social conflict. Sarah Keith and Sung-Ae Lee explain that "interspecies love thus functions as a metaphor for other social boundaries, such as class, economic privilege (or lack thereof) or otherness in general" in their article, "*Legend of the Blue Sea*: Mermaids in South Korean Folklore and Popular Culture" (69).[1] *Secret Garden* makes this connection for mermaid lore as well when Joo-Won chooses "The Little Mermaid" over "Cinderella" as the fairy tale he turns to for guidance. By trying out the plot of "The Little Mermaid," the characters create a fairy-tale map that must be redrawn multiple times before it can reflect the personal landscape of the characters. This metafictional and metaphoric use of the tale overlays the show's use of fairy tales to chart the complex social landscape of South Korean society in the wake of rapid economic and technological growth following the Korean War. This chapter focuses on the direct references to fairy tales in the show and how the characters attempt to apply fairy-tale logic and fairy-tale paths to their own lives, creating a metaphoric map.

Joo-Won and Ra-Im use fairy tales to both navigate and circumvent their own situation, to communicate desire, and to bridge the gap between their different places in the world. Once their understanding of each other is transformed by a magical soul swap, the fairy tale is still the touchstone to which they return to try to navigate their exceedingly complicated relationship, but it is an ineffectual map until it is rewritten and the characters devise for themselves a different ending to the story. I explore how the metafictional use of fairy tales by the characters to address personal conflict works with and against the metaphoric use of tales in depicting the social conflict of a rapidly changed Korean society. Early in the series, the characters reject the story of "Cinderella" as a metaphor for their relationship and engage "The Little Mermaid" instead. The metafictional rejection of Cinderella outright as a template for the fairy-tale love story is important in understanding generally how fairy tales function as discourse in the series and specifically how "The Little Mermaid" frames questions of class difference in the show.

Secret Garden is an example of the metafictional use of fairy tales in contemporary media that does not just retell fairy tales but engages them as texts and interrogates their usefulness for a twenty-first-century world that differs greatly from the sociohistoric periods in which the source tales originated. *Secret Garden* additionally addresses cross-cultural use of fairy tales, as the translation from Danish culture to South Korean culture adds another layer of distance, which is mirrored in the choice of fairy tale. The culture of the mermaid's underwater kingdom differs greatly from her land-bound prince's. In both retelling "The Little Mermaid" for a twenty-first-century Korean Wave audience and critiquing the inability of the tale to be useful as is, *Secret Garden* reaffirms both the need for fairy tales as a genre and the need for the genre's adaptability.

Social and Genre Landscapes in Korean Dramas

Secret Garden is an extremely popular Korean drama written by Kim Eun-Sook, bringing in high ratings when it aired and winning numerous awards in South Korea.[2] Much of the show's appeal comes from its quirky combination of fantasy and romance, as well as its compelling melodrama balanced with light humor. As with many Korean dramas, the romance plot centers on two people from different class statuses whose relationship is not socially sanctioned, and audiences should expect to cry. An important theme in *Secret Garden* is the changing South Korean social rules, and how young people are struggling to change when their parents want to enforce older social norms.

Secret Garden falls into a genre of Korean dramas that Suk-Young Kim refers to as *chaebol* dramas in "For the Eyes of North Koreans? Politics of Money and Class in *Boys Over Flowers*" (96, 105 n8). *Chaebol* are large, family-owned conglomerates that arose after the Korean War in the latter half of the twentieth century. The families that control these multinational corporate groups are frequently powerful, obscenely wealthy, and often politically involved. Kim explains that these families are quite divorced from the realities of the average Korean citizen:

> Members of *chaebol* live in a privileged universe segregated from the workers of their commercial empire, who are also consumers of their products. Their actual lives are veiled in mystery for the most part, but they have provided a rich terrain for a dramatic imagination. Seasoned with both fascination with the unknown and abhorrence of unlimited power, stories involving *chaebol* abound on Korean TV, especially as the fates of these financial elites become entangled with those of the ordinary citizens. (96)

This extreme class disparity lends itself to a standard romantic plot: rich boy loves poor girl, ending in the elevation of the girl in a happily-ever-after union. In "The Fairy-Tale Film in Korea," Sung-Ae Lee notes that cross-class love stories and "the breakdown of class barriers" are common themes in Korean film (207). The connection to "Cinderella" is obvious, and allusions to the fairy tale proliferate in fan and scholarly discussions of shows of this genre, in their advertising, and in the shows themselves, both directly and indirectly.

This extreme class disparity is a product of the considerable instability that has marked Korea for the last century, and Lee has argued in "Memory, Trauma and History: Fairy-tale film in Korea" that folktale films respond to this trauma:

> [Folktale] films have predominantly used the material to represent or allude to Korea's history of colonization, war and military dictatorship over the past century and the struggles of its people to deal with consequent traumatic memory, post-traumatic stress and their continuing impact in a milieu in which the wealthy constantly unsettle the country's proto-democracy movements. (356)

In 1910, Imperial Japan annexed Korea into its empire following two wars, between China and Japan and then Russia and Japan, which were fought for control of the Korean peninsula. From 1910 to 1945, Korea was an occupied state under Japanese control and hundreds of thousands of Korean citizens were relocated to Japan, both forcibly and not, and during World War II Koreans were conscripted into Japanese military service and support roles, which included prostitution for the military.[3] Many Japanese immigrated to Korea as well, and by the end of the occupation, over half of Korean land was owned by Japanese citizens. During the occupation, Japan accelerated the industrialization and modernization of Korea to benefit the Japanese empire and oppressed Korean language and culture. In 1945, Korea gained independence from Japan at the end of World War II, but it was occupied by the Russian and American militaries who backed different governing bodies, leading to the peninsula being divided into North and South Korea by 1948. The conflict between the northern and southern governments claiming sovereignty over the entirety of the peninsula amidst the escalation of the Cold War between the Soviet Union and the United States led to the Korean War from 1950 to 1953, but the peninsula remains divided. The years after the war have been marked by political and military skirmishes and loss of life, and the South Korean government has been overturned multiple times through coup, assassination, and impeachment, as well as through peaceful elections. Seoul hosted the Olympics in 1988 and the FIFA World Cup in 2002, both events that contributed to Korea's economic growth in addition to its fast recovery from the Asian financial crisis in 1997.

Many scholars discussing Korean drama point to the 1990s as a crucial period in understanding the cultural context of the Korean Wave—the export of South Korean music, film, and television to a pan-Asian audience that includes North Korea.[4] In "Cultural Policy and the Korean Wave: From National Culture to Transnational Consumerism," Hye-Kyung Lee points to the elimination of music censorship policies in 1996 as a factor in the boom of Korean media production, as it allowed for the dispersal of music and film that did not align with state-sanctioned ideological messages (189). This period marks an economic shift to incorporate a culture industry into South Korea's economy, with companies and government investing in local media productions and exporting them as cultural products (as opposed to the state controlling cultural production and emphasizing traditional Korean culture). It comes on the heels of the rapid economic development in South Korea from the 1960s to the 1990s, enabled by postwar industrialization, an emphasis on education that included the working class, and cooperation between the government and the *chaebol*, which developed and thrived in this period. The *chaebol* are a crucial part of South Korea's economic recovery, stability, and success, but the creation of these modern economic dynasties has also created immense class stratification. The last sixty years have seen South Korea transition from a country devastated by war to one of the most technologically advanced and economically strong countries in the world.

The turn of the twenty-first century saw an explosion of successful Korean media productions both locally and internationally. The first decade of the twenty-first century saw the popularity of the Korean Wave not just in Asian countries but in Asian diaspora communities as well, facilitated by piracy in those areas of the world where it was not possible to obtain the media legally. The immense popularity of the Korean drama *Winter Sonata* overseas in 2004 marks an important point in the establishment of the Korean Wave as an international phenomenon. YouTube and online streaming sites have been a major distributor of Korean dramas and K-pop to non-Asian audiences in the last decade, leading some scholars to dub the current global phenomenon as Korean Wave 2.0. The history of political instability in Korea is much more complicated than I have summarized here, but my intention with this very brief overview is to indicate the rapid political and socioeconomic changes that have occurred not only between generations in the last century but within a single lifetime.

In *chaebol* dramas, this rapid change often plays out not only in economic disparity and class differences but in generational conflict within families, with parents trying to maintain class divisions and their Western-educated protagonist children seeking to transgress. In *Secret Garden*, Joo-Won is ultimately disowned for his relationship with Ra-Im. The class difference his mother and grandfather object to is so immense that Joo-Won has no frame of reference for Ra-Im's life. He cannot comprehend that she and her roommate together spend the equivalent of $300 per month rent on an apartment. She cannot afford to miss work when she is seriously injured, whereas Joo-Won avoids work because he does not like traffic. With poverty comes deference to one's superiors that includes humiliation. Ra-Im and others of her station are yelled at, belittled, and mocked because of their status. *Secret Garden* depicts this abuse as both normalized and problematic. It is presented not just as character flaw but as systemic, and Joo-Won explains to Ra-Im in an early episode that the "unequal distribution of wealth" results in a "social class system [where the elite] only want two things: inequality and segregation. If they cannot have the power to rule they want a segregated world for themselves" (episode 5). Once Joo-Won has fallen in love with Ra-Im and begins to empathize with her position, he is shown to have a problem with her deference to others and the social humiliation that she enacts and experiences as part of her class. But as the lines above demonstrate, he is acutely aware of the realities of both the fictional and real South Korean class hierarchy and its impact on the organization of society. This class differential is a vital component of *chaebol* dramas and one that facilitates comparison with the "Cinderella" fairy tale, a popular tale in South Korea.

Rejecting "Cinderella"

"Cinderella" is a widely popular tale in Korean media, and the rapid change in economic status of the country over the last century may help explain why. In "Fairy-Tale Scripts and Intercultural Conceptual Blending in Modern Korean Film and Television Drama," Sung-Ae Lee explains that, as with other folk and fairy tales, "Cinderella" has been generalized in Korean drama and film so that the name conjures a collective of motifs rather than specific narrative versions, thus causing it to function more like a tale type than a contextualized tale (276). Lee argues that the popularity of Grimm and Andersen fairy tales in South Korea

> is not simply the impact of Western culture on the East but a matter of tales that have a strong resonance with deep traumas

that underlie modern Korean culture or with cultural changes associated with fluctuations in the economy and shifts in gendering and gender roles since the early 1990s. Of particular interest is the folktale motif of the innocent persecuted child, which is often employed to reflect Korea's extreme socioeconomic stratification and the trauma it disregards. (282)

Lee explains in "The Fairy Tale Film in Korea" that "Cinderella" is one of "a relatively small group of Western fairy tales which have been adapted for the Korean cinema from the Grimms, Charles Perrault, or Andersen. These adaptations are usually at some remove from the Western tales, which circulate as scripts rather than the European originals" (208). "The Little Mermaid" is named as one of the popular tales from Andersen.[5]

At the center of many *chaebol* dramas is socioeconomic class conflict that ultimately reinforces the privileged position of the social and financial elite. In many cases the poor girl is often not awed by the power of the beautiful prince, and the prince's attraction to her centers on her lack of fear in confronting him and her refusal to adhere to social protocols. Though she may defer to others of higher class or social status, the prince is treated as an equal, and she does not show him the expected deference. She treats him as the arrogant jerk he is instead of deferring to his social role of charming prince. And yet, in *chaebol* series that adhere to a Cinderella plot, the plucky heroine must give up her fierce socialist ideals to enter the world of her prince. While shows may criticize the economic disparity, interclass abuse, and *chaebol* control in dialogue and dramatic scenes, the structure that ends in upward class mobility reinforces this disparity as a stable reality. As with many modern Cinderella stories, individuals can transgress class boundaries but the system itself is stable and fixed.

The *chaebol* dramas that have a romance plot are typically discussed in terms of the Cinderella story, and *Secret Garden* is no exception. The advertising calls the series a Cinderella story, and the characters of the show invoke Cinderella as a script. When Joo-Won first proposes to Ra-Im that they becomes lovers, she responds, "Like Cinderella?" To which he replies, "No." Cinderella can't be their story because there is no chance for Ra-Im to transcend the class barrier (episode 5). That is simply fantasy. A metafictional comment on competing Korean dramas, to be sure, this exchange draws critical attention to the class disparity that divides the *chaebol* elite from the average Korean citizen. Rather than a plot point—a barrier or interdiction—for the heroine to overcome, this class disparity is emphasized in *Secret Garden* as an insurmountable and rigid system. Though the disparity is present and crucial to the plot in many other *chaebol* dramas, the rigidity of the system is glossed over by endings that emphasize the ability of individuals to transgress the system. While viewers may still recognize that kind of upward class mobility as fantasy, only possible in the glamorous storyworld of Korean dramas, the shows offer liminal space where the fantastic is possible.

Sung-Ae Lee has examined conceptual blending in *Secret Garden* and other Korean dramas that use European fairy tales and local folktales as both narrative sources and cultural scripts. Lee's analysis of *Secret Garden* is focused on the Cinderella script in the show, and she argues that the "series constantly problematizes [the] fairy-tale script [the main characters] are enacting" ("Fairy-Tale Scripts" 277). She argues, "In quite a complex movement, indeed, the series uses the Cinderella-script to overthrow the Little Mermaid-script and then shatters happy-ever-after by disclosing the Cinderella outcome to be an illusion" (277). Cinderella, she argues, "is evoked as an obvious absence by the repeated assertion that 'The Little Mermaid' is the *second* best-known story in the history of humankind. The first is presumably 'Cinderella,' in that the series obviously follows a Cinderella-script" (277). Lee acknowledges "The Little Mermaid" as a prominent source, but I argue that it is the dominant source over "Cinderella." It is the tale continually referred to by the characters as a map for their love story. Rather than using "the Cinderella-script to overthrow the Little Mermaid-script and then ... [shattering] happy-ever-after," as Lee suggests, I argue that the show uses the narrative logic of "The Little Mermaid" to challenge the notion of "Cinderella" as an appropriate fairy tale for the cross-class love story and to reveal the upward class mobility of the tale to be fantasy. The sad ending of "The Little Mermaid" is presented as more realistic, and the characters engage in an active rewriting of the tale to form an alternate ending that is neither the unrealistic happy ending of "Cinderella" nor the tragic end of "The Little Mermaid."

Even though she is helped by magic, Ra-Im is not able to transcend her class status in *Secret Garden*. In fact, the fantastic elements of the show—namely the magical intervention of Ra-Im's dead father, which induces the two romantic leads to swap souls every time it rains—reinforce the reality of the class system it portrays. The contrast of the fantastic to what is otherwise a mimetic show reconfigures the audience's expected fantasy of class mobility and presents a magic soul swap as the fantastic element of the show instead. This scene of invocation and rejection of the Cinderella plot is an important one for viewers because it directly addresses audience expectations (you think this is Cinderella, but you are wrong) and offers a different fairy-tale map for viewers to follow. Joo-Won offers "The Little Mermaid" as a more appropriate story, and it works in several ways.

Rewriting "The Little Mermaid"

"The Little Mermaid" is a suitable analogy for the series' plot on multiple levels. The obvious one, the one that Joo-Won first picks up on, is that he and Ra-Im are from two different worlds. He is a member of an elite business family, and as such is extremely powerful and wealthy. She is an orphaned stuntwoman living in poverty. The one-sidedness of the little mermaid's love also parallels Joo-Won's obsession with Ra-Im, which is initially unreturned. In Andersen's story, which is the source tale, as opposed to Disney's 1989 film, the little mermaid is desperately in love with the prince and sacrifices her voice to grow human legs, but she does so at great cost—her tongue is cut out as payment to the sea witch, and the transformation that grants her legs also causes intense pain every time she uses her feet. She suffers greatly for love, but the prince clearly does not return her love. He dotes on her, but he loves the mermaid as a child, not as a mate (Andersen, "Mermaid" 16).[6] He firmly states that he can only love the girl he thinks saved him and that he is marrying a princess out of duty. Joo-Won's obsession with Ra-Im is likewise one-sided for the first part of the series, though she finds him to be annoying instead of a cute pet. Joo-Won takes on characteristics of both mermaid and prince, including making a "royal" match out of duty. Ra-Im comes to love him, and it is through the swapping of souls that the two begin to understand each other better. This soul swap is the third parallel between the two stories.

In Andersen's tale the mermaid falls in love with the prince after learning that a human marriage can grant her a soul, something she wants more than anything, and there are several points in Andersen's story that suggest that a soul, not true love, is the mermaid's primary desire. Love is simply the means to an end. Through marriage, souls are joined, and so the mermaid will be able to share the prince's soul. Joo-Won and Ra-Im quite literally share souls, as theirs are swapped every time it rains. By living in the other's body, each lover learns what the other's experiences truly are. There are humorous moments that deal with physically different bodies and threats about not abusing the borrowed anatomy, but more importantly, they learn of the pressures and responsibilities that the other has, which allows them to overcome, or at least face, the obstacles to their relationship. The characters, however, do not connect their soul swap to the mermaid story despite it being a magical, fairy-tale-esque event. *Secret Garden* is not a direct retelling of "The Little Mermaid"; rather it invokes "The Little Mermaid" script, shifting the motifs in different ways. Thus "The Little Mermaid" story is familiar to the characters and provides a logical map by which to navigate their experience.

Joo-Won initially proposes the mermaid analogy when he realizes that he cannot stop thinking about Ra-Im and that he is willing to risk a little humiliation for a fling, but he fully intends to make a business-alliance marriage when the time comes. The scene in episode five begins with Joo-Won questioning Ra-Im about her relationship with her boss, a stunt coordinator, who is secretly in love with her. They are in a hotel room at a Jeju island resort that is the location of a shoot for a stunt and the destination of a weekend with K-Pop star Oska, which Ra-Im has won.[7] The scene alternates between reaction shots of Joo-Won and Ra-Im in conversation and is shot primarily in close-ups of their faces. In confronting Joo-Won about his interest in her personal life, Ra-Im accuses him of harassing her and asks what his intentions toward her are. Joo-Won replies that she knows; they have not changed from his previous proposal. He asks to hug her and explains that "There are two kinds of women for me: one for fun and one for marriage. But you're somewhere between the two, so let me hug you." Ra-Im responds, "What if you like it, what are you gonna do?" His response, "I'll give you a life that's different from now," prompts Ra-Im to suggest a fairy-tale narrative to frame their experience. She asks, "That's awesome, then am I Cinderella?" Joo-Won denies: "Nope. The Little Mermaid. You will probably always be somewhere between the two. Just stay there ambiguously and disappear into bubbles. This is my principle." Ra-Im's lips tremble and she slaps Joo-Won. The song that is associated with the two in romantic or sad moments begins. Joo-Won tells her to "Think about it, then let me know." He leaves, and the scene continues with a teary Ra-Im, who reflects on Joo-Won's words, heard in a voice-over.[8]

Ra-Im finds this proposal insulting. She suggests "Cinderella" as a suitable fairy tale to describe their potential relationship. It is a logical choice, has been used to describe this series, and is associated with *chaebol* Korean dramas. But Joo-Won insists that she cannot enter his world, and she cannot. She does not have the family, the education, or the background to be accepted into his social class. Even at the end of the series when the two find a way to be together, she is not accepted by Joo-Won's mother and grandfather, and his role in the business and his inheritance are cut as punishment for his marriage. The class difference between them is too vast, and the social obligations that Joo-Won must meet to maintain his social position do not allow for a "Cinderella" plot of upward mobility through marriage. While insulting, Joo-Won's rejection of Cinderella is logical and realistic, as opposed to the fantasy expected by fans of this Korean drama genre.

What Joo-Won wants is for Ra-Im to "disappear into bubbles," referring to the end of Andersen's tale in which the mermaid commits suicide and turns into bubbles. Andersen's prince marries a princess, his social equal, which means that the mermaid will die and turn into sea foam, as mermaids do because they have no soul. The mermaid's sisters try to save her from this fate by trading their hair for a dagger from the sea witch. If the mermaid stabs the prince in the heart and then lets the blood fall onto her feet, she will regain her fins. But poised over the sleeping prince with dagger in hand, she cannot bring herself to do this because she loves the prince. She throws herself overboard and turns into bubbles. The version of the tale used in *Secret Garden* stops here. There is an additional scene in Andersen's tale in which the mermaid is turned into a daughter of the air due to her selfless sacrifice and suffering, and she is given the chance to earn a soul through her good deeds. Notably, this extra ending that reinforces the Christian moralizing of Andersen's tale is absent from *Secret Garden*, so that Joo-Won's mermaid simply disappears and is not reborn. Or, rather, he does not concern himself with her; once Ra-Im leaves, he intends to forget her. While I do not think viewers are meant to read Joo-Won as literally wanting Ra-Im to die at the end of their affair, his disregard for her welfare is troubling and selfish, and it is clear why she slaps him. This is a crucial scene in the series for multiple reasons.

First, this scene emphasizes the extremity of the class division. Andersen's little mermaid is a princess in her own right, but her world is vastly different from the prince's. So much so that she has to physically change her body to be able to fit in to the human world. The mermaid cannot be the prince's equal on her own. It takes great sacrifice for her to approach him, and even that is not enough. The social difference between the two is an insurmountable problem, as it is with Joo-Won and Ra-Im. But the comparison also acknowledges that Ra-Im is a princess in her own right. She is a gifted and talented stuntwoman who is basically the best at what she does. Other characters, including Joo-Won and those who hate her, are constantly pointing out how "cool" and "awesome" she is and using English words to do so, so audiences know that it is serious.[9] But the best stuntwoman in the world is still not *chaebol*-quality.

Second, the scene sets boundaries for what is and is not possible in the storyworld. Under a "Cinderella" plot, Ra-Im could marry Joo-Won and become part of his world, but Ra-Im will not become a *chaebol* princess, no matter how cool she is. The happily-ever-after marriage that marks the elevation in class status is not a real option for these characters, and everyone on the show knows it and says so. Rather, the "Cinderella" plot is invoked because of the popularity of that story in Korean media. Fans expect a cross-class love story to be a "Cinderella" story. So in order for "The Little Mermaid" to be *the* fairy-tale metaphor for the series, "Cinderella" must be rejected both directly through metafictional discourse and indirectly through structural differences. This is not to say that "Cinderella" is not a source for the series; it very clearly is, but the rejection of "Cinderella" for "The Little Mermaid" reframes the show's questions of class difference. The show blends "Cinderella" and "The Little Mermaid" scripts and references several other well-known European fairy tales in key fairy-tale moments, such as their first kiss and the end. "Cinderella" invokes issues of justice, and Jane Yolen refers to this tale type as a story of "riches recovered" in "America's Cinderella" (442). There is a social order that has been disrupted, and the magical interference corrects the problem by restoring the servant girl to her proper or higher class. Embedded in the narrative structure of popularized versions of "Cinderella" is the acceptance of class hierarchy. But in "The Little Mermaid," the heroine dies. She does not become a human princess. She does not become wealthy. In the version invoked in the series, which does not include the Christian moralizing at the end of Andersen's story, she does not earn a chance to have a soul. The class division *is* stable, but there are no happy endings here. Joo-Won very clearly sets up the terms of his proposition. They will have a passionate fling, and then Ra-Im will disappear. He will marry someone else more appropriate and forget Ra-Im exists.

Third, the scene sets up the driving metaphor for the show, which is the metafictional use of "The Little Mermaid" as a map. "The Little Mermaid" provides guidance. It charts a path the characters can follow in trying to navigate the impossible social division. It also provides a starting point for their subsequent revisions to the map. As the series progresses, Joo-Won returns to the fairy tale multiple times, revising it in different ways to chart new routes for their relationship. He offers a gender swap in which he is the mermaid who will sacrifice and disappear, and when that fails, Joo-Won offers a reversal of financial status that leaves the prince devoted to the mermaid and in which they live a "boring life." The actual resolution to the series mirrors Joo-Won's final rewrite with him sacrificing his family fortune and position so that he and Ra-Im may live a boring life, but not a poor life; Joo-Won is still wealthy on his own. Ultimately, Joo-Won rewrites the mermaid's story as a way to articulate his own desire to break his social obligations.

Finally, the scene offers a dramatic and cathartic moment when Ra-Im slaps Joo-Won for his suggestion. *How dare he?* And while viewers may react to the slap from its role in the romantic plot—he is cruel to suggest she can be tossed aside after their affair—it also resonates for the background commentary on the class system. The literal comparison of Ra-Im to the mermaid is that her life has no value. It is not worth saving, and it is not a life worth living. His is. Recall that Andersen's mermaid dies because she cannot bring herself to kill the prince who murmurs his bride's name in his sleep. While Andersen's story creates sympathy for the mermaid and her extreme self-sacrifice, the choice between prince or mermaid makes the survivor more valuable—he is more important than she is. It is possible to argue that the mermaid is clearly more important because she is the one whose actions are aligned with the tale's theme, but removing the ending that rewards her sacrifice with the possibility of a soul—as *Secret Garden* does—replaces the hopeful end with one that emphasizes the melancholy of death. It is both noble and devastating that Andersen's mermaid does not kill to save her own life, but her choice—for whatever reason—says his life is worth the cost of hers. The extreme disparity, that the mermaid is literally not human, is invoked in this scene from *Secret Garden*, and it is shocking because it means that Joo-Won sees a woman that he is falling in love with as not his equal in every possible way. She is less important, *less human* than he is, and this is a position that is raised multiple times when their relationships puts pressure on the class system.

The ending proposed by Joo-Won in this scene is a problem, and Ra-Im refuses to engage in a relationship where she will be tossed aside, a relationship that is unequal. In episode 9, when faced with this scenario once again, Ra-Im tells Joo-Won that she cannot be his mermaid "because the Little Mermaid actually loved the man," implying that Ra-Im does not love Joo-Won. She has started developing feelings for him at this point, but his insistence on a romantic relationship built on antiquated patterns that are concerned about the happiness of only the wealthy, male prince is infuriating. Much of the drama in these middle episodes stems from Joo-Won not understanding why Ra-Im is so insulted by his proposal. Like the prince in Andersen's story, he sees being his plaything as a privilege. Faced with a fairy-tale map that is leading him nowhere, Joo-Won tries reversing the directions. He will be the mermaid. The opening scene of episode 12, which continues the closing scene in episode 11, begins with a high-angle long shot over the shoulder of Joo-Won. The two are standing on a street at night, facing each other. The scene alternates reaction shots between the two as the dialogue is given, but the camera stays over the shoulder of each actor, in medium close-up shots.

The opening dialogue is Joo-Won's, and he says, "I'm going to be your Little Mermaid. I'm going to be next to you as if I'm not there. And then I'll disappear like a bubble. So what I'm saying is that I'm desperately hanging onto you." The two argue about this new proposal being "ridiculous," but Joo-Won aligns himself with the mermaid because he recognizes that he is the one feeling the unreturned love. As they continue to argue, Ra-Im raises the impossibility of a future with the mermaid scenario, arguing that reversing the roles does not solve the problem. She asks, "In other words, no matter what kind of sweet time we spend together it will disappear and be forgotten, right?" Joo-Won's response focuses again on his social obligation and the class division:

> Because that's our reality. Sure. We're probably going to argue with my grandfather's siblings who've been totally against my inheriting LOEL, with many investors who've wanted to become part of my family through marriage, and with my mother, who can hurt you. My marriage is a business transaction with the emphasis on mutual interest. Eventually, I'll have to make a decision. Should I disappoint all those people and choose Gil Ra-Im? Or should I forgo Gil Ra-Im, and choose a woman who'll be a good business partner? Do you want me to do the former? Fine. Let's say I give up everything and choose you. We choose our home and pick out our bed. We sleep and wake up together. But . . . for how long would our happiness

last? Do you think the two of us will live happily ever after? I don't have the guts to hate you and resent you but do you feel the same? (episode 12)

Ra-Im agrees with Joo Won's logic here, but also calls him a "fool," arguing that "No woman in this world falls in love thinking of how it'll end." Joo-Won argues that not all relationships succeed, so the lack of a future should not impede their moving forward, but Ra-Im does not give in.

Joo-Won is more accurately reading his fairy-tale map at this point because he has figured out that he is the one who is desperately clinging to an unreturned love like the mermaid does. He is suffering from lovesickness and, in his opinion, has sacrificed his pride and some of his reputation for Ra-Im. But he is still misreading Ra-Im, who is also suffering. Joo-Won does not see how this awkward relationship is hurting her because he does not see how someone who is impoverished and of low class can suffer embarrassment like he does. Ra-Im is also not confessing any of her feelings to him, so he does not know how thoughts of him have been disrupting her work and her relationships with colleagues and friends. Part of the misreading is due to his stubbornness and elitism, but it also reflects the difficulties in transgressing social boundaries and the growing pains of South Korean society in the wake of rapid economic and technological growth following the Korean War.

Joo-Won's misreading of the situation is also due to his inability to let go of the mermaid analogy. His reliance on the fairy tale was not working, so he rewrote the tale by reversing the roles. This gendered role reversal is a very common technique in retelling fairy tales for Western audiences. In the 1980s and 1990s, this was a dominant mode of feminist retelling. However, role reversal is a problematic technique because it preserves the hierarchy of the source tale, maintains distinct categories of gendered behaviors, and leaves the plot of the story intact. Women can be strong and men weak, but this is only a change in representations of gender and not a change that challenges the structural hierarchies and embedded ideologies that script women and men into unequal marriage plots. The reversal does not work for Joo-Won because swapping the gendered roles does nothing to address the problem of the social strictures that doom romance or the underlying belief that he is better than Ra-Im and that her future does not matter. He is still accepting the underlying ideology that says that he cannot marry a stuntwoman and that the prince cannot marry a mermaid. So his new map still leads to suffering and unhappiness. Reversing the directions does not avoid the primary obstacle in his path—outmoded, culturally inappropriate ideology.

Despite this, Ra-Im eventually falls in love and agrees to be with him. At this point the series focuses on battles with Joo-Won's mother over his dating a stuntwoman, hijinks that ensue from more soul swaps, and the overlapping love triangle involving Yoon Suel, Oska, and Jong Soo (the latter being Ra-Im's supervisor). Joo-Won decides to live with Ra-Im and to seriously pursue their relationship, thereby risking his position and inheritance. This shift in his values prompts him to rewrite the ending of "The Little Mermaid" because the ending where one partner disappears is clearly not going to work, but he is still attached to the fairy tale as his guide. So he redrafts the map.

A scene in episode 19 depicts Joo-Won reading his new ending. But because this is a melodrama, the scene is a little more complicated than just presenting a new ending for the mermaid tale. Before this scene, Ra-Im in Joo-Won's body, places the ending of "The Little Mermaid" in one of Joo Won's books. After the two have swapped back into their own bodies, Ra-Im is in a car accident while filming a stunt that results in her being in a coma. Joo-Won finds "The Little Mermaid" page and breaks down sobbing. He decides to take Ra-Im's body into a rainstorm so that they can switch and she can live. This is a touching moment that draws directly on the mermaid's suicide when faced with killing the prince to secure her future in Andersen's tale. Joo-Won chooses to sacrifice himself so that Ra-Im can live, becoming the mermaid he said he would. He is again turning to the story for guidance and direction. But before he swaps their bodies, he writes Ra-Im a love letter detailing his decision and rewrites the ending to the mermaid's story so that they have a happy ending. Joo-Won's soul swap is successful, and he is the one in a coma. His sacrifice is rewarded, and he is revived with magical assistance. However, this is still a melodrama, so it gets more complicated. When Joo-Won awakes, he is suffering from trauma-induced amnesia, believing that he is twenty-one years old, the age when he suffered another trauma that he has been blocking out. He remembers nothing of what has happened in the series, but begins to fall for Ra-Im again, saying many of the same silly and arrogant things. Finding this page triggers his memory of Ra-Im and his failed use of the mermaid map, and so this scene, which reveals his new ending, is also the scene in which he regains his memory.

The scene in episode 19 begins with a full shot of Joo-Won in his library, looking out of the window. A closer shot shows him reflecting on accusations by his mother that Ra-Im used her father (a firefighter who gave his life to save Joo-Won when he was trapped in an elevator in a burning building) to manipulate Joo-Won into loving her. Joo-Won is still suffering from amnesia at this point and does not remember any of his time with Ra-Im, but he has fallen for her again and made the same proposition about having a short-term affair with her. He crosses the room and looks through his books, selecting a copy of *Alice in Wonderland* that contains a printed page of the last page of "The Little Mermaid" story. The final words have been crossed out, and a new ending has been handwritten. The camera focuses on the words on the page: "The knife was shaking in the Little Mermaid's hand but the next moment, she dropped it deep into the ocean." The camera

Joo-Won's rewritten end to "The Little Mermaid," from *Secret Garden* episode 19.

Asking for Directions • 125

switches to a close-up of Joo-Won as he reads, then back to the page as he reads the handwritten addition aloud, then back to a medium close-up to reveal his reaction to the text:

> Just as the Little Mermaid was about to disappear like a bubble the prince discovered the truth and said to the princess 'Is this your best? Are you sure?' He canceled the engagement and ran to the Little Mermaid. From the bubble idea, the Little Mermaid founded a bubble washing machine company and got filthy rich. On the other hand, the prince, who lost all of his savings from unrestrained investments became the secretary of the Little Mermaid and lived boringly ever after. Very boringly. (episode 19)

Joo-Won reacts, asking, "What kind of idiot would do a foolish thing like this?" He looks at the page again and recognizes his own handwriting. He remembers Ra-Im repeating back to him his suggestion about being a mermaid: "Should I just be with you as if I weren't there and then disappear like a bubble? Like the Little Mermaid."[10]

This triggers his memory, and Joo-Won begins to remember making that proposition to Ra-Im. A voice-over gives his voice saying, "Just be with me as if you weren't there and then disappear like a bubble." The scene devolves into rapid flashes of scenes from earlier in the series of Joo-Won and Ra-Im, including the slap from episode 5 discussed earlier. Joo-Won remembers knocking over a vase of flowers and crying as he wrote a letter, which happened as he made the decision to switch bodies with an unconscious Ra-Im. More flashes show Joo-Won remembering switching their bodies, revealing that he is regaining his memory. The scene continues with Joo-Won running down the road and then driving, interspersed with flashes of scenes from the series as he regains his memory completely, including the memories of his accident at twenty-one that he lost with his previous bout of amnesia. The next scene shows Joo-Won confronting Ra-Im and hugging her. After a poorly executed joke where he pretends to still have amnesia, which Ra-Im does not take well, Joo-Won he reveals that he has regained his memory and tells Ra-Im he loves her. Then Joo-Won reveals that he has also regained his earlier lost memories and tells her about how her father died saving him.

In order to make the fairy tale work for their lives, Joo-Won needed to rewrite the ending and change the circumstances of both characters. Rather than transcend social status, Joo-Won's mermaid and prince meet in the middle, with a reversal of financial status that leaves the prince devoted to the mermaid. But important, too, is that they live a "boring life," not happily ever after. A boring life suggests a much more realistic end, to be sure, that floats somewhere between disappearing into bubbles and a strife-free happily ever after.

A key component in the ending to the series is Joo-Won's sacrifice. Andersen's "The Little Mermaid" is concerned with sacrifice, the need to give up something of value to obtain what one wants. The little mermaid sacrifices her voice, her body, her family, her royal status, and ultimately her life in her quest for a soul and/or love (without the Christian moralizing end, the emphasis on the soul in Andersen's original is less obvious, making it easier to read this as a love story). While Ra-Im is not shown sacrificing as much, and therefore may be more easily read as a Cinderella-figure, Joo-Won sacrifices a great deal. He ultimately sacrifices his family, which disowns him, his obscene wealth, and his social status to be with Ra-Im, but before that, he sacrifices his body and life.

When Ra-Im is injured in the accident and left unconscious, Joo-Won initiates a soul swap so that she may live in his body and he be trapped in hers. While he does not actually die, he prepares to by saying good-bye to friends and family and by giving away some of his possessions. He expects to not survive the soul swap. Though Joo-Won does recover, he initially suffers from trauma-induced amnesia, forgetting the last several years and thus sacrificing his life with Ra-Im so that she may live. The ending of the series sees his memory restored and a marriage, but the theme of sacrifice is a major part of the plot that plays into the melodrama genre. Rather than either/or, *Secret Garden* employs a both/and use of the fairy-tale sources, invoking "Cinderella" in the character of Ra-Im and "The Little Mermaid" in that of Joo-Won. The tales share the narrative and geographic space of the series' setting, but they also exist simultaneously in the characters, with the repeated soul swaps confusing the situation so that each body is associated with each fairy tale. The two stories resonate with each other, and their interplay in the series is an important way of interrogating the reliability of these tales in contemporary Korean life. The possibility of "Cinderella" is pure fantasy, but with the sacrifice of "The Little Mermaid," a potential path can be charted; however, it still requires revising the story so that the sacrifice comes from the more privileged person and the happy ending contains a more realistic loss in status, reversing important elements of both stories. "The Little Mermaid" is metafictionally engaged by the characters as a set of directions for how to navigate their circumstances, whereas "Cinderella" is invoked but not directly engaged by the characters. "Cinderella" is also more of a thematic intertext, whereas "The Little Mermaid" lends plot structure in addition to theme.

Sung-Ae Lee concludes that "Conceptual blending, however, also entails the possibility that a script will develop different meanings when carried over to a new cultural context and blended with other scripts" ("Fairy-Tale Scripts" 289). She refers to the scene at the end of the series where, when faced with the impossibility of their relationship being successful, Ra-Im leaves Joo-Won the sad ending of "The Little Mermaid" (i.e., suicide and no soul), and Lee argues that that note "affirms that fairy-tale scripts are also life scripts" (289). Joo-Won's reaction is to rewrite the ending in a move of conceptual blending that draws upon a local variant of Cinderella in which she becomes a businesswoman who doesn't need a prince (289). This combination of Andersen and Korean folktale creates a new script that allows Joo-Won and Ra-Im a different narrative possibility.

The diegetic emphasis on "The Little Mermaid" as the map for the love story means that the audience cannot forget that the class system that causes the major barrier to love is fiercely protected and enforced. Through its metafictional use of "The Little Mermaid" over "Cinderella," *Secret Garden* emphasizes the economic disparity in South Korea and the *real* conflicts it creates. The diegetic focus on the differing perspectives created by that disparity, challenges stories that suggest that swapping places or moving from one class status to another can "fix" the problem. Rather, this is a long process of trial and error in uncharted territory. But *Secret Garden* is a fairy tale as much as it is a melodrama, and it does end with Joo-Won and Ra-Im in a relationship built on sacrifice, a major theme for Andersen. Joo-Won gives up his inheritance and family relationships to marry Ra-Im; he keeps his own money so that they are not poor, but he loses his status, everything that is his family's, and belonging to the *chaebol*. It is not the happily ever after of upward class mobility, but it is also not the tragedy of unrequited love and suicide. They keep the fancy house. The use of "The Little Mermaid" means audiences cannot forget that the class system is stable; the socioeconomic system that benefits a few rich families is constantly showcased and always presented as a problem.

The different worlds analogy invoked by "The Little Mermaid" highlights the extreme class disparity in the socioeconomic positions of the two main characters. The class difference is not presented as just a difference in wealth and social status that can be overcome with a bit of luck and magic. Rather, the difference in experience and point of view is presented as so vast that it is as if the two main characters come from two different worlds. Also important is that when Joo-Won rewrites the ending, his is a business success, not a romantic one. He still cannot decouple love from business even after he rejects the fairy-tale script that has governed his attempts at this relationship. Despite the ability of these characters to find a way to be together, the class system that separates them does not change. Joo-Won's loss of status and wealth does not challenge the system that is the obstacle to the relationship. The systemic problems of Korean society are still in place, and an individual solution is offered to an individual problem. Instead of upward class mobility, downward class mobility is presented as an alternative. The difference is that, at least with this show, the system is challenged as problematic and not accepted by the ascension of the lower-class individual. The system is rigid, but Joo-Won's willingness to leave it suggests that it can be challenged even if it is firmly in place at the ending of the series.

In the final episode, Joo-Won shares his rewritten ending of "The Little Mermaid" with Ra-Im, and the ensuing conversation offers a metafictional commentary on the importance of fairy tales in navigating one's life. A montage of scenes in episode 20 of Joo-Won and Ra-Im living happily together ends with a scene that revisits the fairy-tale metaphors of the show. Joo-Won is sitting on his couch and Ra-Im is lying in his lap. He hands her *Alice in Wonderland* with the altered "The Little Mermaid" ending. She removes the page and reads it, laughing. Then she says, "Hey Secretary Kim. The ending sucks." Joo-Won replies, "I did my best. Do you think you know love?" and he takes the page from her. Ra-Im counters, "Then do you know? What did you say before. . . . The Littler [sic] Mermaid is humanity's first story about fling-relationships." Joo-Won says, "It's true," and Ra-Im asks him about other fairy tales:

RA-IM: "Then what about Snow White?"
JOO-WON: "As a social ruling class she takes care of poor dwarfs and then when kissed by another high-class man she flakes out on the dwarfs."
RA-IM: "How about Sleeping Beauty?"
JOO-WON: "A woman of wealth becomes a social issue from her excessive sleeping and met a wealthy man. The story teaches that if a person does something for a long time, dreams will come true."
RA-IM: "Wow."

The scene continues with the two teasing each other.

Joo-Won and Ra-Im discussing the rewritten end to "The Little Mermaid" and other fairy tales in a happily-ever-after scene, from *Secret Garden* episode 20.

This scene is played for humor as part of the happily ever after of the series, but it highlights Joo-Won's earlier position about the importance of class and social obligations. First, both characters turn to well-known fairy tales to test what they know about love, suggesting that these stories are the scripts by which people learn about love. Joo-Won's response to "Sleeping Beauty" even includes the oft-assumed idea that fairy tales provide a lesson. Fairy tales are clearly positioned as a genre of socialization and one that provides instruction about important concepts. Joo-Won's interpretations are humorous because they configure love as secondary to class: "The Little Mermaid" is about a fling, not true love, because class trumps love in the case of star-crossed lovers, Snow White abandons her charitable work for a "high-class man," and Sleeping Beauty has a wealth-match more than a love-match. In each case, the class of the princess determines her possible ending. These interpretations also reveal both the class ideology embedded in the tales (these are stories of the love lives of the wealthy social elite) and the primacy of class to Joo-Won's way of thinking. His interpretations are cynical, but they serve as a counterpoint in the series to highlight how much his character has evolved to be able to break those scripts and marry beneath his class, forgoing social obligation for love.

And They Lived Boringly Ever After

The very first episode of *Secret Garden* sets up the contrast between an arranged marriage for business and family alliances and marriage for love, with Joo-Won firmly believing that marrying for love is simply not possible for a man in his position. He is the CEO of a prominent department store and heir to a large family fortune. While this tension is present in other Korean Dramas, *Secret Garden*'s combining of the dynastic plots with fantasy makes it unique. The series is sprinkled with touches of magic in every episode, and the magical soul swap that bridges the gap between Joo-Won's and Ra-Im's experiences is a major plot point that is returned to on multiple occasions. Both discreet and prominent magic informs viewers that what we are watching is a fairy tale. With the soap-opera melodrama of family disowning, comas, and traumatic amnesia, the magic is a constant reminder that a happy ending is possible. Soap opera/ melodrama denies a happily ever after due to its serial format, but the fairy tale requires it.

Like *Once Upon a Time*, discussed in chapter 1, *Secret Garden* is a serial melodrama; however, unlike *Once Upon a Time*, which has an open-ended structure, *Secret Garden* is a closed serial with a set ending and a limited number of episodes. Robert C. Allen in the introduction to *To Be Continued . . . : Soap Operas Around the World* explains that "closed serials . . . offer viewers an opportunity after closure to look back upon the completed text and impose upon it some kind of moral or ideological order" (23). While the show still contains false happy endings, where the characters seem to overcome obstacles only to be faced with a new problem, the overarching plot is resolved at the end of the series. Open-ended serials like *Once Upon a Time*, which do not have a set ending for the majority of their airtime, engage in a constant negation of closure to ensure that the various plotlines can continue indefinitely. A predetermined ending, as in the case of *Secret Garden*, allows for short-term negation of plotlines with the promise to audiences of a conclusion that will resolve the emotional drama of the series. In *Complex TV: The Poetics of Contemporary Television Storytelling*, Jason Mittell delineates between the different types of endings television series can have, and he points out that production realities often greatly affect the final episode of a show. Mittell describes a final episode as in the case of *Secret Garden* as a "*conclusion*, when a program's producers are able to craft a final episode knowing in advance that it will be the end" (320). The benefit for audiences is that "Conclusions offer a sense of finality and resolution, following the centuries-old assumption that well-crafted stories need to end" (321). While this is relatively rare in American series, as Mittell points out, it is common in Korean dramas, which are often produced as a completed story with a set number of episodes, a telling difference in the production practices of the two entertainment industries.

Both *Secret Garden*'s closed-serial format and its blended fairy-tale/ melodrama genre are an important context in understanding how the series uses its fairy-tale intertexts. Much of the explicit discussion of "Cinderella" and "The Little Mermaid" is focused on the stories' endings; one leads to a happily-ever-after romance and the other does not. When Joo-Won and Ra-Im discuss the possibility of a relationship in episode 12, this emphasis of the ending is raised, with Joo-Won insisting on the predetermined end for any nonbusiness romantic relationship he has and Ra-Im insisting that women do not begin relationships thinking about how they will end. Joo-Won's preoccupation with endings is a major obstacle to their relationship, and it is the ending of "The Little Mermaid" that seems most logical to him because the two lovers from different worlds are not together. While Ra-Im invokes gender as part of her logic, Joo-Won emphasizes class and socioeconomic status as the primary factors. Yoon Suel, a woman of Joo-Won's social standing and a competitor for his affection, has similar views to Joo-Won, arranging for a business-match rather than a love-match marriage, and her position is presented as a counterpoint to Ra-Im's. While audiences may align with Ra-Im as the morally right character, Yoon Suel as foil shows that Ra-Im does not understand the pressures and social obligations Joo-Won faces as an elite member of society. The preoccupation with endings that is a major part of the drama of the show is only possible because of the closed-serial structure that promises audiences a resolution, and a fairy-tale one at that.

Melodrama and soap operas in the West are often categorized as women's television or feminine genres because of this association with emotion, and Korean dramas are no different. Angel M. Y. Lin and Avin Tong explain in "Crossing Boundaries: Male Consumption of Korean TV Dramas and Negotiation of Gender Relations in Modern Day Hong Kong" the genre terminology in use when discussing Korean dramas in Asian countries:

> In many Asian societies including Korea and Hong Kong, the phrase "TV drama" is used by people instead of "soap opera," referring to the wide spectrum of fictional dramatic programs including both what Americans would call soap operas and other prime time "mini-series" (Shim, 2004). In this paper, the Korean TV dramas discussed possess many important features of the soaps, such as their focus on romance, women's matters and emotional realism. We can see that both soap operas and

> Korean TV dramas possess "feminine characteristics," so they are considered to be "women's genres." (222)

The popularity of feminine genres with male audiences, then, suggests something appealing in the effeminacy of the form. In *Having a Good Cry: Effeminate Feelings and Pop-Culture Forms*, Robyn R. Warhol argues in the context of American media that "to have a *good* cry . . . is to indulge in one of the perquisites of effeminacy, whether the person doing the crying is male or female" (29). Warhol distinguishes between a "good cry" and "cathartic weeping" as a reaction to the sentimentality evoked through narrative techniques in the text and the response to sad or tragic content (*Having a Good Cry* 41). The visual and narrative techniques employed in the genre of melodrama encourage an emotional reaction on the part of the audience. Building on Warhol's work, Mittell argues for understanding *melodrama* as a mode as opposed to a genre and that "incorporating sentimental melodrama and female characters into traditionally masculinist genres has worked to validate effeminate emotional experiences for male viewers and helped destabilize television's long-standing gender hierarchies" (Mittell 251).

Another appeal for Western audiences may be the portrayal of the romantic relationships in the shows, which are typically more chaste than in American soap operas and melodramas, which often contain sexually explicit content. In many Korean dramas, a kiss or an embrace is a mark of intense physical intimacy, and while characters do have sex, it is often implied rather than depicted on-screen. Characters are frequently romanticized more than sexualized, and the camera focuses more on faces than on bodies, thus emphasizing the emotional connection between characters rather than sexual ones. This also offers an interesting alternative to the male gaze as described by Laura Mulvey in "Visual Pleasure and Narrative Cinema," in that both male and female faces tend to be filmed with the same lingering shots that rely on subtle acting to show a range of intense emotions rather than with long shots of the female body. This difference between Korean and American shows in what is being shown on-screen and how it is framed is particularly interesting in light of the research on Korean dramas that focuses on emotional responses. The ways in which the actors' faces and bodies are shot reinforces the plot-level emphasis on intense emotional scenes.

In reception studies that examine the popularity of Korean dramas outside of Korea and the phenomenon of the Korean Wave, many researchers have focused on the appeal of Korean dramas and why they have the fandoms that they do among non-Korean audiences. In an analysis of online fan discussions of Korean drama, Brian Hu suggests in "Korean TV Serials in the English-Language Diaspora: Translating Difference Online and Making It Racial" that "emotion, not politics, is perhaps a more suitable category through which to explore the forums' fan activity" (36). Hu goes on to analyze online Korean drama fan sites as "affective translation communities" for Asian diasporas, but his emphasis on the "emotional investment in Korean television serials" is echoed by many scholars examining the phenomenon of Korean drama (36). One theory is that the melodrama genre and the focus on male emotion is cathartic and inspiring for men in countries with rigid social roles that do not allow for the public expression of emotion.

Lin and Tong argue that for male viewers in Hong Kong, Korean dramas "provide audiences with the pleasure of imaginary identification and emotional release" (223). Lin and Tong argue that the popularity of Korean drama with men challenges gender binaries both because it is a feminized genre and because the content of the shows, which depicts sensitive, emotional men and strong, independent women, upsets the norms in Confucian-based Asian cultures. Of particular interest in their research is the emphasis on crying, on the part of both the male characters and the male audience, which challenges the stereotype of the stoic man who does not show emotion. "All informants," they state, "explicitly assert that men should be able to cry and should have a chance to express their emotions, and Korean TV dramas thus seem to offer them an outlet for emotional release" (Lin and Tong 226). Thus the Korean drama can be for its viewers the fantasy that the fairy tale is for Joo-Won, a means of identification with an emotional experience outside of the bounds of one's normal experience and the ability to experience the emotional release themselves.

Studies of female viewers outside of Korea have likewise focused on the escapist elements of Korean drama. Brenda Chan and Wang Xueli have similar findings in their study of female viewers of Korean dramas in Singapore. For the women interviewed, the "'fairytale-like romance' ... seems to serve as an escape from ... [life's] daily stresses" (294). In particular, the women identify the "self-sacrificing devotion" of male characters who give up "careers, lives or families" for "the one they love" as an appealing fantasy (Chan and Xueli 295). Both male and female viewers noted the frequency of opposite-sex characters in Korean dramas "who were willing to sacrifice everything for their love" as one of the appeals of the genre (Chan and Xueli 294; Lin and Tong 224). The appeal of "The Little Mermaid" story in *Secret Garden*, then, is not surprising, nor is the gender twist in which the man takes on the mermaid role and sacrifices for his love. In their study, however, Chan and Xueli assert that the women recognize the inaccessibility of the fairy-tale romance; they do not expect to replicate those circumstances in their own lives (295–97).

Both studies emphasize the escapist qualities of the dramas as part of their appeal, but equally important to understanding the transcultural appeal of Korean dramas is the idea that the drama actively affects its audience by creating a space in which viewers can engage in emotional responses not necessarily sanctioned by their culture. Both articles discuss the critical distance viewers have from the shows, recognizing when they are engaged with fantasy and nonmimetic portrayals of Korean life, but in both cases viewers also expressed a desire for some of the alternate models for behavior in the shows that would seem to offer more satisfying ways of dealing with daily pressures in their own lives. The transcultural portrayal, even when recognized as fantasy, facilitates a questioning of social norms with which viewers are uncomfortable or suggests an alternative to norms that viewers take for granted as natural. Joo-Won's use of "The Little Mermaid" in *Secret Garden* mirrors this use of fantasy as a discursive space for exploring issues of one's own culture and life, and it conveys both the desire to replicate the fantasy and the recognition that it cannot be done without changing that fantasy to meet one's sociohistorical reality.

4

Following Footsteps

Redrafting Fairy-Tale Maps in Kelly Link's Short Fiction

KELLY LINK HAS WRITTEN several stories that, like the Korean drama *Secret Garden*, depict characters turning explicitly to fairy tales for guidance and finding them lacking. In these and other stories, Link invokes fairy-tale structures that do not play out or have unexpected consequences. Unlike *Secret Garden*, Link's stories rarely have plot resolutions, let alone happy endings, that conform to fairy-tale expectations for genre (as in *Secret Garden*) or a specific tale. While *Secret Garden* turns to pages from a book as the physical reminder of fairy tales as maps for lived experience, several of Link's stories have a recurring motif of fairy-tale shoes and feet. "Travels with the Snow Queen," "Shoe and Marriage," and "The Girl Detective" were each published in Link's first collection of short fiction, *Stranger Things Happen*, and each prominently features fairy tales in which shoes and feet are important and incorporates that element into the short story. "Travels with the Snow Queen" is a retelling of Hans Christian Andersen's "The Snow Queen"; "Shoe and Marriage" draws upon "Cinderella," *The Wizard of Oz*, and the story of Imelda Marcos; and "The Girl Detective" uses "The Twelve Dancing Princesses," the Greek myth of Persephone, and the Nancy Drew mystery series. While each draws upon multiple fairy tales, the primary tales for each feature shoes and feet as prominent symbols.

Rebecca-Anne C. Do Rozario, in *Fashion and the Fairy Tale Tradition: What Cinderella Wore*, suggests that "the shoe is not the heart of the fairy tale, but it is the foundation for many of fairy tale's most cunning and inspiring heroes" (179). She argues that as both "object of fashion, and a method of conveyance," the shoe "navigates the space between the fairy-tale protagonist and the road they travel" (179). The presence of shoes invokes movement and travel, and in Link's trio of stories, the shoes symbolically ground the characters' use of fairy tales as maps for their experiences. In each story, characters engage fairy-tale narratives and motifs directly for guidance and as a way to understand and explain the situations in which they find themselves. The fairy tales are functionally maps, and Link's use of the shoe motifs orient readers to the fairy-tale intertexts of these stories.

Link has written other stories that use these tales, such as "The Cinderella Game" (Cinderella) and "Origin Story" (*The Wizard of Oz*). "The Cinderella Game" focuses more on the stepfamily dynamic of the tale and does not use Cinderella's slipper as a story element.[1] "Origin Story" invokes traveling and paths through its references to the yellow brick road in a broken-down Oz amusement park and the protagonist's ability to float two feet off the ground but not fly, and the story thematically addresses staying home and not venturing forth into the world, with children being an anchor to place. The references to Oz iconography combined with the thematic exploration of leaving versus staying relate this story to the ones I discuss in this chapter; however, the intertextual references and genre-mixed logic of the story are indebted more to superhero stories and tropes than to fairy tales. While both genres of fantasy have overlapping elements, the fairy-tale elements of "Origin Story" do not drive it as they do in the three stories selected for this chapter.

"Catskin" is another fairy-tale inflected short story that touches on the thematic elements of maps and paths I discuss here. At one point, the witch, who is dying, recognizes that her adopted daughter Flora's life was "already laid out, flat as a map" (Link, "Catskin" 127). The witch gives Flora deathbed advice, including to "take the road outside the house and go west" (127). Flora does not follow this advice and heads north with one of her brothers, Jack, who was advised to head east, and they eventually return to their youngest brother without the good fortune that should have resulted in Flora's happily ever after. The implication is that had they followed their mother's advice, they would have had a better life. However, the story also suggests that this outcome is an inevitability: "What child had ever heeded a mother's advice?" (131). Like Little Red Riding Hood, who strays from her mother's advice and suffers for it in the Grimms' version, here fairy-tale advice is ignored and that proves unfortunate for the characters, but the fairy-tale logic is maintained. Children who stray from the path are in danger. In the stories discussed in this chapter, the fairy-tale paths are not presented as paths of safety or good fortune, but rather as paths on inaccurate maps that will not help the characters reach their goals. An important distinction between "Catskin" and the stories discussed here is the metafictional element to the trio of shoe stories. "Catskin" is a fairy tale, but the characters are not aware of fairy tales in the story, whereas in the shoe trio, the characters actively engage fairy-tale tropes and logic and are aware of their existence in and resistance to the fairy tale.

"Travels with the Snow Queen"

Kelly Link's story "Travels with the Snow Queen" is an adaptation of Hans Christian Andersen's "The Snow Queen" that transforms Andersen's story of childhood friendship into a story about adult romantic relationships and questions the effectiveness of fairy tales as maps for real life. Andersen's theme of the transformative power of love and Gerda's devotion to Kay is mirrored and refracted in Link's tale in a way that questions those concepts and the fairy-tale tradition that presents women's sacrifice as normative. While Link's story critiques the fairy-tale tropes of female devotion and transformative love, calling attention to the gender inequity in the tales alluded to, it also engages in a critique of contemporary discourse on relationships and romance. Link's story additionally engages in narrative parody, imitating the second-person address to the reader that begins Andersen's multipart tale and then twisting it so that her second-person narration is maintained throughout the story, addressing both character and reader, and encourages reader-identification with Gerda, who is likewise identifying with the fairy-tale princesses alluded to. The critique of fairy-tale ideologies within the plot is complemented by the parodying of the narrative conventions in Andersen's tale and the use of narrative techniques, like second-person narration and nonsequential plot development, that disrupt readers' expectations for fairy tales. Link's plotting and narration both invoke Andersen's style and disrupt the fairy-tale patterns.

Andersen's story is told in seven distinct episodes. A demon has made a mirror that distorts all that is beautiful with the world. The mirror breaks and falls to earth, and splinters pierce the heart and eye of a boy named Kay, turning him against his best friend, Gerda. Kay, no longer interested in playing with Gerda, eventually leaves for the beautiful and coldhearted Snow Queen. Gerda is devastated and goes to look for him, barefoot, and she encounters several helpful characters before finding Kay frozen blue in the Snow Queen's palace. Gerda hugs Kay; her tears melt the ice and mirror in his heart, and her kisses warm him. Kay's own tears wash out the glass in his eye. They return home overjoyed, "grown up and yet children . . . at heart" ("The Snow Queen" 189).

Like many of Andersen's tales, the Christian moralizing is explicit and the lesson for children is clear. Gerda's great power is her innocence and pure love, and she is to be lauded for her devotion to Kay. The mirror shards have transformed Kay into a jaded, selfish adult, and Gerda's act of selflessness and sacrifice saves him, allowing them both to retain their childlike innocence and joy. This story also includes Andersen's common themes of suffering and extreme sacrifice on the part of an innocent protagonist. Here, as in other stories of his like "The Little Mermaid," this sacrifice is for a seemingly unworthy lover. In "The Snow Queen" this is made explicit when, at the conclusion of the story, the robber girl, who saved and helped Gerda, stops to say to Kay, "I should like to know if you deserve to have somebody running to the end of the world for your sake!" (189). While presented as a rhetorical aside in Andersen's tale, this question of Kay's worthiness becomes a driving force in Link's transformation. Link picks up the theme of suffering and sacrifice for an unworthy lover and compounds it by drawing attention to the many suffering women of fairy tales, both successful and not, who sacrifice for lovers. The emphasis on how difficult fairy-tale plots are on women, coupled with Gerda's rejection of her own expected happily ever after, suggests that fairy tales do not make for very good maps and that women need not follow them.

Link's structure mimics Andersen's, and she repeats the episodes with Gerda and Kay separating, the princess and prince, the robber girl and Bae, the Lapp and Finn women, and Kay in the ice palace. She does not duplicate the exposition about the demon making the evil mirror that warps Kay's heart or the good witch enchanting Gerda with her flower garden and her kindness. The episode with the good witch is replaced by Gerda's hesitance over leaving, her decision to do so, and the early exposition on fairy tales and "travel [being] hard on the single woman" ("Travels with the Snow Queen" 102). The discussion of other fairy tales here—other stories that are similar but not analogous to Gerda's, stories that are not helpful guides for Gerda—mimics the scene in Andersen's witch's garden in which the flowers tell Gerda their own stories, which are explicitly stated to not help Gerda find Kay. Both tales share this concept that other people's stories cannot guide you.

In Link's version, Gerda and Kay are an adult couple. They fight, she throws a glass at him, and it shatters. The next day Kay leaves; Gerda eventually goes to find him because "This is one of the things a woman can do when her lover leaves her" (102). During her journey, multiple characters tell Gerda that "he's not in love with you" (106). Link's robber girl gives Gerda her own thigh-high black leatherette boots and insists she wear them because broken glass as a map is "nonsense" (110, 111). When Gerda does find Kay, frozen blue, he immediately judges her boots as "ridiculous" and "hideous," then asks for a kiss to break the spell (117). She stalls. He asks, "Why did you walk barefoot across half a continent of broken glass if you aren't going to kiss me and break the spell?" (118). Why indeed. Earlier in this scene, Gerda, when confronted with the ice palace, is afraid to enter, "afraid that . . . he will know that you walked barefoot on broken glass across half a continent, just to find out why he left you" (116). Gerda's map is a trail of glass that cuts her bare feet as she follows it:

> The map that you are using is a mirror. You are always pulling the bits out of your bare feet, the pieces of the map that

> broke off and fell on the ground as the Snow Queen flew overhead in her sleigh. Where you are, where you are coming from, it is impossible to read a map made of paper. If it were that easy then everyone would be a traveler. You have heard of other travelers whose maps are breadcrumbs, whose maps are stones, whose maps are the four winds, whose maps are yellow bricks laid one after the other. You read your map with your foot, and behind you somewhere there must be another traveler whose map is the bloody footprints that you are leaving behind you.
>
> There is a map of fine white scars in the soles of your feet that tells you where you have been. . . . Sometimes it is safer to read maps with your feet. (100)

Here maps are presented as difficult and hard to follow, and the protagonist's map of broken glass is grouped with object maps from fairy tales that do not lead their heroes to where they expect. The metonymy of the object maps also positions the maps to stand in for the fairy tales in which they appear, and the map of bloody footprints created in this story marks Link's story as a fairy tale along with the others. The map of bloody footprints becomes a map for the reader. What these fairy-tale maps have in common is that they do not exactly work. The bread crumbs are ephemeral, the stones lead Hansel and Gretel home where they are not wanted, the four winds lead the prince to his destination but he is not happy there, and the yellow brick road leads Dorothy farther away from home. The paths of these fairy-tale object maps end in unexpected and unsatisfying ways.

When the Snow Queen enters the scene, Gerda is surprised by how kind she looks. The Snow Queen suggests that Gerda not kiss Kay, then compliments her on her boots. "Do you love him?" the queen asks (119). And Gerda does not, so she doesn't kiss Kay, leaving him to solve his own puzzle. The Snow Queen brings Gerda on as a guide for Snow Queen Tours, and the story ends with Gerda, standing in her "black laced boots," reflecting on the story her scarred feet tell (120). She says, "Your feet are maps *and* your feet are mirrors. But . . . you have to keep in mind that they are also useful for walking around on. They are perfectly good feet" (120).

Thematically, Link's story emphasizes the broken relationship and Gerda's need to go on this journey to discover what *she* wants. The impression is given that before Kay leaves, Kay and Gerda are simply doing what is expected of them, moving toward their happily ever after. Kay is "the boy next door" and Gerda thinks he loves her (100). Here the story draws on popular culture discourse about marrying the boy next door and the American romanticized ideal of marrying one's high-school sweetheart. It is a cultural construct that defines love by its innocence and has been set up as an ideal in popular films and TV. Link's story critiques this innocent conception of love as Gerda and Kay's relationship is shown to be far more complex and devoid of substantive love. The problems the two experience are realistic—infidelity, disliking the other's friends and family, insecurity, unhappiness, passive-aggressive insults, and the inability to satisfy each other. The list that Gerda carries of things she wants to say to Kay when she finds him paints him as not a very good boyfriend and suggests that before this journey, she had idealized him, something that Andersen's Gerda does as well, believing that her Kay is "sparkl[ing]" and "beautiful" and very "clever" because he can add fractions in his head (Anderson, "The Snow Queen" 176).

In a survey of contemporary retellings of Andersen's work, "The Ugly Duckling's Legacy: Adulteration, Contemporary Fantasy, and the Dark," Naomi Wood explains that this emphasis on Gerda as a betrayed lover is quite common in contemporary retellings (199). Present-day Gerdas, she says, are "updated to reflect contemporary women writers' dislike for passive nineteenth-century ideality," and "no version considers seeking and retrieving the faithless lover as an accomplishment" (Wood 199). While I disagree with Wood's characterization of Link's Gerda as a "companionable Bridget Jones type" and her boots as "tacky," I agree that Link's story "rework[s] what a happy ending looks like to reflect contemporary values and mores" (Wood 199, 200). Indeed, this is one of the few of Link's stories that actually resolves the plot, and Gerda's happy ending becomes her new beginning. I would argue further that Link's transformation of Andersen's story not only critiques the nineteenth-century ideality but also critiques late-twentieth-century romantic ideals that drive characters like Bridget

Jones. Gerda rejects the fairy-tale romance of the twentieth century as well as the Romantic fairy tale on which Link's story is based. And as a guide for Snow Queen Tours, she has become a character who works to lead other women away from using fairy tales and idealized constructions of romance as maps for life.

This thematic rejection of fairy-tale romance and Romantic fairy tales is made explicit by the narration that details the suffering of fairy-tale princesses and other women who are hurt in the name of love. Link's use of second-person narration compels the reader to put herself in the place of these fairy-tale women and to see herself and her own journeys reflected in the broken mirror that guides Gerda. Link's story alternates between two types of second-person narrative address. In the majority of the story, *you* refers to Gerda. For example, the initial use of *you*—"You enter the walls of the city early in the evening, when the cobblestones are a mottled pink with reflected light, and cold beneath the slap of your bare, bloody feet"— clearly refers to a character in the story, the protagonist Gerda (Link, "Travels with the Snow Queen" 99). At other times, in three of the fourteen sections, the second-person address refers to a group of ladies being given a sales pitch for Snow Queen Tours: "Ladies. Has it ever occurred to you that fairy tales aren't easy on the feet?" (100). At the end of the story, Gerda identifies herself as the tour guide. Because this narrator is preoccupied with wear and tear on the feet, just as the protagonist is, readers are encouraged to connect them earlier and see the majority of the second-person narration as self-address. Gerda is the narrator, addressing both herself and other fairy-tale women.

Snow Queen Tours offers special discounts for "older sisters, stepsisters, stepmothers, wicked witches, crones, hags, princesses who have kissed frogs without realizing what they were getting into, etc."—in other words, the fairy-tale women who have not gotten their happily ever afters (103). But the passage that includes the discount also includes a list of fairy-tale women whose tales have damaged their feet: the little mermaid, Karen and her red shoes, Cinderella's stepsisters, Snow White's stepmother, the Goose Girl's maid, and the girl who walked east of the sun and west of the moon. Fairy tales are hard on *all* women. In "Telling Stories of Your Life: The Use of

Second Person Narration in SF," Ruth Nestvold and Jay Lake specifically point to the "Ladies" passages as "appear[ing] to be addressing the female readers of the story" (sec. "'You' in the story," para. 3). While the language in the passage, laden with fairy-tale references and fantastic details, clearly marks the *you* being addressed as other fairy-tale women, the emotional level of reader identification encouraged by the second-person address easily brings the female reader into Gerda's audience. "You've read the fairy tales," says Gerda (Link, "Travels with the Snow Queen" 102). And we have. A later passage reads, "You're sick and tired of traveling towards the happily ever after, whenever the fuck that is—you'd like the happily right now. Thank you very much"—a statement with which many readers can surely identify (112).

The reader is encouraged to identify with Gerda by the second-person *you* address and through Gerda's plot-level reflections on romance. Gerda also identifies with the other fairy-tale women named and alluded to in a way that mirrors how real women identify with fairy-tale women and, in the case of Link's story, with Gerda. Wood, as well as Nestvold and Lake, points to reader identification being encouraged by the plot-level reflections on being a jilted lover in addition to the second-person address that implicates the reader in the story (Woods 200; Nestvold and Lake sec. "'You' in the story," para. 2). Veronica Schanoes, in her analysis of Link's use of the mirror motif in *Fairy Tales, Myth, and Psychoanalytic Theory: Feminism and Retelling the Tale*, explains that this "close" identification between Gerda and the reader "results in Gerda's mirror-as-map becoming the reader's mirror-as-story—'Travels with the Snow Queen' itself" (94). This reader identification is disrupted by the inclusion of the three passages that destabilize the second-person referent. The reader still identifies with the *you* being addressed, in particular because of the content of the passages, but it is unclear who this *you* is. The effect of the change in referent is a jarring one, as it moves the reader out of having a handle on the story—*you* are Gerda—to being unsure what is happening and to whom it is happening. "Travels with the Snow Queen" is certainly a story that reads differently the second time around.

As Monika Fludernik has pointed out in "Second-Person Narrative as a Test Case for Narratology: The Limits of Realism," ambiguity is a central feature of second-person narration (455). *You* could be generic, functioning as a substitution for *one*; it could be "self-address" (455); it could refer to the reader or textual narratee; and as the referent for a protagonist, *you* can be any number of personas. The referent of *you* is unclear when a story begins, and many second-person narratives play with the variety of *yous* that could be addressed before the referent is stabilized. But *you* always has the potential to be destabilized because the narrator can switch to another *you* without signaling to the reader that a change in referent has occurred. According to Fludernik, second-person narration is radical because it bridges the divisions between narrative levels and brings the reader into the text and fictional world (461). The primary effect of the second-person narrative address is to collapse the distinctions among narrator, character, and reader, and in "Travels with the Snow Queen," it also collapses the distinctions among fairy tale, fiction, and reality. The unstable position of the reader in relation to the story is one of the appeals of second-person narration, and it is part of what makes Link's story noteworthy.

Like Choose Your Own Adventure texts and the narration in text-based adventure video games, the use of second-person narration encourages the reader to identify with the protagonist, though it is an unsettling identification because no matter how much we, as readers, want to put ourselves into the position of the protagonist, we are clearly not lost in the Cave of Time nor are we likely to be eaten by a grue. Emotional identification is made, but the second-person referral to the protagonist also constantly reinforces the fictionality of the text. We are reading a fictional story about a woman living a fairy tale and finding her own projections of the fairy tales she has read onto her own life dissatisfying. Given the chance to have her fairy-tale ending, she rejects it and tells a different story. This metafictional effect of the narration in "Travels with the Snow Queen" is thematically mirrored by the commentary in the story about fairy tales not being particularly good maps for the modern woman. The reader identification encouraged through plot elements and the second-person narration encourages a similar rejection of fairy tales by the reader, which is, of course, paradoxical because this advice is coming from a twenty-first-century fairy tale.

While Link's success in using second-person narration shows her skill as a writer, the use of second-person narration in "Travels with the Snow Queen" is not just a neat trick. The metafictional effect of the narration reinforces the metafictional argument of the story—that fairy tales are not particularly good maps and are hard on the feet. Link's transformation of Andersen's tale is, to return to Donald Haase's terms, "simultaneously rejecting and embracing the fairy tale" ("Feminist Fairy-Tale Scholarship" 30). Gerda, who quite literally rejects Andersen's Snow Queen tale and embraces Link's Snow Queen character, embodies this complex relationship to fairy tales that many readers have. The second-person narration invites readers to step into her fabulous boots and find our own maps for navigating this fairy-tale landscape that we, too, inhabit.

"Shoe and Marriage"

There is no stable shoe symbol in "Shoe and Marriage," and each of the four sections of the story uses shoes differently. The primary intertexts are "Cinderella" for "The glass slipper," *The Wizard of Oz* film for "Miss Kansas on Judgment Day," and the story of Imelda Marcos for "The dictator's wife." The final section is without a clear narrative intertext, and references to other fairy tales are mixed into the story well. The first section, "The glass slipper," is written in third person and focalized through the prince character from "Cinderella," who has since married a woman who is not Cinderella—the shoe did not fit, but he fell in love anyway. The story states three times that he loves her (Link, "Shoe and Marriage" 167, 170) and is happy, but he still searches for the girl whose foot will fit the tiny slipper left behind. This conflict is presented as one of expectations. "He loves his wife, but her feet are too big. It wasn't what he expected—his life, it isn't at all what he expected. His wife isn't the one that he was looking for. She was a surprise" (170). The expected narrative is the Cinderella story, where he finds the owner of the missing slipper, marries her, and lives happily ever after. While he does marry a beautiful girl whom he finds covered in soot, the shoe is too small for her feet. He falls in love with her for other reasons: her beautiful smile, laugh, and face are all mentioned multiple times.

The first words spoken to the prince are presented as surprising and break the narrative pattern. After placing the too-small shoe on her sooty foot, he asks, "What size shoe do you wear?" (172). She responds, "'What kind of girl do you think I am?' . . . She sounded as if she were scolding him. When he looked up her face was so beautiful" (172). This scene is presented as both an unfolding of narrative pattern and a subversion of it. When the prince first meets his wife, the onlookers, "his footmen, the lady of the house, her daughters, the other maids," look "as if they knew what was going to happen. They didn't like it one bit, but they weren't one bit surprised" (171). As the prince with a single slipper, looking for its lost owner, his narrative path leads to a cinder girl. He knows it, as do the people around him. But the story—what he expects—is that the shoe will be hers; this is the happily ever after promised to him by the narrative of "Cinderella." But that's not what happens. The shoe does not fit, but they fall in love anyway, and the story is left open with a loose end. There is no narrative closure to the Cinderella plot despite his happy marriage, so he continues looking for the girl who fits the shoe.

The story suggests a foot fetish: two pages describe his past and his interest in women's shoes, or rather seeing women's feet in shoes under long dresses that sweep the floor (168), and John Clute, in his review of the collection titled "Under the Skin of Story," refers to the prince's "obsession with tiny feet." But the paragraphs about the prince's past and childhood do not refer to tiny feet except for in the case of the missing girl. None of the references to feet in these sections mention size unless the single shoe itself or its owner is mentioned. The obsession with tiny feet seems to stem from the shoe itself; it is tiny, so he needs to find a tiny foot to fit it. What this suggests is an obsession with the story more than with the size of feet. It seems as if he has found many girls with tiny feet who fit the shoe, but they are not the missing girl:

> He never found that girl. He finds other girls (Link, "Shoe and Marriage" 168).

> [A]ll these runaway girls—all these women—with their sad faces and their tiny feet (170).
>
> He doesn't expect to find her, but he finds other girls (170).
>
> He was supposed to find it [the shoe]. He was supposed to find her. He never found her (170–71).

While this could suggest a foot fetish for tiny feet, I argue that it suggests a lack of narrative closure. He was supposed to find the shoe, and he did, which means he was supposed to find the girl who lost it, but he did not. He still found happiness with a wife whom he loves and who loves him, but that is not the ending to the story his life was supposed to follow, and so he is left incomplete. His fairy-tale map did not lead him to where he expected, and though he is happy, he is left with a desire to close the story.

At the close of this section, he places the shoe on the foot of a young woman, at what is presumably a brothel, and it fits. She asks, "What do we do now?" a question that is presented in stark contrast to his memory of his wife's shoe fitting: "What kind of girl do you think I am?" (172). "He says to the girl on the bed, 'Take the shoe off. So we can put it on again'" (172). Readers are left questioning what the point is. He finds *a* girl who fits the shoe—but not *the* girl—and the encounter does not lead to romance or sex, but repetition. He is stuck, trying to fulfill the story he cannot. He is happily married, but it is not a happily ever after to the story itself. Happiness and endings are disconnected in the prince's story, and the inability of the fairy-tale narrative to play out is presented as not so much anguishing (he is happily married) as unfulfilling. He is not able to complete the fairy-tale narrative, despite meeting all of the separate steps (marriage to a cinder girl, shoe fitting a foot), because they do not align with narrative expectation. While he is able to have a happy marriage, he is not able to bring his story to a close, and its lack of closure compels him to keep seeking the missing girl. One wonders what would happen if he did find her. That Link does not write that story is telling; instead she presents a story in which a character's path does not follow the fairy-tale map and ends with the dissonance produced by the discord of the two paths.

The second section, "Miss Kansas on Judgment Day," continues the symbolic connection of shoes to marriage, though rather than unmet expectations or a catalyst for romance, shoes and feet are presented as an anchor for the relationship, binding the two newlyweds together. This section is narrated in first person by one partner, revealed to be a woman as the story goes on, and is dominated by the plural pronoun *we*, though *I* and *you* are also used. The gender of the narrator and her partner are ambiguous in the beginning, but references to a wedding dress and a tuxedo jacket suggest a woman and a man. It seems to be narrated to the other married partner, a man, who is the referent of *you*. This section repeats the idea of marriage as a joining:

> Marriage has affected the laws of gravity. We will now revolve around each other. You will exert gravity on me, and I will exert gravity on you. We are one another's moon. You are holding onto my feet with both hands, as if otherwise you might fall right off the bed. I think I might float up and hit the ceiling, splat, if you let go. Please don't let go. (173)

The phrase "Please don't let go" or a variation of that phrase is repeated eight times, and the narrator mentions again that her husband is holding her feet (179). There are additional references to feet—Miss Kansas's ruby red slippers appear multiple times, a judge is "getting his feet wet" (177), and so on—but the repetition of "please don't let go" keeps the emphasis on binding as the main symbol for the section: bound by marriage, bound by holding. The narrator might float away, might lose herself or her partner, should he let go of her feet. The physical closeness is emphasized over the other invocations of foot imagery.

The next most often repeated foot/shoe reference is to the ruby red slippers of Miss Kansas, a contestant in the beauty pageant the couple is watching on television, or possibly dreaming (174). The obvious reference to

The Wizard of Oz film is continued throughout the section, with references to being homesick (173), the Scarecrow (179), and the Wicked Witch of the West (177) in addition to two references to the shoes, including Miss Kansas clicking her heels together (175, 180). These shoes are linked to the couple's new relationship change as well: "I wish I had a pair of shoes like that, you say. I say your feet are too big. But if I had a pair like that, I would let you wear them. Now that we are married, our feet will be the same size" (175).

The shoes in *The Wizard of Oz* and the novel on which it is based (though the red shoes are clearly referencing the film rather than the silver shoes of the book) famously are symbols of Dorothy Gale's journey home and her internal strength and ability. But they are also the source of her strife in the film: they contain the magic to send her home (though not revealed until the end of the film) but are the object the Wicked Witch of the West desires, whether it be for their magic or for their link to her dead sister. By being forced to wear the shoes, Dorothy is also forced to confront the Wicked Witch and embark on a journey that teaches her about herself and creates bonds of friendship (ones that in the book series outlast the confines of the dream ending of the film). The references to the film in Link's story invoke these ideas of being lost and returning home, finding friendship and self. The story's direct commentary on marriage as connecting two people so dramatically that they are gravitationally linked and share everything, including shoe size, build on these themes, but the repetition of "please don't let go" suggests a fragility or tenuous grasp on this connection. A fracture of the bond, as simple as letting go of one's feet, might rupture the connection. Holding onto another's feet becomes an act of grounding the relationship.

The section ends in midsentence, with Miss Kansas literally up in the air, the wind rising, and the narrator saying, "If you were to let go—don't let go—" (180). That the section ends in suspense, with the potential of a tornado ("terrible, noisy, bonecracking air.... The wind is rising" [180]) and its implied separation invoked by *The Wizard of Oz* imagery, suggests that the anchoring and binding connection made to feet is not lasting and reinforces the anxiety of the repetition of "please don't let go" over the narrator's more romanticized vision of marriage as a lasting union and its closeness. The symbolic link of shoes to a way home and grounding is interrupted and left unresolved, and the connection to *The Wizard of Oz* as a compelling path is based not on its happy ending but on its disruption of home and safety.

An additional intertext is Andersen's "The Red Shoes." While not directly referenced in the story, and certainly overpowered by references to *The Wizard of Oz*, it is a present if not intended fairy-tale intertext. The extravagance of material beauty over practicality marked by Karen's red shoes resonates with the beauty pageant of the story. Pageants are a display of beauty and talent that is typically less practical than enjoyable. The pleasure of pageants is in their spectacle, which is also the source of social criticism of them (women objectified for entertainment). Karen's neglect of her Christian duties to care for her ill adoptive mother in favor of dancing in her red shoes is punished in Andersen's story by Karen not being able to stop dancing until her feet are cut off (which, in turn, recalls the Grimms' evil Queen in "Snow White" who dances to death in red-hot iron shoes). Even then she is denied access to the church by her disembodied dancing feet until she is repentant and asks for God's help. She is permitted to enter church at that point, and her heart is filled with such joy at being in the presence of God that it breaks and she dies happy as her soul goes to heaven. While certainly read as a condemnation against "finery and dress, and about being as beautiful as a queen," it is hard to read the story and not see the excess of Karen's suffering and to empathize strongly with her through the focalization that aligns the reader to Karen's perspective (Andersen "The Red Shoes," 66).[2]

While "The Red Shoes" does not exemplify an obvious connection between Andersen's and Link's stories, the excess beauty of Karen's shoes is reflected in the excess of the pageantry in Link's story. Link's use of pageants here is neither an indictment nor an endorsement of beauty pageants, but she uses the beauty-pageant framework for the surreal talents of the contestants. The contestants have weirdly beautiful bodies and talents. Miss Arkansas has "fairy-tale hair, Rapunzel hair," that she braids into lassoes for her act (Link, "Shoe and Marriage" 174); Miss Pennsylvania's dress is a homemade sequined version of Seurat's *Sunday Afternoon at the Boardwalk* (*Un dimanche après-midi à l'Île de la Grande Jatte/ A Sunday Afternoon on the Island of La Grande Jatte*) (175); Miss New Jersey is a devil with red hair teased into horns, pointy teeth, greenish skin, and a tail (175–76);

Miss Nevada was abducted by aliens (176); Miss Texas is a hit woman and exorcist (176); Miss Rhode Island has "too many legs" and performs water ballet (177); Miss Virginia speaks in tongues and is exorcised by Miss Texas (178); Miss Montana has wings and emerges from a fire (178); Miss Oregon walks on water (178); Miss Alaska raises the dead (179); and Miss Kansas bounces naked on a trampoline (180) among other more mundane talents such as Miss Ohio's snake handling or Miss Nebraska's magic tricks. This extravagant pageant show of otherworldly beauties is presented voyeuristically, through the eyes of the narrator as she watches/dreams it with her husband, and it is a distraction for the honeymooners that is interjected with the narrator's concerns about and fears of loss and being lost.

The narrator says, "If only we had a pair of magic slippers. . . . What if we never get home again? . . . Where will we go from here? How will we find our way home again? We should have carried stones in our pockets. Perhaps we will live here forever, in the honey month, on the honeymoon bed" (179). The time and space of the honeymoon is outside of reality, without everyday concerns or problems, and it is contrasted with "home." The honeymoon is like Oz, full of magic and weird beauty, but as a space separate from the mundane, it is also a space separate from responsibility. The narrator's anxiety reflects a concern for the dangers of beauty over responsibility and implies that pageantry is not a replacement for reality. The section is haunted with the idea that this honeymoon cannot last. Recalling the cliché saying "the honeymoon is over," the intertext of "The Red Shoes" whispers the suggestion of duty and responsibility as opposition to beauty.

The third section, "The dictator's wife," is less directly connected to fairy tales and does not retell a specific one. Rather the section recalls Imelda Marcos, First Lady of the Philippines from the mid-1960s to the mid-1980s and wife of Ferdinand Marcos, president and dictator. Imelda Marcos was an active part of her husband's regime and was exiled with him in 1986 following the People Power Revolution; after her husband's death and her return from exile, she was elected congresswoman. She is also known for her immense wealth and extensive fashion and art collections, including a large shoe collection, part of which is housed in the Shoe Museum in Manila. This section of Link's story is anchored on the shoe collection, and begins with the line, "The dictator's wife lives in the shoe museum" (181). The section tells the story of the wife's shoe collection and life with the dictator. It is narrated by an external narrator, but the wife's story is told in dialogue by the woman to a visitor to the museum. Unlike Marcos, who was accused of participation in the corruption of her husband's regime, the dictator's wife is presented as another of his victims. The shoe collection represents not her extravagance and lack of connection to her people but rather a tally of her husband's atrocities. Each pair of shoes in this section of the story belongs to a person the dictator had killed, and the first pairs the dictator's wife collected are those of her fiancé and family, who were executed on her wedding day for trying to prevent the dictator from taking her and forcing her into marriage.

Her story includes a dream life, where she dreams she was married to a nice man and had children who were shoes (186). She tells the visitor that she was happy in her dreams before telling the story of the birth of her own daughter, whom the dictator killed as an infant because she was prophesied to grow up and kill him (187). The visitor asks, "So how did she grow up and kill the dictator?" (187). The woman answers that she didn't, because she was dead, and that the dictator died by stepping on a piece of metal and getting an infection in his foot (187). After his death, the dictator's wife packed up her shoes, sailed far away, and set up the museum with her surviving sister. The section ends with the sister walking the visitor out of the museum, then turning a key on her own wooden sandals, which pop out red wheels, and skating "off down the narrow glass aisle, balanced precariously on her splendid shoes" (188).

Though not directly related to a fairy tale, this section invokes imagery of "Little Red Riding Hood." The dictator's wife is in a bed, "covers pulled up to her chin," and she is "old, fragile, and crumbly" (181). She is "wrinkly like one of those dogs . . . wearing a black wig that's too small for her head" (181). She has false teeth she puts in in the visitor's presence, and it is possible that "her teeth don't fit so well" (181–82). While the initial descriptions of the woman present discomfort at the situation—"In proper museums, you go to stare at the exhibits. They do not stare back at you"—the image of the woman does not suggest a threat (181). The situation is odd, but the dictator's wife is a frail grandmother type. However, as the story progresses, the dictator's wife takes on a more ominous appearance as she is implicated in her husband's actions, not as accomplice but as motivation.

The dictator's wife says, "I killed a lot of men," explaining that the dictator killed men and women who gave his wife too much attention or suggested they were more beautiful than she (184). Immediately preceding this confession is a paragraph that introduces a sinister impression/thought into the woman's telling of her own story: "Underneath the messy wig, the face of the dictator's wife looks like the face of an evil old man and—just for a minute—the visitor may think that it isn't the dictator's wife at all, lying there in the old woman's bed, but the dictator himself, disguised in an old dirty wig" (184). The paragraph serves multiple purposes. It first questions the narrative being told, the perspective of the dictator's wife and her self-positioning as victim rather than coconspirator. It is not so much the events that are questioned, as one would expect a cruel dictator to justify the murders as necessary rather than recount them objectively. Rather the paragraph reminds the reader, through the visitor's lapse in belief as narrated by a seemingly objective external narrator, that this is a single-perspective story. The authority of the speaker is questioned not by providing another version of what happened but by a momentary lapse in confidence in the identity of the speaker. This paragraph also suggests the dictator's wife might have had a more active role in the story than she admits to by her confession of guilt; she feels responsible even if the events as told do not show her as responsible. This same confession of guilt could alternatively be interpreted as reaffirming her status as victim, in that she has internalized the abuse so that she feels culpable for her own abuse as well as that of others.

In terms of the fairy tale, this paragraph complicates the grandmotherly image of the dictator's wife and introduces the possibility of the dictator wolf, which is continued in subsequent descriptions. At one point, the woman licks at tears running down her face (187) and at another it is suggested that she wants to "eat the visitor up": "She stares greedily at the visitor, as if the visitor is delicious. She looks as if she would like to eat the visitor up. She looks as if she would like to eat the visitor up in one bite, spit out the visitor's shoes like peach stones" (188). An old woman in bed in ill-fitting hair and teeth that could be a disguise wanting to eat her visitor recalls the wolf in disguise from "Little Red Riding Hood." But she does not eat the visitor; she just stops talking, and the visitor leaves after an anticlimactic end to the story so the sister can attend a movie with a "happy ending" (188). The invocation of the unfulfilled fairy tale parallels the invocation of the unfulfilled Imelda Marcos reference. This dictator's wife does not go on to resume a political career and amass more wealth; she opens a shoe museum and lives with reminders of her husband's victims, her shoe children. It is a haunting and unsettling end, and not the happy ending that Effie, the sister, skates away to find. The use of the fairy tale does not ground the story or orient the reader; it offers no direction, no path to follow through the forest. It adds a layer of confusion and prevents the sad story of the dictator's wife from being straightforward. As with the other two sections, the fairy-tale patterns and shoe symbols do not offer resolution. Instead the fairy tale is shown to be an inadequate guide for the visitor trying to parse the meaning of the story of the dictator's wife.

The final section is the shortest and is titled "Happy ending." In it an engaged couple is visiting a fortune-teller who reads shoes. She is an expert in "the happy stuff. It's what [she] sees best," and tells the couple that they will grow old together, have a house, smart kids and grandkids, and a garden (190). She sees them in the garden when they are old, drinking lemonade and remembering this encounter. The woman asks follow-up questions about fighting, money, snoring, and dumb jokes, but the fortune-teller resists going into detail, explaining that they will "have a good life" and that if they want their problems read, they will need to see a different fortune-teller (190). This section suggests a happy ending in contrast to the marriages presented earlier in the story, "a good life" in contrast to the happy but unfulfilled marriage of the prince, the anxiety of the honeymooners, and the abuse and trauma of the dictator's wife. But the lack of identity of these and any of the other characters—no names are used for the main characters in the story—opens up this happy ending to be a potential ending for the other couples, at least the first two. The prince certainly claims to have a happy marriage in "The glass slipper," and the honeymooners in "Miss Kansas on Judgment Day" are blissful in their marriage despite anxiety about the change marriage brings and the possibility of it not lasting. The fortune-teller's refusal to disclose problems does not mean the couple will not have them, and her recommendation to "go see the woman next door who reads teas leaves" suggests that there are problems to be seen (190). Her focus on the "good," the "happy," and her vision of the couple in their old age suggests that whatever problems arise can be dealt with.

The last line, "You'll be comfortable together, like an old pair of shoes," equates *happy* and *good* with comfort and configures a happy ending as not one that is perfect but one that works and is comfortable for all involved. The happy ending is not the wedding as many fairy-tale narratives posit it; it is the life that follows. The previous sections all build to this conclusion in their postmarriage focuses: the prince after his wedding, the newlyweds on their honeymoon, and a widow in her old age. The line about the pairs of shoes repeats an idiom, and it also references the actual shoes being read by the fortune-teller—"a pair of old black boots, a pair of canvas tennis shoes"—both seemingly comfortable shoes (189).

The emphasis on ending here—in the title, in the reading by the fortune-teller, and in this section's placement—focuses the reader's attention on endings, including how this one closes "Shoe and Marriage" and the endings of the previous sections. It also draws attention away from a very important line in the first paragraph of this section. The first line of dialogue in the section is from the fortune-teller, who says, "It's just luck that you found each other, you know. Most people aren't so lucky" (189). The invocation of luck cast backward invites different questions about the previous sections. Are the other couples in the story lucky or not so lucky? The dictator's wife would seemingly be unlucky in her marriage arrangements for sure, but the honeymooners are not given enough context for the reader to draw a conclusion. They are locked in the honeymoon moment, full of potential both good and bad, with the impression that as long as they can stay together, all will be well. We know nothing about how they met or what will happen next. For the prince, though, the answer is quite ambiguous. Is he lucky to have found a beautiful cinder girl who makes him happy or unlucky that she is not *the* cinder girl he expected to find? He would seem to be both. But the invocation of luck in this final passage, which, like the comfortable pair of shoes, is a clichéd saying, reminds readers of the lack of fidelity to the fairy-tale narrative patterns invoked in the story.

Many fairy-tale characters seem to be extremely lucky, but there are also many that are very hard working and clever. But that is not what is important here. What is important is narrative desire, narrative pattern. It is like plot armor: things work out for the protagonists because they need to follow the narrative pattern. Readers know that, despite the danger, things will be okay because that is how these stories go, but when the narrative pattern is disrupted, when the fairy tales do not play out as one expects, it is all open. In "The glass slipper" section in particular, the narrative pattern is only partially fulfilled and not in the traditional way. Real life does not have plots, but maybe it has luck. Either way, each section of the story shows failed or averted fairy-tale scripts that do not play out as characters and readers expect. Presented as maps to follow, the fairy tales do not lead the characters to their expected destinations. The dissonance between fairy-tale maps and "lived" experiences produces confusion for the characters and unsettled plots for the readers.

"The Girl Detective"

"The Girl Detective" draws upon the fairy tale "The Twelve Dancing Princesses," the Greek myth of Persephone and Demeter, and the Nancy Drew mystery series. The plot is centered on the girl detective who is looking for her lost mother, and details from the source texts all figure in the telling of her search. The story is told in fragments, subtitled with the subject of each section. The sections are a mix of first- and third-person narration, but assuming they are all linked, a single narrator appears. All of the fragments narrated in third person can logically be read as statements by the narrator of the first-person sections. That said, there are two sections that offer additional layering. One is titled "DANCE WITH BEAUTIFUL GIRLS" and is differentiated from the other sections by its font style—small caps instead of standard. This section is an embedded story told by the fat man, a man who has come to the girl detective for help finding his deceased and missing wife. He is a detective who tells the story of a case he worked on as a young man where he met his wife, and his story is that of "The Twelve Dancing Princesses." The second fragment that deviates from the narration pattern precedes "DANCE WITH BEAUTIFUL GIRLS" and is titled "Why we love the girl detective." The use of the plural pronoun opens up the fragment to ask who "we" are. One reading is that "we" are both the narrator and the fat man, and that this section serves to link the two narrative voices. Alternatively, "we" could represent a larger social group, as the girl detective is presented as a darling of society and her identity a great mystery for the people to solve.

The identity of the first-person narrator is left open—unnamed and gender ambiguous. Early in the story the narrator says, "Someone once suggested that I was the girl detective, but I've never known whether or not they were serious. At least, I don't think that I am the girl detective. If I were the girl detective, I would surely know" (Link, "The Girl Detective" 244–45). This implies a female identity as the girl detective is a girl, but she is also "a master of disguises" and has appeared convincingly male in the story (259, 265). The "we" passage discussed above suggests a more masculine identity by describing the girl detective as "remind[ing] us of the girl we hope to marry one day," and the attributes associated with that are typical of a traditional hetero-patriarchal division of labor, with the wife taking care of a male partner—cooking, finding lost keys, balancing the checkbook, planning vacations, and providing sex (247). The list of things she will do are domestic in nature and confined to the home. The narrator is also a former lover of the girl detective, and the passage "Whom does the girl detective love?" implies a male narrator, but it is not directly textually confirmed. The passage begins with stating, "Remember that boy, Fred, or Nat? Something like that. He was in love with the girl detective," a reference to Ned Nickerson, Nancy Drew's boyfriend (245). This suggests a male love interest for the girl detective though the story does not state that she loved him. That coupled with the dream imagery of plugging a hole in a bottom of a lake with a partially naked waitress implies maleness (255). However, the gender is left ambiguous and is not particularly relevant to the story except that it opens up possibilities and creates further ambiguity about the girl detective and her identity.

Stranger Things Happen by Kelly Link, 2001, cover image by Shelley Jackson.

The Hidden Staircase by Carolyn Keene, 1966, cover image by Rudy Nappi.

In terms of the source texts, she is most closely identified with Nancy Drew, girl detective, through her identifying title. The cover of the short story collection is an image that recreates the covers of the Nancy Drew novels with the girl detective holding her flashlight. Nancy Drew is a fictional teen sleuth and American cultural icon that has been featured in six book series (including one crossover series with the Hardy Boys), two graphic novel series (as crossovers), six feature films, one television movie, three television series (one a crossover), two video game series, various merchandise, and an app. Nancy Drew books have not been out of print since their debut in 1930, and the various texts and products have been marketed to a wide range of age groups of girls and women. While she is not the only girl detective in contemporary fiction and media, she is undeniably a household name and a hero to many girls. The use of "girl detective" to identify the protagonist invokes Drew as a shortcut or template for personality, character traits, and effectiveness. Nancy Drew always solves the case. The "girl detective" phrasing also offers a quick interpretation of the missing mother because Drew's mother died when Drew was very young in all versions of her story, and she is raised by a single father. While Link does not refer to the girl detective's mother as dead, slippage between the terms *missing, lost, forgotten,* and *dead* exists in the story from the first page with the invocation of the Nancy Drew source texts and the introduction of the underworld, which features in both the Persephone myth and "The Twelve Dancing Princesses" fairy tale, though it is a realm of death in the myth and a realm of faerie in the fairy tale.

The first fragment offers the plot and motivation for the story. Titled "The girl detective's mother is missing," the fragment offers a single sentence, "The girl detective's mother has been missing for a long time" (241). The next fragment, "The underworld," describes the underworld as a place "full of things you've forgotten about" (241). While the Drew reference and the name *underworld* both suggest death, Link's description opens up the location to a more metaphorical space of the lost. "Only heroes and girl detectives go to the underworld on purpose" (241). The fourth section is the first to use a first-person pronoun, and it identifies the narrator as one who is trying to figure out the girl detective: "I am detecting the girl detective" (243). The narrator follows the girl detective, but spends most of his time in a tree outside her window, a position that is odd at first, but takes on a more complicated tone when it is revealed that the narrator is a former lover.

The fifth fragment uses second-person address and identifies a narratee as part of the story. The narratee, *you*, lives in the same town and is a witness to "The case of the tap-dancing bank robbers," which references the "The Twelve Dancing Princesses" and features twelve women bank robbers who return lost items from the underworld to the bank. *You* is a witness to the crime and is interviewed on the news, and *you* is quoted in the story. The dancing women are differentiated by their underwear, "embroidered with the days of the week," which is revealed as they dance before the patrons/hostages sitting on the ground (243). The narrator, drawing on the account given by *you*, draws attention to the women's legs and their dancing. While feet are not directly mentioned, the titling of the women as "tap-dancing bank robbers" draws attention to their footwork and the sound of their movement in a way that a reference to other forms of dancing would not. After the women flee, the police discover that the women returned lost items rather than stole, and the first item listed is "several tons of mismatched socks" (244).

This is the first of three significant references to "The Twelve Dancing Princesses" in the story, including the embedded "DANCE WITH BEAUTIFUL GIRLS" mentioned above. The second comes in section nine and is a direct metafictional reference to the story:

> The girl detective doesn't care for fiction. The girl detective doesn't actually read much. She doesn't have the time. Her father used to read fairy tales to her when she was little. She didn't like them. For example, the twelve dancing princesses. If their father really wants to stop them, why doesn't he just forbid the royal shoemaker to make them any more dancing shoes? Why do they have to go underground to dance? Don't they have a ballroom? Do they like dancing or are they secretly relived when they get caught? Who taught them to dance?

> The girl detective has thought a lot about the twelve dancing princesses. She and the princesses have a few things in common. For instance, shoe leather. Possibly underwear. Also, no mother. This is another thing about fiction, fairy tales in particular. The mother is usually missing. (245–46)

This section contrasts the genres of the two primary source texts, detective fiction and fairy tale. The girl detective's practical questions in response to the fairy tale show a rejection of fairy-tale logic and a refusal to enter into the "Once Upon a Time" land invoked by the opening gesture that accompanies most fairy tales and folktales. This fragment also precedes the fat man's story and links the differing "Twelve Dancing Princesses" references by contextualizing them through the girl detective's logical perspective, despite her illogical quest for her dead mother. But the fairy-tale logic, and that of myth, also enable the girl detective's quest. The dead do not continue to live, nor is the underworld a real place in Nancy Drew's world. Her quest is that of fairy tale and myth, though her approach is one of detective reasoning.

The mystery of the "The Twelve Dancing Princesses" (ATU 306 The Danced-Out Shoes), because it is, after all, a mystery-driven fairy-tale, is that of worried parents trying to find out why their daughters are exhausted all day, and the only clue they have to go on is the shoes that are danced to pieces. In the Grimms' version, "The Worn-Out Dancing Shoes," the king hires a series of men, detectives if you will, to solve the mystery. After a series of ineffectual princes and other royalty fail, a soldier solves the case by using the advice and items gifted to him by an old woman.[3] His reward, for revealing that the princesses were enchanted and venturing through a portal to a faerie realm to dance with fairy princes, is to marry one of the princesses. In the fairy tale, the shoes are emblematic of a problem. It is not just that the princesses are using up too many shoes, suggesting excess, but that they are not able to be princesses during the day. They are too tired to fulfill their social roles in the kingdom to which they were born. That the princesses seem to be enjoying themselves and are not under duress in the most popular versions of the story does not factor into the problem.

Their desires, their thoughts, are not under consideration by any of the men in the story who make decisions about their well-being. Their rescue is considered as such because it restores the social order, and the worn-out dancing shoes represent the disruption to that order.[4]

"The Girl Detective" challenges this fairy-tale logic by transferring the emphasis from the worn-out dancing shoes to the dancing feet and by not rescuing the women. The shift from shoe to dancing feet emphasizes movement. The worn-out shoes from the fairy-tale represent ruin and using something up, even if joyfully. The end result is shoes that no longer function and that appear to be too far gone to be repaired (at least, I have not encountered a version where someone tries to resole the dancing shoes).[5] They are an endpoint, even if a temporary end. Dancing suggests movement and continuation. The shift is to the path or the journey, rather than its end, and because dancing is often associated with joy (and worn-out shoes with exhaustion), the implication is a pleasant journey, if a tiring one. The dancing women return things that are lost, but they are not presented as being lost themselves. Finding the princesses and the girl detective's mother does not result in restoring the world to what it was before. Rather, it is the reunion of the family and lost items that is presented as restoration.

The girl detective's mother is aligned with the dancing princesses through description. Near the end of the story, the narrator describes a photo in the girl detective's room that the girl detective "suspects . . . is her mother" (260). The woman is dancing and is described as wearing "a pair of worn dancing shoes" (260). In this section, the narrator speculates on the mother's disappearance, and it is suggested that she was hit by a van, or perhaps got in a van, that matches the getaway van of the tap-dancing bank robbers (260). Death is mentioned as a possibility but quickly followed by an alternative option reminiscent of denial in grief. A few fragments later, the girl detective enters the underworld via an entrance hidden in a bathroom stall in a Chinese restaurant (262). There she and the narrator discover a nightclub with a large sign that says "DANCE WITH BEAUTIFUL GIRLS," and the girl detective finds her mother (263). Though the dialogue tags lack identity, ensuring a level of ambiguity, plot context and the fairy-tale promise of a happy ending suggest a mother-daughter reunion: "Someone says, 'Mom?' Someone embraces someone else. Everyone is dancing. 'Where have you been?' someone says. 'Spring cleaning,' someone says" (263). The ambiguity of the exchange mirrors the interchange of mother and daughter roles from the invoked Persephone myth. Demeter searches for her daughter Persephone, and this plot is reversed in "The Girl Detective." "Spring cleaning" recalls Persephone's time in Hades, but again in reverse. The mother is in the underworld for spring cleaning whereas Persephone can leave Hades in Spring. "Spring cleaning" also incorporates the work of the tap-dancing bank robbers who return lost items from the underworld to where they belong. This section ends in confusion as a line of dancers are moving so fast they cannot be differentiated: "Is that a dancing princess, or a bank robber? Is that a fat old man, or an alligator, or a housekeeper? I wish I knew. Is that the girl detective or is it her mother? . . . I look, and in the mossy glow they all look like the girl detective. Or maybe the girl detective looks like all of them" (264). Schanoes points to this moment as a polyphony of selves marked by joy (132). As the dancing carries them away, the narrator calls out for the dancers to wait, but he falls out of his tree and blacks out. When he awakes, he is back in his tree outside the girl detective's window but cannot see into her room because the blinds are closed.

After not seeing the girl detective for a while, the narrator thinks he spots her at the airport. She is "disguised as a fat old man" or "the kid in the overalls" who gives the man a napkin or perhaps a waitress (Link, "The Girl Detective" 265). This is in the penultimate fragment, "The return of the girl detective." The previous fragment, "The end of the girl detective?," states, "Some people say she never came back from the underworld" (265). Her return is ambiguous and open, and suspicious. Is she back or is the narrator wishing to see her? The final section, "Why I got down out of the tree," further confuses the ending: "She came over and stood under the tree. She looked a lot like my mother. Get down out of that tree this instant! Don't you know it's time for dinner?" (266). The initial referent for *she* appears to be the girl detective, as that is who the previous *she* referred to, and earlier in the story, the girl detective speaks to the narrator in the tree on a couple of occasions. But the final two lines, which are dialogue from "she" even if not marked by quotation marks, are motherly statements, policing behavior and providing nourishment. What this final segment suggests is that the narrator is still a child—or at least a teenager—which opens up the story to be more an imagined game than realistic. The narrator could actually be the girl detective, as stated earlier, if this is indeed all a fantasy s/he is creating. Or this "she" in question could be the girl detective, perhaps in disguise.

This ending does not so much challenge the previous knowledge built by the reader as it returns the reader to the earlier state of confusion. The ambiguity of the identity of the narrator and the girl detective introduced in the final fragment reaffirms the instability from the beginning of the story. The solving of the mystery and the reliance on "The Twelve Dancing Princesses" tale offers stability and logic to the reader, which is unsettled by reprising questions of identity presumed to have been settled. As we read the story, we piece together clues drawn from the source texts—the Nancy Drew series, "The Twelve Dancing Princesses" (ATU 306), and the myth of Persephone—all of which contain a mystery as a core plot element, even if only the Nancy Drew books are detective fiction in genre. The story begins with a mystery—"The girl detective's mother is missing"—and the rest of the story appears to be structured around solving that mystery (241). The importance of the mother's disappearance is foregrounded by the repetition of the title of the first fragment and its one-sentence content. The next fragment about the underworld hints at the mother's death, and as the story continues, more information is revealed to affirm that possibility. The allusions to Nancy Drew and Persephone and the direct referencing and embedded retelling of "The Twelve Dancing Princesses" function as clues for the reader to solve the mystery. The texts are a guide for how readers should interpret the details, and the fairy tale offers a plot onto which those details can be mapped. It is a guide for the story, and it is a guide that the girl detective rejects in the text as being unrealistic. Yet it is a guide that proves fairly accurate until the end.

The lack of rational logic that turns the girl detective away from the fairy tale is necessary for the story "The Girl Detective" because it is the fairy-tale logic that emphasizes wonder over reason and provides closure for the mystery. The plots of the girl detective's mystery, the story "The Girl

Detective," and the "The Twelve Dancing Princesses" do not align exactly, making the fairy tale an imperfect map. It serves more as a compass, pointing in a direction, than a map with a path to follow clearly marked.

Fairy-Tale Maps

Link herself has explained how references to other genres can shape tone and pattern. In an interview for the *Journal of the Fantastic in the Arts* with Brian Attebery, Link explains that "pattern is story. Fairy tale/folkloric or mythic pattern overlays contemporary narrative and the way that we see our own lives. So if you are interested in writing contemporary fantasy, the reader is going to supply a lot of the basic structure for you. This is especially useful in short stories, where you have so little space" (415–16). In another interview with Michelle Dean for *The Guardian*, Link adds that "fairy tales are a very useful kind of storytelling shorthand. . . . You can use fragments of them in ways that add dimension and weight to whatever other kinds of story you're telling" (qtd. in Dean). In "Travels with the Snow Queen," the protagonist's rejection of the fairy tale whose narrative pattern she follows offers a contradiction not resolved by the story. The result is a both/and configuration: the fairy tale as a genre is needed, but the specific version of the fairy tale invoked is not an adequate map for the experiences of the contemporary characters. Fairy tales can ground desire or create unfulfillable expectations, as in "Shoe and Marriage." They can provide structure to help shape the telling of a story, as in "The Girl Detective." But as the girl detective recognizes, they are not logical or rational. When presented with fairy-tale maps and shoes to take them on their journeys, the protagonists of these three stories discover that the paths laid out by the fairy tales are not quite right. Even when the maps lead to the expected places, the characters do not react in expected ways and find that they are neither happy nor at the end of their story. To paraphrase Angela Carter in "Notes from the Front Line," these are new feet in old shoes, and the pressure of the new feet sends the shoes off in a new direction, off the map.

Conclusion

Collapsing Borders in the Age of the Internet

THIS PROJECT, BY ASKING questions about how twenty-first-century fairy tales share narrative space, does not so much create a new fairy-tale map as recognize that maps are drafted and drawn. The shared geography of the texts in part 1 reflects a recognition of the shared space and interconnectivity of the twenty-first century, and the dissolution of narrative borders invites further study of its relationship to the shifting view of real-world borders. Lee Haring explains that "hybridization in folktales and fairy tales are symbolic enactments of the realities of social and cultural conflicts. Hybrid or Creolized folktales and fairytales are a window into worldwide processes of globalization" (470). The pastiche technique that brings together disparate tales into one location enacts the loosening of borders and the collapsing of distances among people scattered across the world. While the internet certainly existed in the late twentieth century, with the World Wide Web making it more accessible to the public in the early 1990s, the early years of the twenty-first century resulted in rapid adoption of the internet for everyday tasks and worldwide communication. Advances in the early part of the first decade of the twenty-first century affected speed, variety, and affordability, making the internet accessible for large numbers of the world's population. The internet has been so transformative that it marks a generational shift—those who have always had easily accessible internet engage the world differently from those who remember the before times. It is not surprising that the dissolution of fairy-tale borders would be popular in the twenty-first century, as changes in everyday life make the dissolution of borders comfortable for contemporary audiences.

The ease of cross-cultural exchange in the age of the internet has resulted in scholars of Korean media dubbing the period after 2010 as the Korean Wave 2.0 in recognition of how the internet enabled expansive, instantaneous, and viral distribution of Korean media outside of the country. The internet has also enabled a level of fan engagement with media, its creators, and fellow fans not possible in an age dominated by physical mail and in-person conventions. Websites like Heidi Anne Heiner's *SurLaLuneFairyTales.com* and D. L. Ashliman's *Folklore and Mythology: Electronic Texts* have made multiple versions of tale types easily accessible for anyone with an internet connection. It is not necessary to purchase anthologies or visit libraries to find a good fairy tale, and sites like *Project Gutenberg* make public domain texts freely available. The increased accessibility of source material makes it easier to create a pastiche.

A truly amazing effect of the internet is the way in which it modifies the geographic (both physical and political) boundaries of the world. International communication is quick, and the cost is covered in one's internet service. Not only can one access information about anywhere in the world at any time, but one can, at three o'clock in the morning, log onto a multiplayer online game and team up with friends in Alaska, New Zealand, and France to battle virtual bad guys and at the same time discuss the Korean drama the team is watching as they play. Physical distance and national borders may separate the players, but the online community transcends those barriers. This connectivity shapes how those in the age of the internet see the world, and this is reflected in the texts analyzed in this project. While the geographic barriers that separate people persist, they are diminished and can frequently be circumvented with internet access. That is not to say that internet access is ubiquitous and democratic. Poverty, government censorship, and physical remoteness are very real barriers to internet access, even in developed nations, but the virtual nature of the internet and the use of satellites also grant access in areas where older methods of communication can be difficult. While geographic borders have remained (relatively) stable, their relevance to our daily lives has fluctuated widely in the context of the internet.

The opening of the narrative borders of the source tales in texts like *Once Upon a Time* and *Indexing*, and to a lesser extent *The Lunar Chronicles*, reflects an understanding of borders as constructed and ideological. This narrative act raises questions about what is being separated by the borders recognized and then ignored by the texts. As these narrative borders are revealed to be flexible and fluctuating, what does that mean for the other borders encountered by twenty-first-century audiences? The narrative borders in many of the texts examined in this project are bypassed by bridges, plot and fragment similarities that invite connections and transgressions rather than separation. The exploration of these connections as a means of moving beyond narrative borders can be a powerful metaphor for explorations of real-world borders. This narrative worldview is emboldened by the global connectivity made possible by the internet, which raises practical questions about the purpose and stability of physical, geographic, and political borders. If one sees borders and barriers as abstract rather than concrete, then traversing them becomes conceivable and preserving them less necessary. Pastiche (and mash up, collage, assemblage, etc.) is not a distinctly twenty-first-century technique, but it is meaningful in the twenty-first century in ways not possible before. The diminishing of barriers that separate people brought about by the internet results in a sort of open-borders worldview. The borders exist, but the ease of movement across them renders them descriptors of difference rather than barriers of separation. If the borders of nations and physical place are more navigable, then that viewpoint can be applied to metaphoric borders, narrative ones included. Why keep tales or genres separate when bridging them is so much fun?

The internet has changed our geographic metaphors because it has changed how we understand space. Adding a virtual dimension to everyday activities shapes how we engage the space around us and how we think about that space. A logical extension of that way of thinking is seen in the stories we tell. While these stories still reflect their places, they also reflect their connection to a world beyond the immediate landscapes of their origin. *Secret Garden* is a good example of a text that both reflects its location and recognizes that location as one point on a map that is connected to multiple other points along varying paths. The international scope of the settings in *The Lunar Chronicles*, the range of folk narrative genres invoked in *Once Upon a Time*, the multiplicity of tale variants referenced in *Indexing*, and the wide range of source texts in Kelly Link's short fiction all point to recognition of shared space and simultaneous habitation. Individual fairy tales do not exist in isolation, and the shared settings of *Once Upon a Time*, *Indexing*, and *The Lunar Chronicles* literalize this always present, always relevant simultaneity. The collapse of narrative borders in the settings of these texts and the crossover of fairy-tale logic from fantasy to fictionalized reality in *Secret Garden* and Link's stories reflects an epistemological shift built upon postmodern conceits that reality is constructed. We understand that genre divisions are made up. We know that the classification system in the ATU is invented, not innate. And our stories reflect this knowledge that we have constructed the barriers that separate us. While some postmodern texts focus on dismantling these barriers, the texts in this project imagine worlds shaped by connections, not divisions.

Connection is also at the core of the direct, metafictional engagement with fairy tales as maps in the texts in part 2. Fairy tales connect us to each other and offer ways of negotiating conflict and loss. They can provide guidance and hope, but they can also lead us astray. As Kelly Link suggests, fairy tales are patterns, and they are tempting shortcuts. Turning to fairy tales as maps for lived experiences in fiction recognizes the long critical history of understanding fairy tales for their socializing function. The greater access and proliferation of fairy-tale material in the age of the internet includes critical perspectives on fairy tales, both formal and not. As Vanessa Joosen's excellent study *Critical & Creative Perspectives on Fairy Tales: An Intertextual Dialogue between Fairy-Tale Scholarship and Postmodern Retellings* shows, the critical discourse surrounding fairy tales is pervasive, and the tales talk back. Critical opinions on tales have become fragmented from their sources and entered into popular culture memory, much like wicked stepmothers and glass slippers. The didactic thrust of children's fairy tales means that "everyone knows" that fairy tales have morals and teach lessons. When fictional adult characters turn to fairy tales, they are reflecting long-standing popular attitudes about the roles of fairy tales in society. In actively rewriting the tales, the characters in *Secret Garden* and Link's stories demonstrate our continued attachment to a genre steeped in hope and wonder. Fairy tales are a fantastic space, open for exploring issues of one's own culture and life, and fairy-tale maps need not lead in the same directions as they have in the past.

Notes

Introduction: Remapping a Genre

1. The earliest recorded variant of "Cinderella" is often identified as Duan Chengshi's "Ye Xian" from approximately 850 CE China, though the motifs of Cinderella have been noted in first- and second-century BCE Greek and Egyptian tales. There are several collections of Cinderella tales that trace its international variants, notably Marian Roalfe Cox's *Cinderella*, Anna Birgitta Rooth's *The Cinderella Cycle*, Alan Dundes's *Cinderella: A Casebook*, and Heidi Anne Heiner's *Cinderella Tales From Around the World*. *Cinderella Across Cultures: New Directions and Interdisciplinary Perspectives*, edited by Martine Hennard Dutheil de la Rochère, Gillian Lathey, and Monika Woźniak, offers new critical frameworks for engaging the range of Cinderella tales that exist.
2. Collections of women-centered traditional tales include those by Angela Carter (*The Old Wives' Fairy Tale Book* and *Strange Things Sometimes Still Happen*), Rosemary Minard (*Womenfolk and Fairy Tales*), Ethel Johnston Phelps (*Tatterhood and Other Tales* and *The Maid of the North: Feminist Folk Tales from Around the World*), and Kathleen Ragan (*Fearless Girls, Wise Women, and Beloved Sisters: Heroines in Folktales from Around the World*).
3. See my articles "Who's Wicked Now? The Stepmother as Fairy-Tale Heroine" and "Ambiguous Villains and Fairy-Tale Monsters in Kelly Link's 'The Cinderella Game'" for discussion of using the term *fragment* over *motif* when working with postmodern retellings.
4. Joosen lists chronotope, attitude to supernatural, characterization, optimism, action versus character development, style, and narratological features as avenues of disruption (13–16). Chronotope would be the element most disrupted in pastiche. Identified as "time space" by Mikhail Bakhtin in "Forms of Time and Chronotope in the Novel: Notes toward a Historical Poetics," chronotope is the "intrinsic connectedness of temporal and spatial relationships that are artistically expressed in literature" (84). Bakhtin identifies time as "the dominant principle in the chronotope" (86), and Joosen's examples of transposition

similarly emphasize time over space though the two are inexorably linked in her examples (13). For Bakhtin, chronotope refers to the way time moves in different genres, differentiating between, for example, adventure-time and everyday-time. However, Bakhtin asserts that "in any meeting the temporal marker . . . is inseparable from the spatial marker" (97). In pastiche, space becomes the focus of the disruption to the fairy-tale chronotope. The interplay of fairy-tale elements from different narratives in a single space disrupts expectations for discrete tales while simultaneously drawing upon these multiple narratives to establish the fairy-tale feel evoked by the multiple references to tales.

5 See Cristina Bacchilega's *Postmodern Fairy Tales: Gender and Narrative Strategies*, Stephen Benson's *Cycles of Influence: Fiction, Folktale, Theory*, and Merja Makinen's "Theorizing Fairy-Tale Fiction, Reading Jeanette Winterson" for discussions of postmodern fairy tales.
6 See Brian McHale's *Postmodernist Fiction* and *Constructing Postmodernism* and Steven Connor's *Postmodernist Culture: An Introduction to Theories of the Contemporary* for an overview of this conversation.

Chapter 1: Genre and Geography

1 This raises some biological questions that are not answered on the show. How does Henry age if none of the adults do? He is shown as both an infant and as a teen. Do the other children—Henry's school friends—age? At the end of the curse, there is a baby boom. Was Cinderella pregnant for twenty-eight years? The obvious answer to these questions is magic. As Henry is Regina's adopted son, the curse isolates him so that he can have a normal childhood, and the illusion of aging classmates is part of that. Or children are not affected by the aging aspect of the curse and no one notices the lack of physical aging for adults. Other theories are possible, but the show simply offers "magic" as the answer.
2 Disney did release a short film of "Little Red Riding Hood" in 1922, but it has not been adapted to a full-length film and is not as well-known as other Disney shorts. See Jack Zipes's *The Enchanted Screen: The Unknown History of Fairy-Tale Films* and Sandra L. Beckett's *Red Riding Hood for All Ages: A Fairy-Tale Icon in Cross-Cultural Contexts*. The version of "Little Red Riding Hood" in the show draws more upon werewolf folklore and the French folktale tradition, and it likely nods to Angela Carter's "Little Red Riding Hood" trio of short stories published in *The Bloody Chamber*.

3   Belle's story is an interesting one, as it embraces the idea of books as journeys and escape, further entwining fiction with physical space. Belle is inspired to be a compassionate hero by a book given to her by her mother, and she turns to books to solve her problems, making library research her most powerful weapon.

4   See, for example, Liz Medendorp's "The 'Frozen' Characters' Mix in 'Once Upon a Time—Season 4' Creates Quite the Slush," Sarah Caldwell's "The Highs and Lows of *Once Upon a Time's Frozen* Episodes," and Jessica Rawden's "11 Reasons Once Upon A Time's Frozen Story Is Flipping Weird." These writers all point out the oddities of the use of *Frozen*, suggesting that it is a miss-fit to the series specifically to capitalize on the film's success.

5   Some of the other non-fairy-tale texts referenced on the show include *The Count of Monte Cristo* by Alexandre Dumas; *Twenty Thousand Leagues Under the Sea* and *The Mysterious Island* by Jules Verne; *The Prince and the Pauper*, *A Connecticut Yankee in King Arthur's Court*, and *The Adventures of Tom Sawyer* by Mark Twain; and *The Scarlet Letter* by Nathaniel Hawthorne. Many of these novels are referenced in season five, where the characters live in the Land of Untold Stories, a mysterious place where characters go to avoid their unhappy endings. The nineteenth-century novels are also very closely linked with an overlapping Victorian London that is the base for some, but not all, of the novels invoked. The Londons of Alice and Dr. Jekyll are the same, for example. This overlapping geography asserts a genre connection among these period texts that bridges fantasy and realism and suggests that these living fictional worlds are not only derived from the realms of fantasy and magic.

Chapter 2: Genres Overlaid

1   As I discuss in "Novels," while the genre of fairy tale and the medium of the novel have long been intertwined, the popularity of long-form fairy tales at the turn of the twenty-first century invites deeper explorations of the productive relationships between the two.

2   Veronica Schanoes (*Fairy Tales, Myth, and Psychoanalytic Theory: Feminism and Retelling the Tale*), Kevin Paul Smith (*The Postmodern Fairytale: Folkloric Intertexts in Contemporary Fiction*), and Jessica Tiffin (*Marvelous Geometry: Narrative and Metafiction in Modern Fairy Tale*) have examined *Witches Abroad* for its metafictional reflection on the power of stories to shape the worlds in which they are told. The novel follows the trio of Discworld witches

as they travel through land distorted by misapplied fairy tales until they reach the epicenter of the distortion. The stories try to warp the world around them to fulfill their narratives, which is a concern in McGuire's *Indexing* series as well. Referred to as "as pastiche of disrupted fairy tales" by Schanoes (77), "relentlessly intertextual" by Smith (135), and "an exercise in literary pastiche" by Tiffin (160), *Witches Abroad* combines different fairy tales in the same landscape. The tales are first encountered discretely as the witches stop in locations marked by individual tales and then as interwoven threads as multiple tales are in play in the city at the center of the disturbance, though the narrative focuses on "Cinderella."

3   Other notable examples include Hines's Princess series, which addresses issues of sexual violence and identity in the source tales, and Michael Buckley's children's mystery series *The Sisters Grimm*, which, like the television show *Grimm*, treats fairy tales as real and the Grimm family as keepers of the tales. *The Sisters Grimm*, like *Once Upon a Time*, connects fairy tales to other fantastic texts, like Shakespeare's *A Midsummer Night's Dream*, eliding divisions that separate fairy tales from other classic texts.

4   In later novels, it is revealed that shells are not actually killed but are experimented on to create the plague, a biological weapon, and its antidote.

5   Meyer addresses fan questions about character appearance on her blog and identifies Cinder as "Lunar (mixed ethnicity—Asian/Caucasian?)" ("A Guide to Lunar Chronicles Character Traits"). Several fans pushed back in comments insisting that Cinder is white because she is identified as being from Europe. Meyer responded in a comment on the post that "Lunars are descended from many Earthen ethnicities and so come in a wide range of skin colors, hair types, facial features, etc."

6   See Ann Schmiesing's "Disability" and *Disability, Deformity, and Disease in the Grimms' Fairy Tales* for discussions of disability in fairy tales.

7   There is not a number for the Pied Piper in the AT index, perhaps because it is a legend, but both 570 The Rabbit-Herd and 570B* The Sheep and the Magic Flute are tale types identified with pipes magically calling animals.

8   The use of 171 is perhaps because AT 171B* Various Conflicts with Bears offers a catch-all category for bear-conflict tales; however, none of the descriptions listed resemble the Goldilocks story. The ATU revision collapses 171B* under 179* Tales about Men and Bears (previously Men and Bear-miscellaneous) but notes that these tales are primarily ones in which "the bear is generally hurt [killed]" (Uther 123). "Goldilocks and the Three Bears" is typically considered to be a literary tale originating with Robert Southey in

1837, not a traditional oral tale, which would explain the lack of indexing by Aarne and Thompson, but the lack of an oral tradition has been contested by Joseph Jacobs and Katherine Briggs, who trace oral variants that precede Southey's tale (see Iona and Peter Opie, "Goldilocks and the Three Bears"; and Alan C. Elms, "'The Three Bears': Four Interpretations"; and Rose Williamson, "The European Sources of the Fairy Tale: A Case Study of ATU 171, 'The Three Bears'" for a discussion of the history). Nevertheless, it is not easily cataloged using the AT/ATU index even when broadening one's search to fox tales to account for variants featuring a vixen rather than a girl or an old woman. The Goldilocks example is unique in that there is a bit of a mystery wrapped up in its tale-type designation. This is clearly not an invention of McGuire's as it is also used by reliable online resources and scholars, and McGuire is following a popular (mis)typing of the tale.

9 Lundell examines the gender bias in the AT index in regard to the absences of gender identity, the misrepresentation of female characters, and the disregard of female activity, in terms of both categorization and linguistic construction of titles and entries. Alan Dundes surveys critiques of the index in "The Motif-Index and the tale Type Index: A Critique," which includes its Eurocentric focus and its representation of the tale types as discrete despite frequent overlap. Francisco Vaz da Silva also discusses epistemological concerns with a system that presents tale types as fixed in "Hybridity." In his introduction to the 2004 expansion of the index, Hans-Jörg Uther lists multiple criticisms of the work, including those listed above, and claims that his revision "has eliminated or mitigated these faults" (8). While much improved, the ATU system still contains limitations, some of which are acknowledged by Uther, but which include geographic and linguistic restrictions and some lack of nuance in regard to gender. Despite these criticisms, the index is an invaluable tool for folklorists aware of its limitations.

Chapter 3: Asking for Directions

1 Keith and Lee recognize that "Korean folklore is not well known internationally" and survey the representation of mermaids in Korean folklore and popular culture (69). Keith and Lee distinguish between traditional *ineo* (fish people) and mermaids, noting that *ineo* typically have legs in traditional tales as opposed to the Western-styled mermaid with a fish's tail. They note that Andersen's tale, translated into Korean in 1935 but available in Japanese since 1904, "exerted a considerable influence on contemporary mermaid stories and

images in South Korea" (70). They explain that "There are no extant mermaid stories in Korean folklore that conclude as tragedies of thwarted love and sacrifice," as in Andersen's tale (81). Keith and Lee also link mermaids and mermaid tales to Korean folktales of *gumiho* (fox spirits).

2. The show has won six Seoul Broadcasting System Drama Awards, four Baeksang Arts Awards, and three Seoul International Drama Awards.

3. See Erik Ropers, "Historical Narrative and the Misrepresentation of Wartime Labor Recruitment in *Kenkanryū*."

4. See Joseph Nye and Youna Kim, "Soft Power and the Korean Wave" and Hye-Kyung Lee, "Cultural Policy and the Korean Wave: From National Culture to Transnational Consumerism."

5. This group of adapted Western fairy tales is the second type of fairy-tale film identified by Lee. The first type is adaptations of Korean folktales and legend, and the third type "blends tales from the two traditions—Korean and European" ("Fairy-Tale Film" 208). According to Lee, the third type is rare in film but more common in television drama.

6. The edition of Andersen's "The Little Mermaid" I use translates this tale's title as "The Mermaid."

7. The stunt is for Oska's music video, and Oska is also Joo Won's cousin and participates in overlapping love triangles as a longtime crush of Ra-Im. Oska and Ra-Im flirt in front of Joo-Won regularly to annoy him.

8. All quotes from the show are taken from the English subtitles translated by DramaFever.

9. Western education is greatly valued on the show and is a mark of success for the younger generation, with multiple characters speaking in English to prove their worth at key moments. The use of English by the characters is often in situations in which one character is asserting dominance or superior experience over another, establishing hierarchal relationships. Alex Baratta argues in "The Use of English in Korean TV Drama to Signal a Modern Identity" that "switching to English in this context [Korean dramas] is often a means to reflect an identity of power for the characters" (54). He builds on earlier research, such as that of Jamie Shinhee Lee in "Linguistic Constructions of Modernity: English Mixing in Korean Television Commercials," that links English in Korean media to "connotations of modernity and power" (Baratta 54). But the parent generation, while still valuing Western education, tries to enforce traditional social codes on their heirs to stave off the cultural Westernization of the children.

10. Joo-Won is suffering from amnesia at this point, and Ra-Im anticipates his comments to her by rephrasing the proposition he made to her before.

Chapter 4: Following Footsteps

1. See my article, "Ambiguous Villains and Fairy-Tale Monsters in Kelly Link's 'The Cinderella Game,'" for a discussion of this story.
2. Do Rozario also explains that Karen's final pair of red shoes is associated with social mobility both in the symbolic connection to Cinderella's slipper and in the context of the story as they were intended for an Earl's daughter and reminiscent of a princess's shoes (190). Her analysis is grounded in Hilary Davidson's study "Sex and Sin: The Magic Red Shoes." Davidson traces the sociocultural history of red shoes as an important context for Andersen's tale, identifying their connection with "authority, wealth, and power" (273). Davidson explains that "Karen literally steps above her station into aristocratic shoes" (278).
3. In Andrew Lang's version, which shared the "The Twelve Dancing Princesses" title, he is a cowboy turned gardener, and the magic aid comes from a lady in a gold dress who comes to him in his dreams.
4. Criticism of "The Worn-Out Dancing Shoes" variants reads the tale in terms of its sexual desire (see Sheldon Cashdon, *The Witch Must Die: The Hidden Meaning of Fairy Tales*) and patriarchal control (see Hayley Thomas, "Undermining a Grimm Tale: A Feminist Reading of 'The Worn-Out Dancing Shoes' [KHM 133]," and Jago Morrison, *Contemporary Fiction*).
5. Hilary Davidson recognizes the "realities of material eighteenth-century shoes' increasingly delicate soles" in "Holding the Sole: Shoes, Emotions, and the Supernatural" (79).

Bibliography

Primary Sources

The 10th Kingdom. Directed by David Carson and Herbert Wise, NBC and Hallmark, 2000.
Aladdin. Directed by Ron Clements and John Musker, Walt Disney, 1992.
Andersen, Hans Christian. "The Mermaid." *Andersen's Fairy Tales*, Longmeadow, 1988, pp. 1–21.
———. "The Red Shoes." *Andersen's Fairy Tales*, Longmeadow, 1988, pp. 62–67.
———. "The Snow Queen." *Andersen's Fairy Tales*, Longmeadow, 1988, pp. 160–89.
Ashliman, D. L. *Folklore and Mythology: Electronic Texts*. 1996–2020, http://www.pitt.edu/~dash/folktexts.html.
Barrie, J. M. *Peter Pan (Peter and Wendy)*. 1911. Project Gutenberg, https://www.gutenberg.org/ebooks/26654.
Baum, L. Frank. *The Wonderful Wizard of Oz*. 1900. Project Gutenberg, https://www.gutenberg.org/ebooks/55.
Beauty and the Beast. Directed by Gary Trousdale and Kirk Wise, Walt Disney, 1991.
Black, Holly. *The White Cat*. Margaret K. McElderry Books, 2010.
Brave. Directed by Mark Andrew, Brenda Chapman, and Steve Purcell. Pixar, 2012.
Brontë, Charlotte. *Jane Eyre*. 1897. Project Gutenberg, https://www.gutenberg.org/ebooks/1260.
Buckley, Michael. *The Sisters Grimm* series. Abrams Books, 2005–12. 10 vols.
Buffy the Vampire Slayer. Created by Joss Whedon, WB and UPN, 1997–2003.
Carroll, Lewis. *Alice's Adventures in Wonderland*. 1865. Dover, 1993.
Carter, Angela. *The Bloody Chamber and Other Stories*. 1979. Penguin, 1993.
———, editor. *The Old Wives' Fairy Tale Book*. Pantheon, 1990.
———, editor. *Strange Things Sometimes Still Happen: Fairy Tales from Around the World*. Faber and Faber, 1993.

Cinderella. Directed by Clyde Gernimi, Wilfred Jackson, and Hamilton Luske, Walt Disney, 1950.

Cinderella. Directed by Kenneth Branagh, Walt Disney, 2015.

Coover, Robert. *Briar Rose*. Grove, 1996.

———. *Stepmother*. McSweeney's, 2004.

D'Aulnoy, Marie-Catherine. "The White Cat." Translated by John Ashbery. *Wonder Tales*, edited by Marina Warner, Oxford University Press, 2004, pp. 19-63.

Dumas, Alexandre. *The Count of Monte Cristo*. 1888. *Project Gutenberg*, https://www.gutenberg.org/ebooks/1184.

Ende, Michael. *The Neverending Story*. 1979. Translated by Ralph Manheim, Penguin Books, 1983.

Ever After: A Cinderella Story. Directed by Andy Tennant, Twentieth Century Fox, 1998.

Frankenstein. Directed by James Whale, Universal Pictures, 1931.

Frozen. Directed by Chris Buck and Jennifer Lee, Walt Disney, 2013.

Goldman, William. *The Princess Bride*. 1973. 30th anniversary ed., Ballantine, 2003.

Grimm. Created by Stephen Carpenter, David Greenwalt, and Jim Kouf, NBC, 2011–17.

Grimm, Wilhelm, and Jacob Grimm. *The Complete Fairy Tales of the Brothers Grimm*. 1857. Edited and translated by Jack Zipes, Expanded ed., Bantam, 1992.

Hawthorne, Nathaniel. *The Scarlet Letter*. 1850. *Project Gutenberg*, https://www.gutenberg.org/ebooks/25344.

Heaney, Seamus. *Beowulf: A New Verse Translation*. Farrar, Straus and Giroux, 2000.

Heiner, Heidi Anne. *SurLaLune Fairy Tales*.1998–2020, http://www.surlalunefairytales.com/.

Hines, Jim C. *The Princess series*. DAW, 2009–11. 4 vols.

Hoodwinked! Directed by Corey Edwards, Todd Edwards, and Tony Leech, The Weinstein Company, 2005.

Into the Woods. Directed by Rob Marshall, Walt Disney, 2014.

Keene, Carolyn. *The Hidden Staircase*. 1930. Grosset and Dunlap, 1966.

Keene, Carolyn. *Nancy Drew Mystery Stories* series. Grosset and Dunlap, Simon and Schuster, 1930–2003. 175 vols.

Lang, Andrew, editor. "The Twelve Dancing Princesses." *The Red Fairy Book*. 1890. *12 Books in 1: Andrew Lang's Complete "Fairy Book" Series: Traditional*

Folk Tales and Fairy Stories From Around the World. Shoes and Ships and Sealing Wax, 2006, pp. 87–90.

Link, Kelly. "Catskin." *Magic for Beginners*, Harcourt, 2005, pp. 125–55.

———. "The Cinderella Game." *Troll's-Eye View: A Book of Villainous Tales*, edited by Ellen Datlow and Terri Windling, Firebird, 2009, pp. 185–200.

———. "The Girl Detective." *Stranger Things Happen*, Small Beer Press, 2001, pp. 241–66.

———. "Origin Story." *Get in Trouble*, Random House, 2015, pp. 153–85.

———. "Shoe and Marriage." *Stranger Things Happen*, Small Beer Press, 2001, pp. 167–90.

———. *Stranger Things Happen*, Small Beer Press, 2001.

———. "Travels with the Snow Queen." *Stranger Things Happen*, Small Beer Press, 2001, pp. 99–120.

The Little Mermaid. Directed by Ron Clements and John Musker, Walt Disney, 1989.

Little Red Riding Hood. Directed by Walt Disney, Laugh-O-Gram, 1922.

McGuire, Seanan. *Indexing*. 47North, 2013.

———. *Indexing: Reflections*. 47North, 2015.

———. *Indexing* series. 47North, 2013–15. 2 vols.

Men in Black. Directed by Barry Sonnenfeld, Sony, 1997.

Meyer, Marissa. *Cinder*. Square Fish, 2012.

———. *Cress*. Square Fish, 2014.

———. "The Little Android." 2014. *Wattpad*, https://www.wattpad.com/story/11861703-the-little-android.

———. *The Lunar Chronicles* series. Square Fish, 2012–15. 4 vols.

———. *Scarlet*. Square Fish, 2013.

———. *Winter*. Square Fish, 2015.

Minard, Rosemary, editor. *Womenfolk and Fairy Tales*. Houghton Mifflin, 1975.

Mulan. Directed by Tony Bancroft and Barry Cook, Walt Disney, 1998.

The Neverending Story. Directed by Wolfgang Petersen, Warner Brothers, 1984.

Once Upon a Time. Created by Edward Kitsis and Adam Horowitz, ABC, 2011–18.

Once Upon a Time in Wonderland. Created by Edward Kitsis, Adam Horowitz, Jack Estrin, and Jane Espenson, ABC, 2013–14.

Perrault, Charles. *Perrault's Fairy Tales*. 1697. Translated by A. E. Johnson, illustrated by Gustave Doré, Dover, 1969.

Peter Pan. Directed by Clyde Geronimi, Wilfred Jackson, and Hamilton Luske, Walt Disney, 1953.

Phelps, Ethel Johnston, editor. *The Maid of the North: Feminist Folk Tales from Around the World*. Owl, 1981.

———, editor. *Tatterhood and Other Tales*. The Feminist Press, 1978.

Pratchett, Terry. *Discworld* series. HarperCollins, 1983–2015. 41 vols.

———. *Witches Abroad*. 1991. Corgi, 1992.

The Princess Bride. Directed by Rob Reiner, 20th Century Fox, 1987.

Project Gutenberg. https://www.gutenberg.org/.

Ragan, Kathleen, editor. *Fearless Girls, Wise Women, and Beloved Sisters: Heroines in Folktales from Around the World*. Norton, 1998.

Rowling, J. K. The *Harry Potter* series. Scholastic, 1997–2007. 7 vols.

Secret Garden. Created by Eun-Sook Kim, Seoul Broadcasting System, 2010–11.

Sexton, Anne. *Transformations*. 1971. Mariner, 2001.

Shakespeare, William. *A Midsummer Night's Dream*. n.d. Project Gutenberg, https://www.gutenberg.org/ebooks/1514.

Shelley, Mary. *Frankenstein, or The Modern Prometheus*. 1818. Project Gutenberg, https://www.gutenberg.org/ebooks/84.

Shrek. Directed by Andrew Adamson and Vicky Jenson, DreamWorks Animation, 2001.

Sleeping Beauty. Directed by Clyde Geronimi, Walt Disney, 1959.

Snow White and the Seven Dwarfs. Directed by David Hand, William Cottrell, Wilfred Jackson, Larry Morey, Perce Pearce, and Ben Sharpsteen, Walt Disney, 1937.

Sondheim, Stephen. *Into the Woods*. 1986.

Star Wars Episode IV: A New Hope. Directed by George Lucas, Twentieth Century Fox, 1977.

Stevenson, Robert Louis. *The Strange Case of Dr. Jekyll and Mr. Hyde*. 1886. Project Gutenberg, https://www.gutenberg.org/ebooks/43.

Twain, Mark. *The Adventures of Tom Sawyer*. 1884. Project Gutenberg, https://www.gutenberg.org/ebooks/74.

———. *A Connecticut Yankee in King Arthur's Court*. 1889. Project Gutenberg, https:/www.gutenberg.org/ebooks/86.

———. *The Prince and the Pauper*. 1882. Project Gutenberg, https://www.gutenberg.org/ebooks/1837.

Verne, Jules. *The Mysterious Island*. 1874. Project Gutenberg, https://www.gutenberg.org/ebooks/1268.

———. *Twenty Thousand Leagues under the Sea*. 1870. Project Gutenberg, https://www.gutenberg.org/ebooks/164.

Willingham, Bill. *Fables* series. Vertigo, 2002–15. 150 vols.

Winter Sonata. Directed by Yoon Seok-Ho, Korean Broadcasting System, 2002.

Winterson, Jeanette. *Sexing the Cherry*. Grove, 1989.

The Wizard of Oz. Directed by Victor Fleming, MGM, 1939.

Secondary Sources

Aarne, Antti, and Stith Thompson. *Types of the Folktale: A Classification and Bibliography*. Academia Scientiarum Fennica, 1961.

"ABC's 'Once Upon a Time' Opens as the Season's #1 New Drama." 24 Oct. 2011, *The Futon Critic*, http://www.thefutoncritic.com/ratings/2011/10/24/abcs-once-upon-a-time-opens-as-the-seasons-number-1-new-drama-581505/20111024abc02/. Accessed 15 Aug. 2020.

Allen, Robert C. Introduction. *To Be Continued . . . : Soap Operas Around the World*, edited by Robert C. Allen, Routledge, 1995, pp. 1–26.

Attebery, Brian. "A Conversation with Kelly Link." *Journal of the Fantastic in the Arts*, vol. 23, no. 3, 2012, pp. 415-417.

Bacchilega, Cristina. *Fairy Tales Transformed? Twenty-First-Century Adaptations & the Politics of Wonder*. Wayne State University Press, 2013.

———. *Postmodern Fairy Tales: Gender and Narrative Strategies*. University of Pennsylvania Press, 1997.

Bacchilega, Cristina, and John Rieder. "Mixing It Up: Generic Complexity and Gender Ideology in Early 21st-Century Fairy-Tale Films." *Fairy Tale Film and Cinematic Folklore: Visions of Ambiguity*, edited by Pauline Greenhill and Sidney Eve Matrix, Utah State University Press, 2010, pp. 23–41.

Bakhtin, Mikhail. "Forms of Time and the Chronotope in the Novel: Notes toward a Historical Poetics." 1973. *The Dialogic Imagination*, edited by Michael Holquist, translated by Caryl Emerson and Michael Holquist, University of Texas Press, 1981, pp. 84–258.

Baratta, Alex. "The Use of English in Korean TV Drama to Signal a Modern Identity." *English Today*, vol. 30, no. 3, 2014, pp. 54–60.

Beckett, Sandra L. *Red Riding Hood for All Ages: A Fairy-Tale Icon in Cross-Cultural Contexts*. Wayne State University Press, 2008.

Benson, Stephen. *Cycles of Influence: Fiction, Folktale, Theory*. Wayne State University Press, 2003.

Caldwell, Sarah. "The Highs and Lows of *Once Upon a Time*'s *Frozen* Episodes." *Vulture*, 15 Dec. 2014, https://www.vulture.com/2014/12/once-upon-a-time-frozen-highs-lows.html.

Campbell, Joseph. *The Hero with a Thousand Faces*. 3rd ed., New World Library, 2008.

Campbell, Josie. "*Lost*'s Kitsis, Horowitz Start at the Beginning with *Once Upon A Time*." *CBR.Com*, 25 Aug. 2011, https://www.cbr.com/losts-kitsis-horowitz-start-at-the-beginning-with-once-upon-a-time/.

Cashdon, Sheldon. *The Witch Must Die: The Hidden Meaning of Fairy Tales*. Basic, 1999.

Carter, Angela. "Notes from the Front Line." *Shaking a Leg: Journalism and Writings*, edited by Jenny Uglow, Vintage, 1998, pp. 36–43.

Chan, Brenda, and Wang Xueli. "Of Prince Charming and Male Chauvinist Pigs: Singaporean Female Viewers and the Dream-World of Korean Television Dramas." *International Journal of Cultural Studies*, edited by Kai Khiun Liew and Jinna Tay, vol. 14, no. 3, 2011, pp. 291–305.

Clute, John. "Under the Skin of Story." *Scores*, Kindle edition, Gollancz, 2016.

Conner, Steven. *Postmodernist Culture: An Introduction to Theories of the Contemporary*. Basil Blackwell, 1989.

Cox, Marian Roalfe. *Cinderella: Three Hundred and Forty-Five Variants of Cinderella, Catskin, and Cap o'Rushes*. Edited by Andrew Lang, David Nutt, 1893.

Davidson, Hilary. "Holding the Sole: Shoes, Emotions, and the Supernatural." *Feeling Things: Objects and Emotions through History*, edited by Stephanie Downes, Sally Holloway, and Sarah Randles, Oxford University Press, 2018, pp. 72–93.

———. "Sex and Sin: The Magic of Red Shoes." *Shoes: A History from Sandals to Sneakers*, edited by Giorgio Riello and Peter McNeil, Berg, 2006, pp. 272–88.

Dean, Michelle. "Kelly Link: Freaky Fairytales." *The Guardian*, 14 Feb. 2015, https://www.theguardian.com/books/2015/feb/14/kelly-link-freaky-fairytales-get-in-trouble.

Do Rozario, Rebecca-Anne C. *Fashion in the Fairy Tale Tradition: What Cinderella Wore*. Palgrave, Macmillan, 2018.

Duggan, Anne E. *Salonnières, Furies, and Fairies: The Politics of Gender and Cultural Change in Absolutist France*. University of Delaware Press, 2005.

Dundes, Alan, editor. *Cinderella: A Casebook*. University of Wisconsin Press, 1988.

———. "The Motif-Index and the Tale Type Index: A Critique." *Journal of Folklore Research*, vol. 34, no. 3, 1997, pp. 195–202.

Elms, Alan C. "'The Three Bears': Four Interpretations." *The Journal of American Folklore*, vol. 90, no. 357, 1977, pp. 257–73.

"Fairy Tale Land." *Once Upon a Time Wiki*, https://onceuponatime.fandom.com/wiki/Fairy_Tale_Land. Accessed 15 Aug. 2020.

Fludernik, Monika. "Second-Person Narrative as a Test Case for Narratology: The Limits of Realism." *Style*, vol. 28, no. 3, 1994, pp. 445–79.

Foster, Michael Dylan, and Jeffrey A. Tolbert, editors. *The Folkloresque: Reframing Folklore in a Popular Culture World*. Utah State University Press, 2016.

Haase, Donald. "Feminist Fairy-Tale Scholarship." *Fairy Tales and Feminism: New Approaches*, edited by Donald Haase, Wayne State University Press, 2004, pp. 1–36.

———. "Hypertextual Gutenberg: The Textual and Hypertextual Life of Folktales and Fairy Tales in English-Language Popular Print Editions." *Fabula*, vol. 47, no. 3–4, 2006, pp. 222–30.

Hale, Sierra. "Soldering Together Young Adult Science Fiction: The Cyborg and Implicit and Explicit Racial Spaces in Marissa Meyer's *Cinder*." The 36th International Conference on the Fantastic in the Arts, 18–22 March 2015, Orlando, FL.

Haraway, Donna J. "A Cyborg Manifesto: Science, Technology, and Socialist-Feminism in the Late Twentieth Century." *Simians, Cyborgs, and Women: The Reinvention of Nature*, Routledge, 1991, pp. 149–81.

Haring, Lee. "Hybridity, Hybridization." *Folktales and Fairy Tales: Traditions and Texts from Around the World*, edited by Anne E. Duggan and Donald Haase, with Helen J. Callow. 2nd ed., ABC-CLIO, 2016, pp. 467–71.

Harries, Elizabeth Wanning. *Twice Upon a Time: Women Writers and the History of the Fairy Tale*. Princeton University Press, 2001.

Hay, Rebecca, and Christa Baxter. "Happily Never After: The Commodification and Critique of Fairy Tale in ABC's *Once Upon a Time*." *Channeling Wonder: Fairy Tales on Television*, edited by Pauline Greenhill and Jill Terry Rudy. Wayne State University Press, 2014, pp. 316–35.

Heiner, Heidi Anne. *Cinderella Tales From Around the World*. SurLaLune Press, 2012.

———. "The Story of the Three Bears." By Robert Southey. July 2018. *SurLaLune Fairy Tales* https://www.surlalunefairytales.com/book.php?id=22&tale=607. Accessed 15 Aug. 2020.

Hennard Dutheil de la Rochère, Martine, Gillian Lathey, and Monika Woźniak, editors. *Cinderella Across Cultures: New Directions and Interdisciplinary Perspectives*. Wayne State University Press, 2016.

Hu, Brian. "Korean TV Serials in the English-Language Diaspora: Translating Difference Online and Making It Racial." *The Velvet Light Trap*, no. 66, 2010, pp. 36–49.

Hutcheon, Linda. *Narcissistic Narrative: The Metafictional Paradox*. Wilfrid Laurier University Press, 1980.

———. *A Poetics of Postmodernism: History, Theory, Fiction*. Routledge, 1988.

———. *A Theory of Parody: The Teachings of Twentieth-Century Art Forms*. Methuen, 1985.

Jameson, Fredric. "Postmodernism and Consumer Society." 1988. *The Cultural Turn: Selected Writings on the Postmodern, 1983–1998*. Verso, 1998, pp. 1–20.

Jorgensen, Jeana. "A Wave of the Magic Wand: Fairy Godmothers in Contemporary American Media." *Marvels & Tales: Journal of Fairy-Tale Studies*, vol. 21, no. 2, 2007, pp. 216–27.

Joosen, Vanessa. *Critical and Creative Perspectives on Fairy Tales: An Intertextual Dialogue between Fairy-Tale Scholarship and Postmodern Retellings*. Wayne State University Press, 2011.

Keily, Karl. "NYCC: *Once Upon a Time* Pilot Screening and Panel." *CBR.Com*, 15 Oct. 2011, https://www.cbr.com/nycc-once-upon-a-time-pilot-screening-and-panel/.

Keith, Sarah, and Sung-Ae Lee. "*Legend of the Blue Sea*: Mermaids in South Korean Folklore and Popular Culture." *Scaled for Success: The Internationalisation of the Mermaid*, edited by Philip Hayward. Indiana University Press, 2019, pp. 69–88.

Kim, Suk-Young. "For the Eyes of North Koreans? Politics of Money and Class in *Boys Over Flowers*." *The Korean Wave: Korean Media Go Global*, edited by Youna Kim. Routledge, 2013, pp. 93–105.

Kukkonen, Karin. "Popular Cultural Memory: Comics, Communities and Context Knowledge." *Nordicom Review*, vol. 29, no. 2, 2008, pp. 261–73.

Lee, Hye-Kyung. "Cultural Policy and the Korean Wave: From National Culture to Transnational Consumerism." *The Korean Wave: Korean Media Go Global*, edited by Youna Kim. Routledge, 2013, pp. 185–98.

Lee, Jamie Shinhee. "Linguistic Constructions of Modernity: English Mixing in Korean Television Commercials." *Language in Society*, vol. 35, no. 1, 2006, pp. 59–91.

Lee, Linda J. "Fairy Tales and Fairy Folk: Evolving Expectations of Contemporary Fairy Tales." Popular Culture Association/ American Cultural Association Annual Meeting, 20 March 2008, San Francisco, CA.

Lee, Sung-Ae. "The Fairy-Tale Film in Korea." *Fairy-Tale Films Beyond Disney: International Perspectives*, edited by Jack Zipes, Pauline Greenhill, and Kendra Magnus-Johnston. Routledge, 2016, pp. 207–21.

———. "Fairy-Tale Scripts and Intercultural Conceptual Blending in Modern Korean Film and Television Drama." *Grimms' Tales Around the Globe: The Dynamics of Their International Reception*, edited by Vanessa Joosen and Gillian Lathey. Wayne State University Press, 2014, pp. 275–93.

———. "Memory, Trauma and History: Fairy-tale Film in Korea." *The Fairy Tale World*, edited by Andrew Teverson. Routledge, 2019, pp. 356–67.

Lin, Angel M. Y., and Avin Tong. "Crossing Boundaries: Male Consumption of Korean TV Dramas and Negotiation of Gender Relations in Modern Day Hong Kong." *Journal of Gender Studies*, 16, no. 3, 2007, pp. 217–32.

Lundell, Torborg. "Gender-Related Biases in the Type and Motif Indexes of Aarne and Thompson." *Fairy Tales and Society: Illusion, Allusion, and Paradigm*, edited by Ruth B. Bottigheimer. University of Pennsylvania Press, 1986, pp. 149–63.

Makinen, Merja. "Theorizing Fairy-Tale Fiction, Reading Jeanette Winterson." *Contemporary Fiction and the Fairy Tale*, edited by Stephen Benson. Wayne State University Press, 2008, pp. 144–77.

Masters, Megan, and Matt Webb Mitovich. "Real Truths Behind ABC's *Once Upon a Time* (Including That Pesky *Fables* Comparison)." *TVLine*, 7 Aug. 2011, https://tvline.com/2011/08/07/5-real-truths-once-upon-a-time/.

McHale, Brian. *Constructing Postmodernism*. Routledge, 1992.

———. *Postmodernist Fiction*. Routledge, 1987.

McRobbie, Angela. "Postmodernism and Popular Culture." 1986. *Postmodernism and Popular Culture*. Routledge, 1994, pp. 1–22.

Medendorp, Liz. "The 'Frozen' Characters' Mix in 'Once Upon a Time—Season 4' Creates Quite the Slush." *PopMatters*, 19 Aug. 2015, https://www.popmatters.com/196503-once-upon-a-time-the-complete-fourth-season-2495495861.html.

MetaCritic. "*Once Upon a Time*." https://www.metacritic.com/tv/once-upon-a-time. Accessed 15 Aug. 2020.

Meyer, Marissa. "A Guide to Lunar Chronicles Character Traits." 31 July 2014, http://www.marissameyer.com/blogtype/a-guide-to-lunar-chronicles-character-traits/.

Mitchell, Jennifer. "'A girl. A machine. A freak': A Consideration of Contemporary Queer Composites." *Bookbird*, vol. 52, no. 1, 2014, pp. 51–62.

Mittell, Jason. *Complex TV: The Poetics of Contemporary Television Storytelling*. New York University Press, 2015.

Morrison, Jago. *Contemporary Fiction*. Routledge, 2003.

"Mulan." *Once Upon a Time Wiki*, https://onceuponatime.fandom.com/wiki/Mulan. Accessed 15 Aug. 2020.

Multilingual Folk Tale Database. http://www.mftd.org/index.php?action=atu. Accessed 17 Sept. 2018.

Mulvey, Laura. "Visual Pleasure and Narrative Cinema." *Feminism and Film*, edited by E. Ann Kaplan. Oxford University Press, 2000, pp. 34–47.

Nestvold, Ruth, and Jay Lake. "Telling Stories of Your Life: The Use of Second Person Narration in SF." *The Internet Review of Science Fiction*. Bluejack, Mar. 2007, http://www.irosf.com/q/zine/article/10375. Accessed 29 Oct. 2012.

Neumann, Birgit, and Ansgar Nünning. "Metanarration and Metafiction." *the living handbook of narratology*, edited by Peter Hühn. Hamburg University Press, 24 Jan. 2014, https://www.lhn.uni-hamburg.de/node/50.html.

Nye, Joseph, and Youna Kim. "Soft Power and the Korean Wave." *The Korean Wave: Korean Media Go Global*, edited by Youna Kim. Routledge, 2013, pp. 31–42.

"Once Upon a Time Wiki: Map Making Contest." *Once Upon a Time Wiki*, https://onceuponatime.fandom.com/wiki/Once_Upon_a_Time_Wiki:Map_Making_Contest. Accessed 15 Aug. 2020.

Opie, Iona, and Peter Opie. "Goldilocks and the Three Bears." *The Classic Fairy Tales*. Oxford University Press, 1974, pp. 199–200.

Preston, Cathy Lynn. "Disrupting the Boundaries of Genre and Gender: Postmodernism and the Fairy Tale." *Fairy Tales and Feminism: New Approaches*, edited by Donald Haase. Wayne State University Press, 2004, pp. 197–212.

Propp, Vladímir. *Morphology of the Folktale*. Edited by Louis A. Wagner, Translated by Laurence Scott. 2nd ed. University of Texas Press, 2001.

Radish, Christina. "Co-Creator/Executive Producer Adam Horowitz ONCE UPON A TIME Interview." *Collider*, 23 Oct. 2011, https://collider.com/adam-horowitz-once-upon-a-time-interview/.

Rawden, Jessica. "11 Reasons Once Upon A Time's Frozen Story Is Flipping Weird." *Cinemablend*, 28 Sept. 2014, https://www.cinemablend.com/television/11-Reasons-Once-Time-Frozen-Story-Flipping-Weird-67560.html.

Rooth, Anna Birgitta. *The Cinderella Cycle*. C. W. K. Gleerup, 1951.

Ropers, Erik. "Historical Narrative and the Misrepresentation of Wartime Labor Recruitment in *Kenkanryū*." *Forum for World Literature Studies*, vol. 3, no. 1, 2011, pp. 70–80.

Rose, Margaret A. *Parody//Meta-Fiction: An Analysis of Parody as a Critical Mirror to the Writing and Reception of Fiction*. Croom Helm, 1979.

Rowe, Karen E. "To Spin a Yarn: The Female Voice in Folklore and Fairy Tale." *Fairy Tales and Society: Illusion, Allusion, and Paradigm*, edited by Ruth B. Bottigheimer. University of Pennsylvania Press, 1989, pp. 53–74.

Rudy, Jill Terry. "Broadcast (Radio and Television)." *The Routledge Companion to Media and Fairy-Tale Cultures*, edited by Pauline Greenhill, Jill Terry Rudy, Naomi Hamer, and Lauren Bosc. Routledge, 2018, pp. 367–75.

Rutledge, Amelia. "Science Fiction and Fairy Tales." *The Oxford Companion to Fairy Tales: The Western Fairy Tale Tradition from Medieval to Modern*, edited by Jack Zipes. Oxford University Press, 2000, pp. 451–56.

Schanoes, Veronica. *Fairy Tales, Myth, and Psychoanalytic Theory: Feminism and Retelling the Tale*. Ashgate, 2014.

Schmiesing, Ann. "Disability." *The Routledge Companion to Media and Fairy-Tale Cultures*, edited by Pauline Greenhill, Jill Terry Rudy, Naomi Hamer, and Lauren Bosc. Routledge, 2018, pp. 104–12.

———. *Disability, Deformity, and Disease in the Grimms' Fairy Tales*. Wayne State University Press, 2014.

Schwabe, Claudia. "Getting Real with Fairy Tales: Magic Realism in *Grimm* and *Once Upon a Time*." *Channeling Wonder: Fairy Tales on Television*, edited by Pauline Greenhill and Jill Terry Rudy. Wayne State University Press, 2014, pp. 294–315.

Seifert, Lewis C. *Fairy Tales, Sexuality, and Gender in France, 1690–1715: Nostalgic Utopias*. Cambridge University Press, 1996.

Smith, Kevin Paul. *The Postmodern Fairytale: Folkloric Intertexts in Contemporary Fiction*. Palgrave Macmillan, 2007.

"The Snow Queen." *Once Upon a Time Wiki*, https://onceuponatime.fandom.com/wiki/The_Snow_Queen_(Fairytale). Accessed 15 Aug. 2020.

Thomas, Hayley. "Undermining a Grimm Tale: A Feminist Reading of 'The Worn-Out Dancing Shoes' (KHM 133)." *Marvels & Tales*, vol. 13, no. 2, 1991, pp. 170–83.

Thompson, Stith. *Motif-Index of Folk-Literature: A Classification of Narrative Elements in Folktales, Ballads, Myths, Fables, Mediaeval Romances, Exempla, Fabliaux, Jest-Books, and Local Legends*. Revised and enlarged ed., Indiana University Press, 1975.

Tiffin, Jessica. *Marvelous Geometry: Narrative and Metafiction in Modern Fairy Tale*. Wayne State University Press, 2009.

Uther, Hans-Jörg. *The Types of International Folktales: A Classification and Bibliography*. Academia Scientiarum Fennica, 2004.

Vaz da Silva, Francisco. "Hybridity." *The Routledge Companion to Media and Fairy-Tale Cultures*, edited by Pauline Greenhill, Jill Terry Rudy, Naomi Hamer, and Lauren Bosc. Routledge, 2018, pp. 188–95.

Warhol, Robyn R. *Having a Good Cry: Effeminate Feelings and Pop-Culture Forms*. The Ohio State University Press, 2003.

———. "Making 'Gay' and 'Lesbian' into Household Words: How Serial Form Works in Armistead Maupin's *Tales of the City*." *Contemporary Literature*, vol. 40, no. 3, 1999, pp. 378–402.

Warner, Marina. *Once Upon a Time: A Short History of the Fairy Tale*. Oxford University Press, 2014.

Williams, Christy. "Ambiguous Villains and Fairy-Tale Monsters in Kelly Link's 'The Cinderella Game.'" *The Journal of the Fantastic in the Arts*, vol. 29, no. 1, 2018, pp. 68–85.

———. "Novels." *The Routledge Companion to Media and Fairy-Tale Cultures*, edited by Pauline Greenhill, Jill Terry Rudy, Naomi Hamer, and Lauren Bosc. Routledge, 2018, pp. 565–71.

———. "Who's Wicked Now? The Stepmother as Fairy-Tale Heroine." *Marvels & Tales: Journal of Fairy-Tale Studies*, vol. 24, no. 2, 2010, pp. 255–71.

Williamson, Rose. "The European Sources of the Fairy Tale: A Case Study of ATU 171, 'The Three Bears.'" *The Fairy Tale World*, edited by Andrew Teverson. Routledge, 2019, pp. 391-401.

Wood, Naomi. "The Ugly Duckling's Legacy: Adulteration, Contemporary Fantasy, and the Dark." *Marvels & Tales: Journal of Fairy-Tale Studies*, vol. 20, no. 2, 2006, pp. 193–207.

Yolen, Jane. "America's Cinderella." *The World Is a Text: Writing, Reading, and Thinking about Culture and Its Contents*, edited by Jonathan Silverman and Dean Rader, 2nd ed. Pearson/ Prentice Hall, 2006, pp. 441–48.

Young, Katharine. "Storyworlds/Narratology." *The Routledge Companion to Media and Fairy-Tale Cultures*, edited by Pauline Greenhill, Jill Terry Rudy, Naomi Hamer, and Lauren Bosc. Routledge, 2018, pp. 213–21.

Zipes, Jack. *The Enchanted Screen: The Unknown History of Fairy-Tale Films*. Routledge, 2011.

———. *Fairy Tale as Myth/ Myth as Fairy Tale*. University Press of Kentucky, 1994.

———. *Fairy Tales and the Art of Subversion: The Classical Genre for Children and the Process of Civilization*. 2nd ed. Routledge, 2006.

———. *The Irresistible Fairy Tale: The Cultural and Social History of a Genre.* Princeton University Press, 2012.

———. *Relentless Progress: The Reconfiguration of Children's Literature, Fairy Tales, and Storytelling.* Routledge, 2009.

Zolkover, Adam. "Corporealizing Fairy Tales: The Body, the Bawdy, and the Carnivalesque in the Comic Book *Fables*." *Marvels & Tales: Journal of Fairy-Tale Studies*, vol. 22, no. 1, 2008, pp. 38–51.

Index

Aarne-Thompson (AT) index, 80–81, 82–89, 90, 94, 103, 178–79nn8–9
Allen, Robert C., 132
Andersen, Hans Christian: "The Little Mermaid," 88–89, 95–96, 116–17, 118–19, 121, 127, 179–80n1; "The Red Shoes," 152–53, 181n2; "The Snow Queen," 45–46, 139–40, 147
Arabian Nights, 36
authors, fairy-tale, 50–51, 53–54, 59–62

Bacchilega, Christina, 1–2, 9, 11, 36
Bakhtin, Mikhail, 175–76n4
Baratta, Alex, 180n9
Baxter, Christa, 58–59
"Beauty and the Beast," 44, 83, 94, 177n3
beauty pageants, in "The Red Shoes" and "Shoe and Marriage," 152–53
bloody footprints, map of, in "Travels with the Snow Queen," 141–42
body dysmorphia, 71–72
Brave, 40
broken glass, map of, in "Travels with the Snow Queen," 141–42
Buckley, Michael, 178n3
Buffy the Vampire Slayer, 18–19

Campbell, Joseph, 97
Carter, Angela, 4, 168, 176n2
"Catskin" (Link), 138–39

chaebol and *chaebol* dramas, 110–11, 112–13, 114–15, 118. See also *Secret Garden*
Chan, Brenda, 135–36
chronotype, 175–76n4
Cinder (Meyer), 67–76, 79, 104
"Cinderella": allusion to, in *Indexing*, 85; and connection of plot to place, 102; earliest recorded variant of, 175n1; expectations for, 68–69; rejection of, in *Secret Garden*, 108–9, 113–16, 118, 119–20, 127–28; retellings of, 5–6; and "Shoe and Marriage," 147–49; and stacking of narratives, 101. See also *Lunar Chronicles, The* (Meyer)
Cinderella (Disney, 2015), 15
"Cinderella Game, The" (Link), 138
cinematic classics, as *Once Upon a Time* source material, 60–61
class disparity, in *Secret Garden*, 108, 109–13, 114–15, 116, 119–21, 122–23, 128–29, 131
closed-serial format, 132, 133
closure, delayed, in *Once Upon a Time*, 58–59. See also happily-ever-after ending
Clute, John, 30, 148
compact fairy tales, 12
complex fairy tales, 12
conceptual blending, 115, 128
Cress (Meyer), 72, 75–76

cross-cultural exchange, 170. *See also* globalization; Korean dramas; Korean Wave
crying: and emotional reaction to melodrama, 134; and emotional release from Korean dramas, 135
cyborg imagery, 72–73, 75. *See also Lunar Chronicles, The* (Meyer)

dancing, in "The Girl Detective," 163–65
Davidson, Hilary, 181nn2,5
Demeter, 166
detective fiction, 158–68
Discworld series (Pratchett), 65
Disney: *Brave*, 40; *Cinderella* (2015), 15; *Frozen*, 45–46; and *Once Upon a Time* content, 28, 29, 31, 38, 40, 44–49, 60–61; releases "Little Red Riding Hood" short film, 176n2
Do Rozario, Rebecca-Anne C., 137–38, 181n2
Duan Chengshi, 175n1
Duggan, Anne E., 4
Dundes, Alan, 179n9
duplication, versus revision, 11, 12, 15

emotional release, from Korean dramas, 134–35, 136
English, in Korean dramas, 119, 180n9
escapism, and Korean dramas, 135–36
Ever After, 15

fairy-tale authors, 50–51, 53–54, 59–62
fairy-tale borders, dissolution of, 169–72
fairy-tale fragments, 8; children's exposure to, 30–31; Link on, 168; in *Once Upon a Time*, 50
fairy-tale novel series, 64–65. See also *Indexing* (McGuire); *Lunar Chronicles, The* (Meyer)
fairy-tale parodies, 30–31

fairy tales: audience of, 68; continued attachment to, 172–73; feminist retellings of, 4, 5; functions of, 69; interconnection of, 1–2, 3–4; as literature, 61; as metafictional, 64; multiplicity in study of postmodern, 10–12; newness in, 5–7; retellings of, 4–5, 91–94. *See also* mixing fairy tales
fairy-tale structure, of *The Lunar Chronicles*, 69–72
fan engagement, 170
feet: in "Shoe and Marriage," 147–49; in "The Girl Detective," 163, 165; in "The Red Shoes," 152; in "Travels with the Snow Queen," 144–45. *See also* shoes
feminine genres, 133–35
feminist retellings of fairy tales, 4, 5
Fludernik, Monika, 145–46
folkloresque, 40
Foster, Michael Dylan, 40
fragments. *See* fairy-tale fragments
Frankenstein (Shelley), 60–61
Frozen, 45–46

gender bias, in AT index, 179n9
gender identity: in *Indexing: Reflections*, 97–98; in "The Girl Detective," 159
genre mixing/hybridity, 9–10; as common in contemporary fairy tales, 69; and dissolution of narrative borders, 169; in *Indexing*, 90–91; in *The Lunar Chronicles* and *Indexing*, 66
"Girl Detective, The" (Link), 158–68
globalization, 169–70. *See also* Korean dramas; Korean Wave
"Goldilocks and the Three Bears," 88, 178–79n8
Goldman, William, *The Princess Bride*, 13
Grimm, 5

Haase, Donald, 2, 16, 147
Hale, Sierra, 72
happily-ever-after ending, 18–19; delayed, in *Once Upon a Time*, 58–59; in *the Lunar Chronicles*, 74, 78–79; and multiplicity of character functions in *Once Upon a Time*, 50–54; in *Secret Garden*, 126–27, 128–33; in "Shoe and Marriage," 147–50, 156–57; in "Travels with the Snow Queen," 143, 145
Haraway, Donna, 72
Haring, Lee, 10, 11, 169
Harries, Elizabeth Wanning, 12, 30
Hay, Rebecca, 58–59
Hines, Jim C., 101, 178n3
horizon of expectations, 8, 18, 48, 58, 68
Horowitz, Adam, 6–7, 29, 30–31
Hu, Brian, 135
Hutcheon, Linda, 11, 17, 20

Indexing (McGuire), 65–66; dissolution of narrative borders of source tales in, 171; fairy-tale retellings in, 91–94; genre mixing in, 90–91; geographic pastiche and AT index in, 80–81; literary classics referenced in, 88–89; memetic incursions in, 92–93; monomyth in, 95–97; narrative landscape of, as organized by tale type, 94–100; note on AT index in, 86–87; pastiche in, 66; publication of, 21, 81–82; references to tale types in, 87–88, 89; shared setting of, 172; as showcasing academic study of fairy tales, 103; stacking of narratives in, 102–3; structure of, 21, 82–84; urban legends referenced in, 89–90

Indexing: Reflections (McGuire): fairy-tale retellings in, 91–94; genre mixing in, 90–91; memetic incursions in, 92–93; monomyth in, 95–97; narrative landscape of, as organized by tale type, 94–100; note on AT index in, 86–87; references to tale types in, 87–88, 89; role reversal in, 97–99; as showcasing academic study of fairy tales, 103; stacking of narratives in, 102–3; typing of Sloane in, 85–86
ineo (fish people), 179n1
internet, 169–70

Jameson, Frederic, 10, 12–14, 29
Japanese occupation of Korea, 110–11
Joosen, Vanessa, 8, 172, 175–76n4
Jorgensen, Jeana, 9, 10
justice, evoked by Cinderella tale type, 120

Keith, Sarah, 108, 179–80n1
Kim, Suk-Young, 110–11
Kitsis, Edward, 6, 29
Korea, Japanese occupation of, 110–11
Korean dramas: English in, 119, 180n9; genre terminology used for, 133–34; popularity and appeal of, 135–36; sex and sexuality in, 134–35; social and genre landscapes in, 109–13, 114–15, 116, 119–21, 122–23, 128–29, 131. See also *Secret Garden*
Korean folklore, 179–80n1
Korean Wave, 111–12, 170
Kukkonen, Karin, 8, 90

Lake, Jay, 144–45
Lee, Hye-Kyung, 111
Lee, Jamie Shinhee, 180n9
Lee, Linda J., 30

Lee, Sung-Ae, 108, 110, 113–14, 115, 128, 179–80n1, 180n5
lesbian relationships, in *Once Upon a Time*, 47–48
LGBTQ+ representation, 47–48, 71–72
Lin, Angel M. Y., 133–34, 135
Link, Kelly, short fiction of, 21, 137–39; "Catskin," 138–39; "The Cinderella Game," 138; and continued attachment to fairy tales, 173; crossover from fantasy to fictionalized reality in, 172; "The Girl Detective," 158–68; "Origin Story," 138; "Shoe and Marriage," 147–58; shoes in, 137–38; *Stranger Things Happen*, 137; tone and pattern in, 168; "Travels with the Snow Queen," 137, 139–47, 168
literary classics: as *Once Upon a Time* source material, 60–61, 177n5; referenced in *Indexing*, 88–89
literature, fairy tales as, 61
"Little Mermaid, The": as analogy for *Secret Garden* plot, 107–9, 116–31; in *Indexing*, 88–89, 94, 95–96; in Korean folklore, 179–80n1; and rejection of "Cinderella" in *Secret Garden*, 115–16
"Little Red Riding Hood": allusion to, in *The Lunar Chronicles*, 75, 76–78, 101; and connection of plot to place, 102; Disney short film of, 176n2; evoked in "Shoe and Marriage," 154–56
long-arc plot serials, 18–19. *See also Once Upon a Time*
loss, in "The Girl Detective," 162–63
Lunar Chronicles, The (Meyer), 65–66; character appearance in, 178n5; *Cinder*, 67–76, 79, 104; *Cress*, 72, 75–76; cyborg imagery and identity in, 72–73, 75; dissolution of narrative borders of source tales in, 171; fairy-tale structure of, 69–72, 74–79; hybridity as core concept of, 67–69; pastiche in, 66; *Scarlet*, 72, 75, 76, 102; shared setting of, 172; stacking of narratives in, 100–101; structure and context of publication of, 21; themes in, 66–67, 73–74; *Winter*, 75, 76, 78–79, 101
Lundell, Torborg, 88, 179n9

magical realism, 32
Makinen, Merja, 11, 12, 14
Marcos, Imelda, 147, 153–56
marriage: American cultural construct of, 143; in "The Little Mermaid," 117, 118; in *Secret Garden*, 117–18, 122, 131, 133; serialization as undermining, plot, 58; in "Shoe and Marriage," 147–50, 151, 156–57
mash ups, 6–7, 14. *See also* mixing fairy tales; pastiche
McGuire, Seanan. *See Indexing* (McGuire)
McHale, Brian, 15
McRobbie, Angela, 14
Medendorp, Liz, 45, 46
melodrama: categorized as feminine genre, 133–35; in *Once Upon a Time*, 58; in *Secret Garden*, 124–25, 127, 128–29, 131–32. *See also Once Upon a Time*
memetic incursion, 80–81, 90, 91, 92, 96
Men in Black, 90
mermaids, in Korean folklore, 179–80n1. *See also* "Little Mermaid, The"
metafictional narrative strategies, 16–20, 57–63, 64
Meyer, Marissa. *See Lunar Chronicles, The* (Meyer)
Mitchell, Jennifer, 72
Mittell, Jason, 18–19, 57, 132, 134

mixing fairy tales: in *Indexing*, 80–81, 83–84, 93–95; in *The Lunar Chronicles*, 75–78; in *Once Upon a Time*, 27–28, 47, 59; and stacking of narratives, 100–104. *See also* mash ups; *Once Upon a Time*

monomyth, 95–97

motifs, 8

multiplicity: of character functions in *Once Upon a Time*, 49–57; in *Indexing*, 91–92; and metafictional element to fairy tales, 17; pastiche and, 14; and plurality of fairy tales in *Once Upon a Time*, 46; shift toward, 5; in study of postmodern fairy tales, 10–12

multivocality, 15–16

Mulvey, Laura, 134

Nancy Drew mystery series, 158, 159, 162, 164, 167

narrative borders: dissolution of, 169–72; interaction of characters across, in *Once Upon a Time*, 35–37, 42–43

narrative complexity, 18–19, 57

Nestvold, Ruth, 144–45

Neumann, Birgit, 17

newness, in fairy tales, 5–7

nostalgia, pastiche as, 12–14, 29–31

novels. *See* fairy-tale novel series

Nünning, Ansgar, 17

object maps, in "Travels with the Snow Queen," 142

Once Upon a Time, 27–28; and audience understanding of fairy-tale genre, 31; Belle's story in, 177n3; conflicts grounded in specific locations in, 33–35; dissolution of narrative borders of source tales in, 171; division of location by magic in, 31–32; Enchanted Forest setting of, 32–33, 38–39, 41–42; Fairy Tale Land setting of, 39–41; fairy-tale parodies and fragments and, 30–31; interaction of characters across narrative borders in, 35–37, 42–43; multiplicity of character functions in, 49–57; and newness in fairy tales, 5, 6–7; nostalgia in, 29–30; pastiche in *Indexing* versus, 93; production of, 21; and serialization and metafiction, 57–63; shared setting of, 172; source material for, 37–38, 40–41, 44–49, 60–61, 177n5; stacking of narratives in, 101; Storybrooke setting in, 28–30, 42–43; transformation of shared genre into shared geography in, 41–42, 48–49; unanswered biological questions in, 176n1

open-serial format, 132

oppression, in *The Lunar Chronicles*, 73–74, 78

optimism, 18–19

"Origin Story" (Link), 138

Otherness, in *The Lunar Chronicles*, 67–68, 73, 75

pageants, in "The Red Shoes" and "Shoe and Marriage," 152–53

parody: pastiche versus, 10–11; as type of metafiction, 20

pastiche, 7–16; approaches to geographical, 103–4; chronotype as element most disrupted in, 175–76n4; and dissolution of narrative borders, 169, 171; in fairy-tale novel series, 65–66; in *Indexing*, 80–81; and metafiction, 19–20; through mixing fairy tales, 27; as nostalgia, 12–14, 29–31; in *Once Upon a Time* versus *Indexing*, 93; parody versus, 10–11; and serialization in *Once Upon a Time*, 59

Index • 201

pattern, Link on, 168. *See also* fairy-tale fragments
Persephone, 166, 167
Pied Piper, 91, 178n7
postmodernism, 15
Pratchett, Terry, *Discworld* series, 65
Preston, Cathy Lynn, 8, 40
Princess Bride, The, 13
Propp, Vladímir, 49, 52

racial identity, in *The Lunar Chronicles*, 72
"Rapunzel," 75, 76, 85
"Red Shoes, The" (Andersen), 152–53, 181n2
revision, versus duplication, 11, 12, 15
Rieder, John, 9
role reversal: in *Indexing: Reflections*, 97–99; in *Once Upon a Time*, 54–56; in *Secret Garden*, 117, 120, 122–25, 127, 131
romance, thematic rejection of fairy-tale, 143–44
Rose, Margaret, 20
Rowe, Karen E., 1–2
Rudy, Jill Terry, 19
Rutledge, Amelia, 69

sacrifice: in Andersen works, 140; and escapism of Korean dramas, 136; in *Secret Garden*, 124–25, 127–29; in "Travels with the Snow Queen," 139, 140. *See also* suffering
same-sex relationships, in *Once Upon a Time*, 47–48
Scarlet (Meyer), 72, 75, 76, 102
Schanoes, Veronica, 145, 166, 177–78n2
Schwabe, Claudia, 32

second-person narration: ambiguity in, 145–46; in "The Girl Detective," 163; in "Travels with the Snow Queen," 144–47
Secret Garden: conclusion of, 131–33; connection of original location to world in, 171–72; and continued attachment to fairy tales, 173; crossover from fantasy to fictionalized reality in, 172; versus Link's short stories, 137; "Little Mermaid" as analogy for plot of, 116–31; overview of, 21–22, 107–9; rejection of "Cinderella" in, 108–9, 113–16, 118, 119–20, 127–28; social and genre landscapes in, 109–13
Seifert, Lewis C., 4
self-consciousness, of fairy-tale genre, 64
serialization, 18–19; of *Indexing*, 81–82; and metafiction, 57–63; open-ended versus closed-ended serials, 132. *See also* fairy-tale novel series; *Once Upon a Time*; *Secret Garden*
sex and sexuality. *See also* LGBTQ+ representation
sex and sexuality, in Korean dramas, 134–35
Sexton, Anne, 4
Shelley, Mary, 60–61
"Shoe and Marriage" (Link), 147–58
shoes: in Link short fiction, 137–38; red, 181n2; in "Shoe and Marriage," 147–52, 153–54, 156, 157; in "The Worn-Out Dancing Shoes," 164–65. *See also* feet
short-arc plot series, 18–19
Sisters Grimm, The (Buckley), 178n3
slavery, in *The Lunar Chronicles*, 73–74
Smith, Kevin Paul, 177–78n2

"Snow Queen, The" (Andersen), 45–46, 139–40, 147
"Snow White": allusion to, in *Indexing*, 82, 83, 96–97; allusion to, in *The Lunar Chronicles*, 75, 78, 79, 101; and innate knowledge of fairy tales, 30–31; and interaction of characters across narrative borders in *Once Upon a Time*, 36–37
soap operas, 18–19; categorized as feminine genre, 133–35; conventions in *Once Upon a Time*, 57–58; happily-ever-after ending in, 132. *See also* Korean dramas; *Secret Garden*
social landscape, in *Secret Garden*, 108, 109–13, 114–15, 116, 119–21, 122–23, 128–29, 131
spheres of action, 52–53
stacking narratives, 100–104
Star Wars, 12–13
Stranger Things Happen (Link), 137
structuralist approach to narrative, 52–54
suffering: in Andersen works, 140; in Link short fiction, 140–41; in "The Little Mermaid," 116, 119; in *Once Upon a Time*, 51, 56–57, 62; in *Secret Garden*, 123–24; in "Travels with the Snow Queen," 144–45. *See also* sacrifice

Thumbelina, 89
Tiffin, Jessica, 14, 17–18, 64, 177–78n2
Tolbert, Jeffrey A., 40
Tong, Avin, 133–34, 135
transgender representation, in *The Lunar Chronicles*, 71–72

"Travels with the Snow Queen" (Link), 137, 139–47, 168
"Twelve Dancing Princesses, The," 158–59, 162, 163–65, 167–68

underworld, in "The Girl Detective," 162–63, 164, 165–66, 167
urban legends, 89–90
Uther, Hans-Jörg, 179n9

Vaz da Silva, Francisco, 10, 179n9
villains: in *Indexing*, 97–99; and multiplicity of character functions in *Once Upon a Time*, 49–57

Warhol, Robyn R., 19, 58, 134
Warner, Marina, 1, 3–4
Winter (Meyer), 75, 76, 78–79, 101
Winterson, Jeanette, 4
Witches Abroad, 177–78n2
Wizard of Oz, The, 147, 150–53
women heroes, in *Once Upon a Time*, 44–45, 48
Wood, Naomi, 143, 145
"Worn-Out Dancing Shoes, The" (Grimm), 164–65

Xueli, Wang, 135–36

"Ye Xian" (Duan Chengshi), 175n1
Yolen, Jane, 120
Young, Katharine, 8

Zipes, Jack, 4, 11, 12, 44
Zolkover, Adam, 9, 10

www.ingramcontent.com/pod-product-compliance
Lightning Source LLC
Chambersburg PA
CBHW031833230426
43669CB00009B/1339